LEE & KIRBY:

THE WONDER YEARS

(Jack Kirby Collector #58)
written by Mark Alexander

TwoMorrows Publishing
Raleigh, North Carolina

Lee & Kirby: The Wonder Years

(a.k.a. *Jack Kirby Collector* #58)

Written by Mark Alexander (1955-2011)
Edited, designed, and proofread by John Morrow, publisher
Softcover ISBN: 978-1-60549-038-0
First Printing • December 2011 • Printed in the USA

The Jack Kirby Collector, Vol. 18, No. 58, Winter 2011 (hey, it's Dec. 3 as I type this!). Published quarterly by and ©2011 TwoMorrows Publishing, 10407 Bedfordtown Drive, Raleigh, NC 27614. 919-449-0344. John Morrow, Editor/Publisher. Four-issue subscriptions: $50 US, $65 Canada, $72 elsewhere. Editorial package ©2011 TwoMorrows Publishing, a division of TwoMorrows Inc. All characters are trademarks of their respective companies. All artwork is ©2011 Jack Kirby Estate unless otherwise noted. Editorial matter ©2011 the respective authors. ISSN 1932-6912

(above and title page) Kirby pencils from What If? *#11 (Oct. 1978).*
(opposite) Original Kirby collage for Fantastic Four *#51, page 14.*

Acknowledgements

First and foremost, thanks to my Aunt June for buying my first Marvel comic, and for everything else. Next, big thanks to my son Nicholas for endless research. From the age of three, the kid had the good taste to request the *Marvel Masterworks* for bedtime stories over *Mother Goose.* He still holds the record as the youngest contributor to *The Jack Kirby Collector* (see issue #21).

Shout-out to my partners in rock 'n' roll, the incomparable Hitmen—the best band and best pals I've ever had. Thanks for canceling practice for a month so I could finish this text.

There's not enough room on this page to adequately express my gratitude to John Morrow and the zany bunch (how's that for a mid-sixties Marvelism?) at TwoMorrows Publishing. The meteoric rise of the TwoMorrows Universe, which started with a phantasmagoric fanzine called *The Jack Kirby Collector* #1, is living proof of what someone with a Kirbyian work ethic can achieve in a very short time.

Thanks to Rhonda Rade who paved the way for the Stan Lee interviews, and who never once acted like she was sick of my endless requests for more pieces of the puzzle. Without her, this book would not exist. See ya on the tour, Ro-Ro.

Thanks to Carol "Kay-Ro" Dixon, whose internet research was invaluable (especially the bit about the Marx Brothers). Big thanks to Tracy Stubblefield for prints and M.U., and particularly to Laura Bruns who opened several doors that were closed to me. Besides this, Laura's willingness to sacrifice her weekends on behalf of this manuscript is the only reason we made the deadline.

Thanks to Mark Evanier for his exclusive FF info and for decades of unselfishly helping comic book scribes everywhere while asking nothing in return. Jack Kirby couldn't have picked a better historian or a better friend.

Thanks to author Gerard Jones for encouragement, inspiration, and especially for the tips on Charles Dickens, The Lower East Side and ANC. This book might have been a "revoltin' development" without his help. Thanks to Mike Gartland and Will Murray for their much appreciated input. They've always been my favorite *TJKC* writers. Thanks to Larry Lieber for his friendly and informative phone calls. And thank you Mr. Roy Thomas for providing your 1965 Marvel map.

Huge thanks to Dr. Michael J. Vassallo, Tom Lammers and Jim Vadeboncoeur for pulling us from the quicksand of Timely/Atlas contradictions. The pre-Marvel era of Martin Goodman comics is alive and well because of these visionary historians. Do yourself a favor: read Tom's book *Tales of the Implosion* and "Doc V's" forthcoming book on artist Joe Maneely.

Thanks to Joe Sinnott for providing exclusive info on the final Kirby *FF* issues.

And more than anyone else, thanks to Fabulous Flo Steinberg for being so generous with her Marvel memories, for proofreading, and for drawing maps of all the 1960s Marvel offices. She's beyond fabulous—she's one of the superheroes of this story.

Thanks to Queen Roz Kirby for being the woman behind the man. And speaking of The Man, thanks to Stan Lee for the exclusive FF interviews. And last but most, thanks to Jack Kirby who (along with Stan) gave me the best moments of my childhood.

To offer a cliché, 'NUFF SAID.

Mark Alexander, May 2011

[The editor wishes to add special thanks to Rand Hoppe of the Jack Kirby Museum and Research Center (www.kirbymuseum.org), Glen Gold, Larry Houston, David "Hambone" Hamilton, Cheryl Urbanczyk, Heritage Auctions (www.ha.com), and the Jack Kirby Estate for their help supplying imagery for this book.]

Copyrights

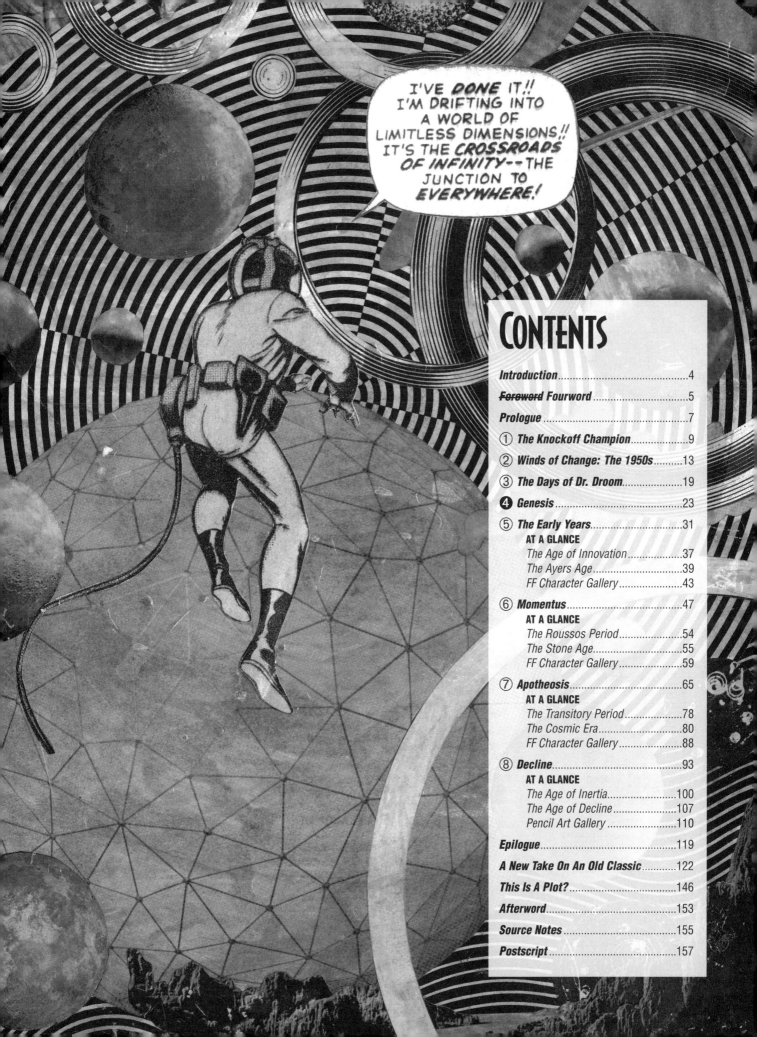

CONTENTS

INTRODUCTION

by editor John Morrow

Mark Alexander (1955-2011)

This publication started life as a lengthy *Jack Kirby Collector* article entitled "A Universe A'Borning" that Mark Alexander had spent many, many months writing in the early 2000s. After turning in the final draft of his manuscript, Mark would regularly send me updates on it, and ultimately asked me to pull it entirely from the schedule, as he was going to re-tool it into something else. You now hold that "something else" in your hands (although his original "A'Borning" article will likely see print in an upcoming issue of *TJKC*). He was absent from *TJKC*'s pages for several years, largely because he had spent countless hours refining the original "A'Borning" article, and then literally years crafting it into this book.

Seeing how well it turned out, I made the decision, in consultation with Mark, to turn one issue of *TJKC* into a king-sized book instead of the usual magazine, featuring only Mark's revised article, then called "Fantastic Four: The Wonder Years." Since the book was as much about Stan and Jack as it was the *FF*, we decided to modify the title to better reflect the content.

But don't get the idea that Mark stopped working on this book once he'd handed in his "final" manuscript. Starting in early 2010, for weeks and months after he first said it was done, I'd get "Stop the Presses!" updates by Priority Mail Flat Rate Envelope—at times on a weekly basis—saying he'd just discovered some new tidbit or factoid that was essential to the book. He'd always ask if there was still time for "just one more revision", and since we'd planned this book well in advance, there was always more time—or so I thought.

Mark didn't use e-mail regularly, so he usually had his friend Rhonda Rade post messages for him (thanks, Rhonda!), and I'd e-mail notes back for Rhonda to pass on to him. She also sent me the various digital versions of his presumably completed manuscript. The last e-mail I got was the *FINAL* "final" version on May 16, 2011, just three days after the *previous* "final" manuscript; this one was titled *"Final Wonder Years May 16 please delete all others"*. I also received one last Priority Mail envelope from Mark, sent on May 11, 2011 containing his suggestions for some illustrations to run with the text.

Knowing this book wasn't due on press for several months (and figuring I'd get at least one more "final" version, knowing what a perfectionist Mark was),

EXPANDED BOOK-PROPOSAL!
John—this is so that you can see how the project is shaping up.

"FANTASTIC FOUR--THE WONDER YEARS"
A Book proposal for TwoMorrows Publishing
By Mark Alexander
ROUGH DRAFT #2 (11-29-09)
PLEASE DESTROY THE PREVIOUS COPY

R.E: BIG NEWS FROM STAN LEE!

I put it all aside for more pressing deadlines, and finished prepping for the 2011 Comic-Con International in San Diego, California. The theme this year was the FF's 40th Anniversary, and the con folks had asked me to contribute something for their Program Book. I immediately thought of *this* book, and they were delighted to run an excerpt from it, which Mark put together back in April 2011 from one of his "not quite final" final manuscripts.

I headed off to Comic-Con last July, and made sure to snag a few extra copies of the Program Book to send to Mark, so he could see his work there. But the week after the Con, while vacationing with my family in Los Angeles, his sister, Cheryl Urbanczyk, sent me an e-mail with the shocking news: Mark had died on June 30, a month prior. He'd had a heart attack and been in a coma for a week before he passed away.

I don't know if Mark somehow knew his time was near, but in the month between this last "final" manuscript and his passing, I didn't get any more updates, so I know he must've been pretty happy with it. And now, knowing it will see print after his passing, this manuscript feels as rare and valuable to me as an early *FF* page, and I wanted to treat it with the utmost respect.

Cheryl reiterated what I already knew—that Mark was immensely proud of this book, and very excited for it to see print. So despite my original plan to present it at our usual tabloid size, I decided to hark back to the first 30 issues of *TJKC* when Mark was a regular contributor, and revert to our old size. It just felt right.

We discussed this book back and forth through the many revisions, and I pointed out some errors that he corrected. While I don't agree with all his conclusions, I think it's a pretty amazing look at the Lee/Kirby collaboration—where they came from, how they worked together during those years, and how they affected us all.

So here's to you, buddy. Thanks for all you've done for this publication, and Kirby fandom, over the years. Rest well, and say "hey" to Jack and Roz for us all. ★

by Mark Alexander

he Wonder Years was a hit TV series from the 1980s about a young boy's coming of age in the 1960s. The undercurrent of this unerringly accurate portrayal of life in the American suburbs was the disembodied voice of its narrator, the lead character's adult personification.

More than anything, *The Wonder Years* is about the baby-boomer narrator's attempt to make sense of his childhood memories. His conclusion is that no mater how terrifying and anxiety ridden his childhood had been, it wasn't so bad compared to his present incarnation. He's grown up to be a smart-ass, self-conscious observer who can only make wisecracks about the human experience instead of partaking in it as he'd done in his youth.

Isn't this how most of us, to some extent, usually end up?

The incomprehensible slide from the virtues of our Wonder Years to our present confusion of national identity partly stems from our current lack of worthy heroes, either fictional or flesh and blood. Today's kids have no Neil Armstrong, no John Lennon, and no Martin Luther King. For that matter, are there any 21st century comic book heroes equal to Captain America or Reed Richards?

Superheroes were originally created to reflect the best in all of us. But today's comic books are full of snarling, violence-crazed anti-heroes with dubious moral codes. The women have exploding muscles and basketball size breasts. The men look like angry steroid cases. Such characters are dangerously narrow symbols of heroism. They are a reflection of our nightmares more than our dreams.

This is a tale of four superheroes from a bygone era when heroes were noble and incorruptible. It's about the two pop-culture visionaries who created them, and a decade that was more tumultuous

AT A GLANCE
FF #1-102

INTRODUCTION:

Throughout this book, we've inserted **AT A GLANCE** sections, offering overviews of *Fantastic Four* #1-102. Critical analysis and strong opinions are an essential response to any art. But unlike traditional literature, where a huge body of example and theory have set forth the modes of criticism, the critique of a large comic book omnibus has had few guidelines. Still, the essence of any type of literary appraisal remains the same: The reviewer carefully studies the material in question, ponders its aesthetic qualities, and offers his humble judgment.

In trying to define the styles and principals of our subject matter, we've attempted to add a little structure by dividing things up into somewhat arbitrary categories. The Lee/Kirby *Fantastic Four* cannon can be discerned, with hindsight, as a series of roughly classifiable periods interspersed with hiatuses of consolidation and/or hesitancy. For the comprehensive survey of issues #1 through #102 which forms the **AT A GLANCE** segments of this book, these periods will be addressed generally as follows:

FF #1-6 will be called *The Age of Innovation;* scattershot innovation to be specific. Issues #7-20 and *FF Annual* #1 will be called *The Ayers Age,* knowing full well there's a Ditko-delineated issue in that group. *FF* #21-27 will be noted as *The Roussos Period,* and *FF* #28-38 and *FF*

Annual #2 will be labeled *The Stone Age* with no attempt at witticism.

FF #39-43 and *FF Annual* #3, the period that bridges the Kirby/Stone era of cartoon art to the Kirby/Sinnott era of "cosmic" art, will be called *The Transitory Period* because it was the gap between two major phases. The series was virtually reborn after *FF* #43.

The debut of Gorgon began *The Cosmic Era*, spanning *FF* #44-67 along with *FF Annuals* #4 and #5. This was the apotheosis, the Gilded Age when the magazine reached its stunning apex.

Somewhere around *FF* #68, after Kirby got fed up with Lee changing his plots, Jack began incorporating simpler storylines and more straight-ahead battle scenes. As a result, *The Age of Inertia* began.

Finally, beginning with *FF* #95, there's *The Age of Decline*, a period of lassitude and resignation that set in after the art devolved and the mandate of "no more continued stories" was issued.

It's not the intent of this publication to suggest that these "periods" are carved-in-stone epochs or that others should adhere to them. This is merely one way to see the development of *Fantastic Four* down through the years. It's easier to address the overall body of work by these divisions.

Numerous other comic book writers have dealt with this subject matter in much more solemn terms; as sociology or subculture, mythopoeia or High Art. The **AT A GLANCE** segments treat the Lee/Kirby *FF* cannon like a series of record reviews, but without the 5-star rating system. Personal prejudices were inescapably left in because as much as anything, this is a bittersweet backward glance at the idyllic landscapes of the author's suburban childhood.

Above all, these sections are an effort to analyze the most crucial elements of each new stage as *Fantastic Four* developed—to convey the different flavors of different phases, how they felt, the ways in which they changed, grew more complex, diversified, and the ways in which they remained the same; the same yet never, ever, dull.

That comforting core of changelessness has always been the key to *Fantastic Four's* longevity.

and awe-inspiring than any before or since.

It's about a time unlike any other, a time of signs and wonders. If you were a kid who loved superheroes, it was the best time there's ever been.

For many baby boomers, the 1960s were the Wonder Years, the Marvel Years. It was a luxurious time when life was marked by suburban ease and middle-class optimism. Most young kids in the suburbs weren't overly concerned with campus riots, overpopulation, urban decay, racial unrest or destructive industrialism. Such things were a mere curiosity; a sideshow of fragmentary black-and-white images that flickered from Walter Cronkite's evening news report.

This was a world where no drudgery existed and summer vacation seemed to last forever. Those were the most peaceful summers imaginable. No school, no work, no bills and no taxes. Imagine yourself on a beautiful clean summer morning with a Technicolor sunrise under the blue suburban skies of the 1960s. Picture yourself perched beneath a huge willow tree in the cool and musty recesses of its deep shade. There you lie, contentedly reading a Lee/Kirby *Fantastic Four,* filled with wonders you hadn't dared to dream existed.

Lying in that shade, you were inviolate. Nothing could reach you, nothing could touch you. Those old Marvel comics offered both privacy and escape. They were like a refuge, an atmosphere so calm and cosseted that reading them was like stepping back into the womb. As long as you stayed inside you felt safe from all catastrophe. It was an insulated childhood fantasy and it went beyond anything that can be described in words.

Nothing will ever be that simple or that good again.

The ancient Romans had a saying: "May you be blessed enough to live in exciting times." The 1960s were truly exciting times. They were The Wonder Years, the Lee/Kirby years, the last decade of optimism in superhero comics.

Time can't wreck the perfection of those old *Fantastic Four* comic books. They were flawless, incomparable, and full of The Right Stuff.

Those comics went straight to the heart of everything.

(above) Cover and splash from Astonishing *#56 (Dec. 1956), Kirby's first job after returning to Timely/Marvel.*

IRONY (A PROLOGUE)

If there was a secret to his greatness, it was probably rage.

In the Lower East Side of New York, you needed anger to survive. You needed even more to transcend. Jack Kirby's fury might have come from his childhood, or even from some previous incarnation, some past life. It wasn't important. What mattered was the energy he drew from it.

The King of all comic book artists was a short, cantankerous man who rose from the Lower East Side of Manhattan, one of the toughest and most overcrowded neighborhoods America has ever produced. The millions of immigrants who poured through Ellis Island at the turn of the last century and filled the Lower East Side, Kirby's parents among them, endured some of the most abject conditions that overpopulation and neglect had ever contrived anywhere.

At that time the Lower East Side was the densest neighborhood on Earth, the densest in history—half a million people in a square mile, with anywhere from 1,500 to 1,800 people crammed into a single block.

The young Jacob Kurtzberg, as he was then known, came of age during the Great Depression when the idea of making a living as an artist was an unrealistic and impractical notion. Fighting bullies, rival gang members and anti-Semites all through his formative years made him tough, temperamental and full of fury. He eventually channeled his rage into the most powerful action art anyone had ever seen. When we see superhero art today, no matter who rendered it, we're looking at some variant of Jack Kirby's anger: teeth-gnashing, forward-thrusting characters, brutal punches and bodies hurtling through space. From any angle, it all channels back to one man.

Stan Lee, the son of two Jewish-Romanian immigrants, grew up wanting to write The Great American Novel. All his life he was agonizingly sensitive, desperate for approval and easily influenced by others. Fresh out of high school, he lucked into a cush, well-paying job in a relative's magazine firm—just until he could launch a career as a "serious" writer, he told himself.

By 1940, both Lee and Kirby were working for Martin Goodman's Timely Comics where Stan prospered and quickly moved up the corporate ladder. Kirby, on the other hand, managed to get himself fired in less than two years. Shortly thereafter, when America entered World War II, both Jack and Stan patriotically volunteered for the Army.

There is no greater analogy to underscore the contrasting fortunes of these two men than their wartime experiences. When Stan told his commanding officer he worked in the comic book industry, Lee was assigned to draw cartoon training manuals and venereal disease awareness posters. When Kirby mentioned that he had drawn *Captain America* prior to the war, his C.O. ordered him to become an advance scout, and draw reconnaissance maps detailing German artillery points. It was one of the most dangerous jobs in the military.

So instead of drawing posters, Kirby dodged bullets and almost had his feet amputated as a result of hypothermia. Lee on the other hand remained stateside the entire war, and supplemented his military paycheck by writing for Goodman through the mail. At one point Stan was arrested and jailed for breaking into the mailroom to procure a writing assignment. Lee was facing court martial and prison time in Leavenworth, but in the end the eternally lucky Stan Lee was freed with no consequences.

After the war Kirby continued to battle his way through the comic book industry, creating new genres and pissing off publishers. Out of necessity, sixteen years after being fired by Martin Goodman, Kirby had to swallow his pride and ask Stan if he could come back and work for him. At this point Timely Comics (now called "Atlas") was teetering on the cusp of insolvency, and Goodman was ready to jump ship at the next sign of trouble.

This is when irony reared its absurd head.

Lee and Kirby both had proletarian Jewish backgrounds. They were both fast, indefatigable workers who could produce stories of remarkable quality and quantity without ever missing a deadline. Other than that, they were diametrically opposite in every possible way. Fate brought them together because Lee was about the only editor who would hire Kirby, and Jack was about the only good artist Stan could afford. They joined forces at midlife, at the nadirs of their careers, and against all odds their contrasting personalities and talents coalesced—creating a synergy that eventually made the comic book medium

(this page) Lee (top) and Kirby in their WWII uniforms, early 1940s.

a force to be reckoned with.

Had it not been for these two iconoclastic mavericks, it's entirely possible that superhero comics would never have budged an inch from the rancid cesspool of the DC-dominated early 1960s; in which case they would be extinct, or only exist as an endangered subspecies of children's entertainment. Kirby and Lee carved out a whole new world for comic book fans. A world that was startling, overwhelming and vivid with life—a world that seemed perfectly tailored to the taste of young readers in the Silver Age of comics.

Kirby's violent ghetto-bred anger and Lee's self-mocking charm were the bed in which the Marvel Universe was conceived. And from day one, Reed Richards and Sue Storm were the Adam and Eve of that Universe.

The Fantastic Four made everything that came before them seem redundant. Their impact was prodigious. They were more complicated, more neurotic, and in every way more interesting than anything comics previously had to offer. They startled the entire industry into a whole new perspective on superheroes. They caused infinite changes and opened new vistas that had been closed by narrow-minded corporate editors with marginal imaginations. They were the sun, the center, the nucleus of the Marvel Universe. Everything ebbed and flowed around them.

The 1960s *Fantastic Four* was the most consistently satisfying superhero series in the history of comic books. For nearly a decade it offered unwaveringly solid craftsmanship juxtaposed with the boldest experiments readers had ever seen. No comic series before or since has changed the *status quo* so much, so fast, so thoroughly and with such style. There may come a time when future comic book creators equal or surpass the majesty of the Lee/Kirby *FF*, but at the time of this writing, it has yet to happen.

Mister Fantastic, the Invisible Girl, the Thing and the Human Torch were the four cornerstones; the foundation on which The House of Ideas was built. They rose above what comic book heroes had been, and dictated what comic book heroes would become. Above all other superheroes they defined their times and epitomized their era.

This is their story.

Kirby recaptures the old days of working with Lee, in this pencil art detail from What If? *#11 (Oct. 1978).*

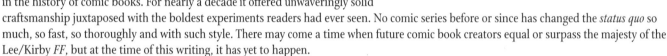

A 1965 distributor's flyer, used to convince newsdealers to carry the Marvel line. With an estimated 32 million copies waiting to be sold, it didn't take much convincing.

THE KNOCKOFF CHAMPION

No one Never accused Martin Goodman of moderation.

From the time he first entered the publishing business in 1931 until he retired in 1975, Marvel's seminal publisher was known for two things: replicating other companies' successful ideas and indiscriminate binge-and-purge marketing strategies.

He certainly isn't an easy character to unravel. His ex-employees describe him as a soft-spoken pleasant looking man of medium height with finely chiseled features and prematurely white hair. He was a dapper dresser who wore wire-rimmed glasses and favored Ivy League bowties. For the most part, Goodman distanced himself from his lower level staff but treated them with polite cordiality. Among the writers who worked for him, he had a reputation for imposing very few editorial controls.

As a publisher Goodman had limited imagination. He didn't plan years ahead and he didn't bother too much about innovation or progression. But he made money, and for the most part he avoided mistakes.

It's been rumored that Goodman never continued in school past the fourth grade, yet he was a remarkably adroit businessman with an uncanny knack for predicting what the public would buy on the newsstand. One of the few things that Stan Lee and Jack Kirby agreed on in their later years was that Martin had a penchant for reneging on deals and promises in the business arena. Be that as it may, Goodman was just as important to the birth of the Fantastic Four as Jack or Stan.

Born in 1908, Martin Goodman was younger than most of the leading publishers of his era—fifteen years younger than DC comic's founder Harry Donenfeld and eight years younger than DC's co-founder Jack Liebowitz. Jack and Harry entered the publishing business in 1932. By 1944, Liebowitz had orchestrated the merger of several Donenfeld-owned publishing, distribution and licensing companies into a single corporate entity called National Periodical Publications. Two of the operations housed by National Publications were Independent News (IND.) and DC Comics, both of which were presided over by Jack Liebowitz. The young Martin Goodman would find Liebowitz to be a tough competitor.

Indeed, it was a tough business. When Donenfeld and Liebowitz were coming up in the world, there was a blood-splattering newsstand circulation war in progress between the monopolistic American News Company and newspaper tycoon William Randolph Hearst. American News Company (ANC) was a mob-connected distribution arm that would one day play a major role in the story of Marvel Comics.

With its outright ownership of countless newsstands across America, ANC had a virtual stranglehold on the circulation of every major newspaper and magazine in the country. The Hearst/ANC rivalry involved hiring mobsters and hit-men who engaged in fire-bombing, beating, and killing rival news dealers. Between 1912 and 1913, twenty-seven newsstand owners were murdered in Chicago alone, with many more wounded.

The circulation war's worst bloodshed occurred when future DC mogul Jack Liebowitz was a young man. Unlike his partner Harry Donenfeld, who in his youth enjoyed hanging out with gangsters, Liebowitz preferred to steer clear of the mob. But he soon realized he'd have to cooperate with such men in order to survive in the cut-throat business of publishing.

As it turned out, Martin Goodman was a survivor too. He'd learned the art of self-preservation during the Depression, the era of Great Hopelessness. When the Wall Street Crash of 1929 short-circuited the U.S. economy, Goodman became a drifter; bumming around the country, living in hobo camps and cooking over blazing campfires. Where Donenfeld and Liebowitz had fought their way up in the capitalist jungle, Goodman had battled his way up from the hobo jungles; up from the drifters, the dregs, the human flotsam and jetsam.

Goodman's knack for survival would serve him well during his forty-year rivalry with DC's Jack Liebowitz. It's a testament to Liebowitz's business savvy that Goodman's Marvel Comics were never in first place until Liebowitz had stepped down from the DC hierarchy. Jack wasn't about to give Martin the satisfaction of outmaneuvering him.

But the story's getting ahead of itself:

(clockwise from top left) Liebowitz, Donenfeld, and Martin Goodman.

In 1932, Goodman borrowed some capital and formed Western Fiction Publishing, a company which specialized in pulp magazines featuring nostalgic tales of the old West. In May 1933, Martin's first pulp publication *Western Supernovel Magazine* hit the stands. When it became a success, Goodman began to show early signs of a suck-and-run marketing mentality, flooding the newsstands with numerous Western titles until public interest waned. Goodman's often-quoted motto was, "If you get a title that catches on, and then add a few more, you're in for a nice profit." True enough, but Martin's sell-and-switch approach was a bad long-term strategy. By jumping from one hot trend to another and exploiting its commercial potential to exhaustion, a publisher can't develop a distinct identity and cultivate a market of loyal, regular readers.

In 1939, right after Donenfeld and Liebowitz had a huge hit with Superman, Goodman decided to add comic books to his publishing line. To achieve this, he enlisted the services of Funnies, Inc., a firm that created comics for publishers who didn't have their own in-house staffs.

The first comic that Goodman and Funnies, Inc. put together was a mixed bag anthology called *Marvel Comics* #1 (Oct. 1939). Its first printing sold 80,000 copies, and a second printing in November 1939 sold another 80,000 units. After that, Goodman was in the comics business in a big way.

The two most historically important characters featured in *Marvel Comics* #1 were Carl Burgos' Human Torch, and the Sub-Mariner, who was created by a struggling, hard drinking Irishman named Bill Everett. The dichotomy of Prince Namor and the Torch was a peculiar paradox. They were the oddest of icons, the least heroic heroes imaginable.

On the cover of *Marvel Comics* #1 (right), the Human Torch looks ugly, repulsive and menacing. He was an android who burst into flame, escaped his maker, then ran amok, spreading terror throughout the countryside.

The Sub-Mariner was arrogant, obtuse and anti-social. He was a troubled rebel with a short temper and a bad attitude and he despised the human race for polluting the ocean. He waged war against the air-breathers more than once, flooding entire cities in the process.

The Torch and Sub-Mariner's early adventures were a marriage of insane violence and sociopathic alienation. These two were both unstable beings, complete misfits. They were astoundingly different from any superheroes on the current scene, and they represented the first blurring of good and evil in superhero comics.

Now that Goodman was producing comics, he chose the name Timely Publications for his comic book line. Timely was located on the west side of Manhattan at 330 West 42nd Street in what was then the McGraw-Hill building, a thirty-three story skyscraper layered with swatches of blue-green terra cotta. The offices were businesslike and unassuming, consisting of six rooms: A small waiting room, a business and bookkeeping room, two editorial rooms, and the staff office. The staff office was a tiny, crowed room with a single window

The murderous phantoms were made out of the tail of the comet— and they'd finally abduct every one of Earth's lovely daughters!

Kirby drew numerous illustrations like this for Goodman's line of pulp magazines in the late 1930s.

where the Timely artists sat at their art boards drawing, inking and lettering comic book pages.

Goodman had a large, comfortable office that contained a swivel chair padded with three cushions, a desk from which he ate his lunch (usually crackers and milk) and a sofa where he took his daily nap. Martin's regular naps were a source of amusement to his staff. Stan Lee felt they proved Goodman wasn't as motivated as he should have been.

In the beginning Timely Publications could aptly be described as a teeming nest of nepotism. Part of Goodman's staff included his three brothers. There was Artie Goodman who did color guides for the comics, Abe Goodman the bookkeeper, and Dave Goodman whose job was taking pictures of scantily-clad models for the company's men's magazines.

Another relative was the much disliked Robert Solomon, a business manager and self-appointed story critic whose main function was to run interference for Martin when he was too busy to deal with people. "Robby" was Martin Goodman's brother-in-law. He was also Stan Lee's Uncle, and he would soon be Stan's ticket into the comic book industry.

While *Marvel Comics* #1 had shown solid numbers on the newsstand, Goodman's efforts to follow it up bombed. Joe Simon, a tall middle-class kid from Syracuse, had been lured away from Funnies, Inc. in late 1939 by Goodman for a five-dollar pay raise. Martin told Simon he needed a new action hero strip and he needed it fast. Joe responded with a jingoistic superhero who looked a lot like another red white and blue comic hero called the Shield. Simon originally called the character "Super American" but quickly decided that "Captain America" would be better. To produce Cap's first issue, Simon enlisted the aid of his pal from the Victor Fox studio, a promising 22 year-old comic book artist from the Lower East Side named Jack Kirby.

Kirby was the first illustrator to realize that in order to create truly exciting superheroes, the artist has to transcend the limitations of realistic human anatomy. Kirby deconstructed the human form, then reassembled it in totally new aesthetic proportions. His action heroes defied all known laws of physics. Their bodies carved endless arabesques in space as they jackknifed, corkscrewed, twisted and turned in impossible contortions. It was the most kinetic, action-packed comic book art anyone had ever seen.

Jack and Joe's first *Captain America* comic (below) was pretty much a fifty-fifty effort. Simon contributed to the plot and the cover design, as well as the inking and lettering. But the energetic figures throughout the story were pure Kirby. After Cap's seven-page origin, the book becomes a high-speed thrill ride with the brakes off. Cap and Bucky pounded their enemies senseless; their high-velocity

 punches hit like artillery shells and sent the bad guys hurtling through space. A Captain America uppercut would launch a Nazi right through the panel borders clear into the next page. It was panel after panel of pounding fists, whizzing bullets, smashed walls, broken glass and Kirby-debris flying everywhere. No one had ever seen power of this magnitude on a comic book page. It was acrobatic action executed with the savage

Simon & Kirby drew this sketch for a young Larry Lieber, during a 1940s visit to the Timely offices with his older brother Stanley Lieber (Stan Lee).

abandon of a barroom brawl, and it instantly changed the way every superhero artist in the business approached his craft.

This was the way to draw action heroes.

Martin wanted to buy Captain America outright, but Simon wasn't that green. He knew he had a red white and blue goldmine on his hands, and there were buyers out there with deeper pockets than Goodman. So Joe and Martin sat down and hammered out a real sweetheart of a deal. Instead of being buried in a Marvel anthology comic, Cap would get his own book. Simon and Kirby would get twenty-five percent of the take (which they would split 15/10 in Simon's favor), and Martin would hire them as his editor and art director.

The deal that Simon and Kirby made with Goodman was big news in the comics industry. It was even bigger news when *Captain America* #1 (March 1941) sold out in days, and the next print run was set at over a million copies. By the end of all this, one thing was clear: Simon and Kirby had arrived.

Soon, Jack and Joe were so busy cranking out Goodman's comics that they needed an assistant. So toward the end of 1940, Robert Solomon brought in his nephew Stan Lee, who was also the first cousin of Jean Goodman, Martin's wife.

For the princely sum of eight-dollars a week, Lee would fetch coffee, proofread, handle the mail and erase pencil lines from Kirby's art after it was inked. Young Stan also had a tendency to horse around. He would climb onto file cabinets, slam doors and play "Yankee Doodle" on his ocarina until Simon and Kirby threw things at him. Jack hated the fact that Lee could goof off all he wanted because he was related to the boss.

Despite their occasional differences, Jack, Joe and Stan all loved working on the hugely successful *Captain America* series. With the patriotic Captain America, Martin finally found the bigger-than-big

Kirby drew this illustration to accompany an early text piece by Stan in All-Winners #2 (Fall 1942).

Fantastic Four inker Frank Giacoia. Because Martin lacked anyone with more experience, Stan became Timely's new editor.

The job, Goodman told him, was temporary.

Meanwhile, Timely Comics sailed through the war years enjoying record prosperity. America loved Goodman's new breed of heroes and anti-heroes. One often overlooked innovation of Timely's "Big Three" is that they were the first comic book stars to take a political stand. The cover of *Captain America* #1 depicted Cap smashing Hitler's face. The Torch burned Germany's air force, and Sub-Mariner single-handedly sank the Japanese fleet. After America entered World War II, *Captain America* sold nearly one million copies per issue. War was good business.

Goodman soon became the most prolific comic book publisher in the industry. But that isn't to say he was the most original. Anytime another publisher had a comic that was selling well, Martin would immediately tell his staff to produce a reasonable facsimile—a "knockoff" version.

During the war Timely Comics was characterized by a wide spectrum of genres. Beginning in April 1942, Goodman branched out into humor with *Comedy Comics* and *Joker Comics*. Then Timely produced a floodtide of funny animal comics that sold almost as well as the superhero books. Teenage girl books like *Patsy Walker*, *Millie the Model* and *Nellie the Nurse* soon followed. Eventually crime comics and romance titles appeared, along with horror books. With *Two-Gun Kid* in 1948, Goodman had come full circle, returning to the Western settings of his first pulps.

By now Timely Comics had morphed into Marvel Comics, a name that wouldn't last very long the first time around. The company's address had changed as well. During World War II, while Stan was busy drawing V.D. awareness posters, Timely moved from West 42nd Street and set up operations in the Empire State Building. One might speculate that Goodman's luxurious new surroundings were funded by Simon and Kirby's *Captain America.*

Tastes were changing in the postwar era, and Timely's superhero comics began to wane. While a fickle comic-buying public was busy reading about monsters, cowboys and funny animals, Goodman's oddly unique superheroes began to lumber into obscurity. By the end of the decade they had all faded away. *Captain America* had somehow become *Captain America's Weird Tales*, a horror mag where Cap himself was nowhere to be found.

As the 1940s ran down, Martin Goodman's comic book line seemed increasingly barren. With the new decade just up ahead, new characters would come up to replace Cap, Namor and the Torch, but they weren't in the same class. And so the final curtain closed on Timely's Big Three. They seemed to have vanished with the same suddenness from which they emerged; blown away like chaff, scattered to the winds.

superhero he'd been looking for—one who could hold his own in the marketplace against Batman, and even Superman. It probably never dawned on him that patriotism has a way of going out of vogue in peace time.

Cap's creators were going out of vogue as well—at Timely anyway. That sweetheart deal they made with Goodman went south after only ten issues of *Captain America.* One of Goodman's accountants, Morris Coyne, told Simon that Goodman was screwing them on their twenty-five percent royalty by piling most of Timely's overhead on *Captain America.* Goodman claimed that Simon trumped up the whole conflict so he could cut a better deal with Jack Liebowitz at DC.

There may be some justification for Martin's allegation because Simon and Kirby were in fact moonlighting for Liebowitz behind Goodman's back. Simon and Kirby eventually let Stan in on their secret, and shortly thereafter Martin confronted Jack and Joe with the issue. When the duo admitted to their clandestine activities, Goodman fired them.

Despite Joe Simon's belief that someone at National tipped Goodman off, Kirby held a lifelong notion that Stan had ratted them out for personal gain. In Joe's version of the story, Kirby told Simon: "The next time I see that little s.o.b., I'm gonna kill him." But he didn't. Instead, Jack and Joe moved on to the beckoning horizons of DC Comics where Jack Liebowitz had promised to double their pay and promote them heavily in the DC house ads: "*These boys are really good*!" he wrote.

Soon after Simon and Kirby's departure from Timely at the end of 1941, Chesler shop veteran Syd Shores became the company's unofficial art director, and young Stan took over Joe Simon's former office where he began writing *Captain America* and other superhero tales like *Jack Frost*, which was occasionally drawn by future

While Stan stayed behind at Timely, Kirby (with Simon) found even greater success with the Boy Commandos and others at National (DC) Comics.

WINDS OF CHANGE: THE 1950s

Winds of change were blowing through the comics industry during the Eisenhower years. But the warm gentle breezes from the beginning of the decade would stand in stark contrast to the cold turbulent gusts at the era's end.

However, in the first weeks of 1950, the era's end was a long way away. And it was probably the last thing anyone would be thinking about if they were sitting in Longchamps, the ground floor restaurant of the Empire State Building, knocking back cocktails with the likes of Bill Everett and Carl Burgos, both of whom worked for Timely Comics and both of whom were Longchamps regulars.

The conversation in the restaurant would often center on the reoccurring rumors about dismissals and restructuring, and the considerable melodrama that a female inker named Valerie Barclay had caused among the staff artists a few months back.

Departing from Longchamps, an elevator ride to the building's fourteenth story would lead to Martin Goodman's publishing operation which took up half of the entire floor and encompassed several rooms. Suite 1401 was a large room called "the Bullpen"—so named for its occupants' love of baseball—with Stan Lee's office up front, near two female proofreaders. Goodman's nearby office was inevitably bigger than Stan's, with a chaise lounge in the corner near the windows. The view from Martin's office was a breathtaking panorama of the Manhattan skyline.

In the Bullpen quarters, cranking out comic art from 9-to-5 at a furious rate, one might see the soft-spoken, constantly smoking Bullpen supervisor Syd Shores, along with artists Mike Sekowsky, Dan DeCarlo, Joe Maneely, Don Rico, Stan Goldberg, Carl Burgos and Gene Colan. But not Bill Everett, who preferred to work at home and never joined the Timely staff. Come noon, the boys would sit around eating brown-bag lunches and playing poker until Shores called them back to their drawing boards.

But not everyone paid attention to Syd Shores. At one point writer/artist Don Rico led an in-house "rebellion" against Shores. For this and various other Rico-related Bullpen problems, Martin Goodman would forever refer to the artist as "Rat Rico."

Another Bullpen artist who Goodman viewed as a troublemaker was the transcendentally beautiful Valerie "Violet" Barclay, an inker who'd studied under Timely artist Dave Gantz. Gantz was a Bronx native who was born the same month and year as Stan Lee. He would soon regret taking the tempestuous ex-hostess under his wing.

Unsurprisingly, once Barclay was entrenched in the Timely Bullpen, she began causing considerable friction among the male staff—particularly between artist Mike Sekowsky and future *Fantastic Four* inker George Klein, both of whom found her irresistible. Violet soon decided that the $35 a week Goodman was paying her wasn't worth the drama. In mid-1949 she left Timely to become a fashion model. After that, the only girl in the throng would be the amiable Marie Severin, who on any given summer afternoon might be seen yelling at Artie Simek, for the umpteenth time, to shut up about the damn New York Yankees.

In late 1949, the Bullpen artists began hearing rumors that the axe was about to drop. Exactly how this all came about is unquestionably vague. The dismantling of the Timely Bullpen is probably the murkiest period in the company's history.

The official reason for the firing of the company's full-time

As the 1950s marched on, Stan found himself in charge of a line of less than original titles.

13

artists was an inventory surplus. Some historians claim this is the sugar-coated version, and the real reason was a tax-maneuver. Others claim that Goodman's decision to dismiss his staff of artists was designed to help fund his own national distribution organization.

Here are the differing viewpoints: Most of the Bullpen artists were on salary, but sometime in late 1949, Goodman's attorney's informed him that due to a recent change in New York State employment laws, it would be more lucrative to have his salaried employees put on outworker status.

Goodman, who avoided confrontation like the plague, left it to Stan to fire the Bullpen. From this point on, the comfortable days of the salaried artist were over. Goodman's comics would hereafter be done almost exclusively by freelancers. Only production assistants and editors would be kept on staff. According to Gene Colan, "They felt they could save some money by not having a staff of artists, but there was still lots of freelance work there—I picked up plenty, and I know the other guys did too."

Another version of the unpleasant episode goes like this: Over the years Stan had amassed an entire closet full of unused art and scripts that had been paid for, but weren't scheduled for release. During this stage Lee had a habit of playing fast and loose with Goodman's money, often buying inventory he didn't need, especially if he had an artist who needed work. According to several Timely artists, anytime Stan got a story he was unhappy with, he would simply pay for it and throw it in the closet.

The practice of keeping finished art on hand for emergencies was a good way to keep from getting behind schedule. In the rare event that an artist couldn't meet a deadline, Stan could pull a story from his back-up pile. But somewhere along the way it grew out of control and kept piling up; thousands of dollars worth of completed stories with no release dates, collecting dust. When Goodman learned of Stan's excess inventory, he was furious. He informed Stan that the surplus would mean more layoffs.

In an exclusive correspondence, comics historian Dr. Michael J. Vassallo reflected on the situation: "Artists who I have interviewed from that time period do remember the story about there being too much inventory building up. A close study of the actual books being published at the time, and what features appeared in 1950, do show a real mess where features were shoved into books where they didn't belong, giving the feeling that inventory was being used up. My guess is that the dismissal of the Bullpen could be a combination of both facts. Leon Lazarus, an editor at Timely in 1948-1950, recalled the same inventory story. The answer could be that Goodman made the decision after learning about the law change and finding all the inventory. He could have decided it would save him money all around."

One of Stan's most unpleasant memories from that era is the day when Goodman found the inventory glut. Lee remembered it like this: "When Martin learned of all the material I had been accumulating for later use, he took an extremely dim view of what I had done. In fact, a dim view is putting it mildly. For starters, he told me that he was running a business, and not a charity operation."

Goodman wasn't running a charity operation, but he *was* planning to run a distribution operation. Goodman's original distribution arm had been Kable News, but at the dawn of the 1950s, with comic book production at an all-time high, Martin wanted to move into self-distribution.

Goodman had long been fascinated with the distribution

process and he displayed a considerable flair for it. He was keen to examine behind-the-scenes reports and rumors about which books were hot. He also loved the guessing game of trying to predict The Next Big Thing. Having his own distribution chain would enable him to respond more aggressively to sales figures and evolving trends.

The costly self-distribution operation that Goodman envisioned would be funded by a two-pronged cost-cutting strategy. The dismantling of the Bullpen had cut back on office overhead and artist's salaries. In mid-1950, additional capital was saved by moving the Timely offices from the posh Empire State Building to a smaller, less expensive headquarters at 60 Park Avenue near 47th Street.

The Park Avenue address was a new building constructed on the site where the old Hotel Margery had been torn down. Stan's Park Avenue office was notably less lavish than his previous digs. It was a windowless cubbyhole with a small electric fan sitting atop a file cabinet in the corner. A manual typewriter was positioned at the right of Lee's desk, and dozens of books spanning every subject imaginable were piled up all over the room. In this new environment Stan went right on editing, writing, art-directing, designing covers, and dealing with Martin's production department.

Now that production was up and costs were down, Goodman was able to set up his own national distribution system. In December 1951, he launched Atlas News Company which was overseen by Arthur Marchand. By the end of the year, a black-and-white globe bearing the name ATLAS would be seen on all of Goodman's comic books. With the luxury of being his own distributor, Martin Goodman was unchained. He could now flood the market to his heart's content.

And he did. At one point Atlas was publishing a staggering eighty-five separate comic book titles. But they weren't the most original comics the world had ever seen. When Al Harvey had a hit with Casper the Friendly Ghost, Goodman published a Casper knockoff called Homer the Happy Ghost. Archie Comics had Archie Andrews, so Goodman produced Homer Hooper. Newspapers had Dennis the Menace, so Goodman published Melvin the Monster. And Martin's answer to TV's Sgt. Bilko was Sgt. Barker. Goodman used to tell Stan that it was never a good idea to be the first with anything.

And so it went, year after year: Shameless, barefaced plagiarism, relentless in its unoriginality. The only reason Goodman didn't get sued back to the Stone Age was because he avoided stealing from DC Comics with its litigation-happy legal department, and because deep down his rivals knew that *their* characters had also been purloined from older comics and pulps.

Just the same, Goodman took the idea of unoriginality to a whole new level. He made it an art form. Hands down, Martin Goodman was the undisputed knockoff champion.

In 1947, Stan shared his comics knowledge in this self-published booklet.

Abandon Ship

Can any comics-history overview that spans the 1950s skip over the Wertham fiasco? The answer, unfortunately, is no. Although it's doubtful, there may be someone reading this who doesn't know the story—maybe an alien from space.

Dr. Fredric Wertham was a New York psychiatrist who was pissed off at comic books and had been for years. His sensationalist 1954 book *Seduction of the Innocent* almost capsized the comics industry. It claimed that funnybooks were ruining the "mental hygiene" of America's youth and enticing them to commit crimes.

Citing Batman and Robin, Wertham was obsessed with what he called the "fundamental indecency" of a grown man cavorting with a young boy whose costume was apparently designed to exploit his smooth bare legs.

Soon there was a televised McCarthy-like Senate Subcommittee investigation on the evils of the comic book culture. Wertham, whose long bespectacled face and high-pitched Teutonic voice made

Kirby's Mainline books were unfortunately doomed from the outset.

him seem like a comic character himself, went before the cameras and informed America that the protruding breasts on Millie the Model might inspire young girls to stuff their bras with tissue paper (which would undoubtedly trigger the end of civilization as we know it). Another committee member, Richard Clenenden, whined about an issue of *Strange Tales* where "thirteen people die violently."

Publisher Bill Gaines, whose beautifully illustrated cutting-edge E.C. comics were the envy of the entire industry, had been watching Wertham's witch-hunt from the sidelines and had seen enough. Gaines volunteered to testify before the committee to tell his side of the story.

The first generation of comic makers, the Simons, the Kirbys and the Everetts knew that silence would be the best tactic against the crusade. But Gaines was a generation removed from the old guard, and the Angry Young Turk felt inclined to speak his piece. He vowed that he would "fix those bastards" once and for all.

On April 21, 1954, after a two-day speed binge, Gaines made the huge mistake of going up before the Senate Committee in a reduced state of awareness. Although his intentions were good, his plan backfired.

As the Dexedrine and No-Doze wore off, Gaines began to crash on national television. When the Committee started grilling him in earnest, he couldn't find the right words. At one point he opined

Dr. Fredric Wertham

that a comic book cover depicting a severed head was in good taste. It was becoming clear to Bill that he was blowing his chance to fix those bastards. It was becoming even clearer that those bastards were fixing *him*. As he sat in his chair fuming, Gaines could feel himself fading away. Meanwhile, America recoiled in horror. Inevitably, Bill Gaines' testimony did as much harm to the comics industry as Wertham's.

At an apartment in midtown Manhattan, Jack Kirby and Joe Simon observed the insanity on television with their friend and collaborator, comics writer Jack Oleck. Simon watched in disbelief, chiding Gaines and muttering to the TV screen, "Stupid, stupid, stupid." Jack Kirby said nothing.

Simon and Kirby's partnership was one of the causalities of the Wertham witch-burnings. In 1954, faced with dwindling commissions by comic book publishers, Jack and Joe tried forming their own company, Mainline Publications. They soon found the Wertham-era business climate too cold to sustain life. The titles they created like *Bullseye* and *In Love* were formidable enough, but all the major comic book distributors declined to take them on.

According to Simon, "We couldn't get a decent distributor with all the protests going on, and all the parents groups raising hell. Our books weren't being sold. They never even got on the newsstands. Jack and I were pulling our hair out. We couldn't afford to keep producing comics that never got unwrapped, so we had to pull the plug on our company."

Soon it was all over. Wertham's attempt to bring down the comics industry ultimately failed, as it was bound to. Throughout American history, anytime the self-appointed watchdogs of public morality go up against Art, and try to muzzle it, or restrict it, or destroy it, they lose. Wertham was no exception. America soon lost interest in Wertham's maniacal ranting and moved on.

Today the name Fredric Wertham is little more than a source of amusement among older comic book fans. But at the time, the Wertham hysteria almost wiped out a classic American art form. Besides that, it destroyed the careers of hundreds of comic book

Kirby ghosts Johnny Reb and Billy Yank *for his neighbor, Frank Giacoia.*

15

professionals who left the industry forever after the purge of the 1950s. What did it all prove?

The comics medium was still bleeding profusely from the wounds of Werthamism in the late summer of 1956, when a free-lance artist named Frank Giacoia paid Stan a visit. Giacoia had penciled the "Jack Frost" story that Lee wrote for *USA Comics* #3, but he was a slow penciler, and these days he was looking for work as an inker. Stan told Frank that he couldn't help. At this point all of Goodman's artists were inking their own pages.

But Giacoia wasn't going to give up that easily. He told Lee he could bring in a friend who lived near him; a great artist who felt that inking his own pages was drudgery. If this worked out, then Frank might have some inking to do. Stan told Frank to bring his friend on board.

Giacoia's neighbor was Jack Kirby, whose comic book career was presently undergoing a series of ups and downs that seemed to mirror the entire industry. Kirby had dissolved his partnership with Joe Simon after Mainline Publications fell to ruin. Despite the setback, Jack and Joe remained friends. Kirby, now solo, was taking work wherever he could find it, trudging around New York with a portfolio, looking for publishers who needed a fast-on-the-draw comic book man.

Kirby's eventual return to Atlas in 1956 was more a lack of options than a choice. It was somewhat humiliating for Timely's ex-art director and Captain America's co-creator to ask his former office boy for page-rate work. Besides this, Kirby didn't want Martin Goodman to think that all was well after Goodman screwed him on *Captain America*.

None of this was an issue with Stan, who was glad to have him back. Lee gave Jack a few issues of *Yellow Claw* to pencil, and a trickle of other work, but nothing substantial. At this point Stan had another artist he preferred over Kirby, a young man named Joe Maneely. Stan and Joe were working together on a comic strip for the Chicago Sun-Times Syndicate called *Mrs. Lyons' Cubs*, which Lee hoped would be the next *Peanuts*.

In immediate terms, Kirby's 1956 return to Atlas didn't amount to much. He was basically testing the waters. He would soon find better paying work at DC, and he would occasionally ghost on Frank Giacoia's newspaper comic strip *Johnny Reb and Billy Yank*. In September 1958, the King would co-produce his own newspaper strip called *Sky Masters*. As it happened, what little work Kirby was getting from Stan would soon dry up because the axe was about to drop once again.

Throughout the 1950s, Atlas Comics had rolled with the punches, experiencing varying vicissitudes of fortune and famine, booms and busts. But it always managed to survive. The main reason for Goodman's endurance was the fact that Martin had his own distribution company and didn't have to worry about getting his magazines to the marketplace. That all changed one day when Goodman took some bad advice from a business manager named Monroe Froelich.

The ambitious Froelich had been trying to expand his power base in Goodman's company to include some control over distribution. But Atlas-boss Art Marchand was thwarting his attempts to do so. Subsequently, Froelich was determined to shut Atlas News down.

By late 1956, the hard times that beset comics had taken their toll. Publishers were folding in droves, and the number of comics being published dropped from about 650 to 250. At this point Goodman was publishing very few titles, which made it easy for Froelich to convince him that his distribution chain had become a liability. Froelich advised Goodman to dismantle Atlas News and cut a deal with American News Company, America's largest magazine distributor. Stan thought this was a foolhardy move, and he was right.

Despite Stan's misgivings, Goodman shut down Atlas News Company on November 1, 1956 and Froehlich negotiated a five-year contract with American News, the decades-old distributor that had once waged war with William Randolph Hearst. In early 1957, six months after Goodman signed on, American News went belly-up.

ANC had been under investigation by the Justice Department for restraint of trade, running a monopoly and alleged mob connections. On April 25, 1957, ANC's biggest client, George Delacorte,

Kirby splash page from Yellow Claw *#2 (Dec. 1956).*

A Joe Maneely caricature of Stan and he.

*After Mainline folded, Kirby scrounged for work in the late 1950s and found it, at DC (*Showcase #6, *Feb. 1957, below), on* Sky Masters *(above, 12/24/58), and even at Archie Comics (*Adventures of The Fly #1, *Aug. 1959, bottom left).*

announced that he would seek a new distributor for his Dell Comics. Immediately after that, most of ANC's remaining clients like *Newsweek*, *The New Yorker* and *Popular Mechanics* also made a dash for the exit door.

On May 6, 1957, Dell filed a fifteen-million dollar anti-trust lawsuit against ANC, and by May 17th it was all over. American News announced it was closing its Wholesale Periodical Division, leaving many publishers, including Atlas, with no means to distribute their magazines. After that, the Mafia-linked American News vanished into nothingness as suddenly as the Timely superheroes had a decade earlier.

When this happened, Atlas Comics didn't so much fall from grace as plummet. Martin's only option was to run with his tail between his legs to Harry Donenfeld's Independent News and plead with them to distribute his books. The once mighty publisher of eighty-five comic book titles was now a serf to DC's distribution arm and to Jack Liebowitz, who was quite happy to take his money along with his self-esteem.

Liebowitz, whose vision was always more far-ranging than Goodman's, undoubtedly saw the wisdom in being able to control his longtime rival. With the industry in crisis, Independent News wasn't about to let Martin pull any of his flash-flood publishing stunts. Liebowitz put Goodman on a strict regimen of eight comic books a month. It was a needed restraint. Some authors imply that Jack Liebowitz was being vindictive toward his longtime rival by only allowing him eight titles a month. In fact, Liebowitz was looking out for the best interests of the near-moribund comics industry,

MILLIONS OF YEARS AGO, MY PEOPLE WERE WISE AND POWERFUL MEMBERS OF EARTH'S INHABITANTS...WE DEVELOPED THE SCIENCE OF MAGIC TO A DEGREE HIGHER THAN THE HUMANS EVEN DREAM ABOUT... BUT GREED AND STRUGGLE FOR POWER DROVE OUR PEOPLE TOO FAR...LIKE YOUR OWN ATOM BOMBS, OUR MAGIC HAD THE FORCE OF GIANTS!!!

which at that point couldn't support any more titles.

The collapse of Atlas was both immediate and immense. The company, which was now nameless, moved to 655 Madison Avenue and Stan found himself working in a tiny two-office space that Gene Colan described as "a closet." It was a long way down from the Empire State Building both physically and psychologically.

Due to the restrictive new ten-year deal with IND., Goodman's comic book line had to be pruned with brutal rapidity. By late April 1957, Goodman had cut back his number of titles from about sixty to eight. The result was a huge amount of excess inventory. Once again Goodman told Stan no new art would be needed until all the unused inventory had been burned off. He ordered Lee to suspend all work until things picked up again, then he left for a vacation in Florida.

Once again it was up to Stan to tell his artists he had no work for them, and to immediately stop whatever they were working on. "They were in shock, I was in shock" Lee recalled. On April 26, 1957, Stan was telephoning his artists, including Jack Kirby, with the bad news.

Joe Sinnott remembers that day very well: "Stan called me and said 'Joe, Martin Goodman told me to suspend operations because I have all this artwork in house and have to use it up before I can hire you again.' It turned out to be six months in my case."

As John Romita later recalled, "I thought I would never be in comics again. When Stan pulled a western book out from me in the middle of a story, I figured that's it. I never got paid for it, and I told my wife if Stan Lee calls, tell him to go to hell."

Dick Ayers remembered it like this: "That was the real low point. Stan called and said 'this is it, we better just abandon ship.'" Each and every layoff made Stan physically ill. He would forever after call this period "the dark days."

After he returned from Florida, Goodman began flinging multiple genres into the marketplace, hoping that something would stick. Only now there was a lot less to throw. In this period Martin decided to increase the number of titles in his line by juggling sixteen bi-monthly books instead of eight monthlies. Stan's "sweet sixteen," as Atlas aficionados now call them, had widely diverse themes. Lee worked on teenage-girl titles and kiddie fare like *Millie the Model* and *Homer the Happy Ghost*. He produced westerns and war mags like *Wyatt Earp* and *Navy Combat*. There were fantasy anthologies such as *Strange Tales* and *World of Fantasy*, and knockoffs of the Simon/Kirby romance books like *Love Romances* and *My Own Romance*.

Most of these comics were vapid, derivative stuff. They paid the bills and kept Goodman's comic book line solvent, but it was a lead-pipe cinch that *Millie the Model's* back-up feature *My Girl Pearl* wasn't going to set the world on fire, even if she was "America's Darling Dim-Wit."

And so for the next four years Stan Lee toiled in obscurity in a neglected corner of Goodman's Magazine Management firm, presiding over the tattered remnants of Martin's comic book line. Sales of funnybooks had tailed-off and the nameless, bottom-drawer operation that Lee spearheaded seemed like a dying concern. Martin's main income now came from his conventional magazines, most of which featured bad jokes and female flesh. Rumors flew that Goodman was getting out of comics, even selling off the office furniture. Sol Brodsky, Stan's production assistant, recalls that Martin was ready to pack it all in at this point.

Some think the only reason Goodman even bothered to hook up with Independent News for one last, low-budget shot at comics was because he didn't want to fire Stan. Others say it was because he didn't want to tell his wife he fired Cousin Stan. Conversely, another individual who worked at Magazine Management, editor Bruce Jay Friedman, felt that Goodman was keeping Lee around to humiliate him into leaving.

Whatever the case, by the end of the 1950s, Stan must have wondered how a decade that began with so much promise and prosperity could have ended up so inhospitable. Lee felt trapped, grinding out the same four-color dross year after year with no hope of creative satisfaction or greater financial reward. That "temporary" job he'd taken from his cousin-in-law twenty years earlier had taken him over. He'd changed from an energetic whiz-kid editor with a large staff to a worn-out drudge with one secretary who seemed to have less and less to do. At thirty-five, he already felt middle-aged. Lee wanted out, but he had a family to support. Perhaps it would be best to just keep his head down, nose to the grindstone, and settle in for a lifetime of safe mediocrity.

Things only got worse. In June, Stan's premier artist Joe Maneely suffered an untimely death. According to Atlas sources, Maneely lost his glasses the previous week in the city and was hopelessly myopic without them. On the night of

Friday, June 7, 1958, after a bout of drinking with Bill Everett and some other laid-off Timely artists, the nearsighted Maneely was heading home to his young wife and two daughters in New Jersey when he stepped off a moving commuter train and fell between two cars. When Maneely's body was discovered, he was still clutching his art portfolio.

Joe Maneely had been an incredibly gifted cartoonist, able to produce high quality work in any genre at lightning speed. Stan said he could pencil and ink seven pages a day. Maneely was Lee's favorite artist by a long shot, and Joe's death upset him greatly.

But something fateful happened after that. Maneely had been the company's workhorse. Because of his death, there was some penciling work available. In addition to this, Goodman had recently ordered Lee to increase production after a long period of using mostly inventory material. Stan now had steady work to offer.

And steady work was exactly what Jack Kirby needed. Because of a financial dispute over *Sky Masters*, Kirby had become enemies with DC editor Jack Schiff, and he no longer felt welcome at National Publications. Al Harvey, who'd been giving some work to Jack and his ex-partner Joe Simon, was suddenly canceling Harvey Comic's superhero titles to publish kiddie books like *Little Dot*, *Baby Huey* and *Casper the Friendly Ghost*.

After these setbacks, Kirby's life seemed to be running parallel to Stan's. He too was at the rock-bottom of his career. He too felt the comics industry was a sinking ship. And like Lee, he too had a family to feed. To Kirby, comic books had become a trap. Even so, he couldn't leave them behind. He had no other trade.

Now, at age 41, Kirby's prospects were bleak indeed. His glory days with Joe Simon were far behind him and most of the comics industry had pretty much written him off. With all this on his mind, the King swallowed his pride and went back to work for Martin Goodman, who paid some of the lowest rates in the industry.

In the fall of 1958, as the decade rushed to a close, Jack Kirby walked back into Stan Lee's life; undoubtedly assuming that the comic book—the oddest American art form—was nearly finished.

Then the 1960s happened.

(left) Kirby added new life to DC's Green Arrow strip (Adventure Comics #256, Jan. 1959), *and (above) launched Archie's* The Fly *and* Private Strong *(1959).*

THE DAYS OF DR. DROOM

At the close of the 1950s, darkening clouds of uncertainty were gathering over Martin Goodman's New York comic book offices. Promisingly, the great Jack Kirby seemed to have settled in for the long haul, and because sales on *Rawhide Kid* picked up as soon as Kirby took it over, Goodman forestalled dropping the axe on his comic book line—for awhile anyway. There was a second reason that Martin stayed his hand from pulling the plug. He'd been hearing rumblings from DC about a couple of their new titles that were selling particularly well.

Was it possible that superheroes were about to make a comeback?

A lot of kids undoubtedly wondered where all the costumed heroes had disappeared to. The Golden Age superheroes, spawned in the late 1930s and early 1940s, had been drawn with an angular, choppy vigor by idealistic young cartoonists in a time when comics were uncontaminated by self-consciousness and significance. Their crudely drawn, wildly exciting adventures were raw, violent and energetic, reflecting the stress of worldwide upheaval and the gathering storm clouds of World War II.

Back then, colorful characters like the Vision, Captain America, Plastic Man, Captain Marvel and the Human Torch blazed from the newsstands with lurid color and insane variety. Fistfights, explosions and death were their calling cards, and in those early, wild days of comics, moral distinctions were a simple clash of absolutes—good versus evil. If a bad guy needed to be killed, the hero killed him. The only thing taboo was boredom.

But by the mid-1950s, the heart had gone out of the comic book industry. All the brash and violent Golden Age superheroes had vanished. Fredric Wertham and his ilk had issued them a passport to literary limbo. The superheroes who managed to survive the do-gooders campaign became squeaky clean and deeply boring. The newly formed Comics Code Authority effectively castrated the Golden Age heroes, and their tales soon approximated the literary equivalent of Sominex. The exclusion of raw, violent action had rendered superheroes dull and feeble. They were gutted, finished, and in no time they became as dead as the Pharaohs.

The Human Torch returns (briefly) in Young Men *#27 (April 1954, above) and #28 (June 1954, left, his final outing of the revival).*

Granted, DC still published nine superhero books, but six of them starred the handsome, pro-social Superman whose adventures had become increasingly flabby. This was due to the rise of DC's "super family" which included Superboy, Supergirl, and a horrific horde of super-powered pets like Streaky the Super-Cat, Beppo the Super-Monkey, Comet the Super-Horse, and their ringleader, Krypto the Super-Dog. These imbecilic characters, by their very banality, seemed to sum up everything that had gone wrong. It was a truly hideous state of affairs.

With these dire developments came a crucial shift of prominence. Now that superheroes no longer held center stage, many of the writers and artists who created them simply switched gears and kept going, cranking out comics in other genres such as westerns, romance stories and funny animal books.

Martin Goodman had likewise given up on superheroes. In 1953, a brief attempt to resurrect Captain America, Sub-Mariner and the Human Torch had gone straight down the mineshaft. Goodman now instructed Stan to have his small team of freelancers produce eerie tales of monsters and alien invaders. Weird stories like these had flourished in the pre-Wertham years when blood, gore and violence went uncurbed. But with the new Comics Code restrictions, Goodman's late 1950s monster comics seemed to have no flair, no flash, and no fiber. Kids who'd plunked down their dimes hoping to buy a cheap thrill were soon bored enough to return to their homework.

Now it was the summer of 1956. Superheroes had declined into near oblivion, readers were bored and comics sold less. By this point there was hardly anything left. Plagued by the Wertham crusade, a new entertainment alternative called television and a distinct lull in overall creativity, comics seemed to be on an irreversible collision course with extinction.

Then suddenly there was a lone splash of light in the wilderness.

Showcase #4 (Oct. 1956, below), was a breath of fresh air in a moribund comics industry that stank of death and decay. The book's cover, attractively rendered by Carmine Infantino, depicted a film strip uncoiling like a cobra. On the film was a red-clad figure running from frame to frame; running so fast that his sheer velocity hurled him right off the film. *PRESENTING THE FLASH! WHIRLWIND ADVENTURES OF THE FASTEST MAN ALIVE!* cried the cover blurbs. This was the magazine that pulled your hand irresistibly to that squeaky, spinning comic book rack. This was the comic that refused to be left unsold.

Showcase #4's interior delivered what its compelling cover promised. In his origin story the Flash is a police scientist named Barry Allen who becomes endowed with supersonic speed after a freak accident. Being a fan of the Golden Age Flash, Allen takes the name of his hero and designs a bright red costume which ingeniously shoots out of his ring. He then makes the obligatory vow to use his powers to fight crime.

Significantly, the magazine wasn't just a nod to older readers who'd been fans of the original Flash. In the nervous wake of the Comics Code Authority, this

(above and next page) Kirby and Lee team on the Dr. Droom strip in Amazing Adventures #3 *(Aug. 1961).*

new Flash was more cerebral, less violent than his Golden Age predecessor, but his adventures were never dull. He used brains, not brutality to subdue his enemies. In this way he was the first post-modern action hero. More important, he was a trampoline from which superheroes began to bounce back.

Basically, *Showcase* #4 got things moving again. It set the stage for a fresh new approach to costumed crime fighters. Unlike the stodgy and predictable Superman and Batman, who were beginning to seem like faded relics from comic's increasingly irrelevant past, this new Flash had a sleekness and vitality that was entirely of the modern age. He proved that if superheroes were going to make a comeback, they couldn't be brought back with the same violent, boisterous aesthetic of the Golden Age heroes.

Meanwhile, at 655 Madison Avenue, Stan Lee and Jack Kirby seemed to be languishing in a state of creative inertia. During the first two years of their partnership they had been dutifully churning out formulated monster tales; comic book equivalents of 1950s Japanese monster movies. Sales were tepid, and after two years of cranking out monsters by the megaton, Jack and Stan had quite enough. Their fortunes stood at low tide and their monster comics were on a fast track to obscurity. With the coming of the new decade, Lee and Kirby were ready to move Goodman's comics line in a different direction.

Jack and Stan's Distinguished Competition at National had shown the way. DC's new revamped version of the Flash had ushered in the "Silver Age" of comics, and the success of the Scarlet Speedster encouraged DC to take a chance on even more costumed characters.

Another Golden Age stalwart, the Green Lantern, was also revamped and reinstated. Aquaman, who'd been collecting dust in second-feature stories, was soon given his own book as well. And

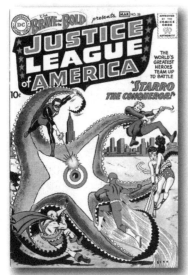

most promising of all was a comic called *The Justice League of America*. The JLA was a new version of the Golden Age Justice Society of America. It corralled all of DC's most popular action heroes into one exciting and overcrowded comic that kids were wild about.

Suddenly, the super-heroes had returned with a roar. Lee and Kirby, still mired in the mediocrity of monster comics, felt the winds of change that were blowing from DC. The only question was how to respond. Now that superheroes were on the rebound, Jack and Stan's options were clear—either create something startling or get off the sinking ship.

Here's what they came up with: An American Doctor named Anthony Droom travels to Tibet to treat an ill lama. Droom is taken to a temple in a remote part of the Himalayan Mountains. Once in the temple, Droom is made to walk barefoot across red-hot coals, and then faces the menace of a "gorlion," part gorilla and part lion. Finally, he meets the aged lama and learns it was all a test to see if he was worthy. Having passed the test, Droom is given the lama's mystical powers and his adventures begin in earnest. "I Am The Fantastic Dr. Droom!" was published in *Amazing Adventures* #1 (June 1961). Lee and Kirby felt this would be a worthy response to the increasingly successful DC superhero revival.

All things considered, they should have stuck with *My Girl Pearl*.

Looking back with fifty years of hindsight, Dr. Droom seems entirely dismissible; an obvious loser. In terms of critical and commercial success, Droom missed the mark by an absurd margin. But that's clear only in view of what came after him. When seen in the context of the times, Dr. Droom's redeeming qualities begin to creep through. First, one must remember this was 1961, and the prevailing belief was that superheroes wore costumes and had secret identities. Dr. Droom didn't, and that in itself was a revelation.

Although the series was fatally flawed, something about its basic premise was oddly impressive. There had never been a superhero series with an Eastern spiritualism angle. There was something eerie and atmospheric about Dr. Droom's realm of hypnotism and alternate realities. The weird, shadowy world of the occult was hip, edgy and innovative. It had a mother lode of potential, and with a stronger lead character a book like this might shape up to something really substantial. The

dark, brooding magnificence of the Lee/Ditko "Doctor Strange" series would prove this soon enough.

Marvel's most recent history book, *Marvel Chronicles*, speculated that the Dr. Droom stories may have been written by Stan's brother, Larry Lieber. But they weren't. At our request Larry reviewed the Dr. Droom material and verified that he has no recollection of ever working on those stories. Given detailed examination, the Dr. Droom dialogue reads like a Stan Lee script more than anything.

Beyond that, Stan undoubtedly co-created the character. Lee has stated that Dr. Droom was based on a 1930s radio drama that he'd loved as a child called *Chandu the Magician*. In the radio series an American named Frank Chandler learned occult secrets from a

yogi in India and became "Chandu." It's notable that one of Chandu's supernatural skills was "astral projection"—a power which Lee would soon give to Dr. Strange, who was clearly based on both Dr. Droom and Chandu.

In the final analysis, Dr. Droom's short-lived series was a mere signpost, a foreshadowing of bigger things to come. The book's final importance wasn't so much in itself as in the effect it would have on Marvel's immediate future. The Droom series facilitated Lee and Kirby's transition from monsters to action heroes. In that sense, Dr. Droom can rightfully be seen as the forefather of the Marvel superheroes, the most potent superheroes since superheroes were born.

The guillotine descended swiftly on Doctor Droom. Kirby drew four issues in *Amazing Adventures* #1-4 (June-Sept. 1961), then he departed from the series. The fifth and final Dr. Droom tale in *Amazing Adventures* #6 featured unattractive art by Paul Reinman, who occasionally inked Kirby's work.

The King had no time to draw the last Dr. Doom story which was dated November 1961, a date which would go down in comics history. Kirby was pulled off *Amazing Adventures* to create an entirely new comic, a second attempt at superheroes.

Now it was crunch time. Dr. Droom had been a sad flop and Goodman's sales had been dropping all through the last half of 1961. Martin's comic book line desperately needed a hit to stay afloat. Back in the Golden Age, Goodman had climbed to the top of the sales heap by sheer volume. But now his old tactic of

Back to the old drawing board, as the duo returns to giant monsters in Amazing Adventures *#6 (Nov. 1961)—the same month that* Fantastic Four *#1 appeared. The art here seems superior to the underdeveloped art in* FF *#1 and #2, which featured sparse backgrounds, simple layouts, and an overall lack of the detail found here.*

finding a winning title by scattershot publication was no longer an option. Jack Liebowitz wasn't about to let him run wild and oversaturate the market, especially now that the comics industry was showing signs of slow recovery.

The fate of Goodman's comic book operation was pretty much in the hands of Lee and Kirby at this point. The pressure was on, and it was imperative that they come up with a hit series. If they didn't, the game would be over.

But Jack Kirby had worked under pressure before, standing solo behind enemy lines sketching Nazi artillery points. Compared to that, this was nothing. He'd make sure his next superhero comic would attain a sense of splendor that the ill-fated Dr. Droom series had only been groping toward.

GENESIS

Given hindsight, it all seems so inevitable.

That a weird, wondrous comic book full of strange characters with dark complexities would appear out of nowhere, at the exact right time, and start a renaissance now seems entirely plausible. In fact, only those who were there at the time can attest to how startling it all was. It's like trying to tell someone born after the 1964 "British Invasion" how impossibly futuristic the Beatles seemed compared to everything before them. You had to have been there.

By the dawn of the 1960s, success and complacency had ruined DC Comics. They were an entrenched establishment tainted by elitism, smug in their place at the top of the mountain. The editors who controlled the content of the books seemed uninterested in change of any kind. Their comics were selling, so they made little effort to try anything new. Mostly, they survived on habit. DC's hands-on editors were notorious for stifling artists with individual vision, opting instead for a refined, easily accessible "house style." The DC house artists drew as if they were working from a laboratory. Sterilized and sanitized, the artwork was dully drawn with no flash, no force, no energy and no speed.

During these years superhero comics were dominated almost entirely by National Periodicals' Superman and Batman lines—nine books in all. Their stories and art were primarily aimed at readers whose average age was ten. Mind you, these comics weren't shoddy by any means. They had a consistent standard of clear, clean artwork, polished but passionless, and painted with bright primary colors. If you were ten, and had been raised on this pabulum, these comics seemed entirely tolerable—mostly because you didn't know anything else.

In fact, almost all of the early 1960s *Superman* and *Batman*

comics had a built-in sense of tedium. The stories were repetitive clichés, remorseless in their banality. They were warm and snug like a blanket. At the end of every *World's Finest* comic, Superman and Batman would defeat the villain then smile and shake hands, chummy as can be. It was dire, it had dragged on for years, and it was beginning to bore everyone blind.

These were bland times for kids who loved action heroes. The new adventures of *The Flash* had begun promisingly enough, but now even the Flash seemed to be mired in DC's outmoded notions of corporate superheroism. Creatively, everything was at a standstill. An acute state of inertia was rotting away at the very core of comics like a creeping paralysis. Everything was frozen, everything was petrified. The time was right for a revolution. What the decaying industry desperately needed was something entirely new, a revelation, a spark, a rallying point; something truly atmospheric that would give the medium a whole new style and direction.

Something had to change, and something did. The Fantastic Four were that something.

Tuesday, August 8, 1961 was a fairly discouraging day for America. In the headlines Cosmonaut Gherman Titov completed a 25-hour trip around the Earth which U.S. newspapers called

The front page of the New York Times *from August 8, 1961—the day* Fantastic Four #1 *went on sale.*
©1961 New York Times

23

"Russia's ticket to the moon." Soviet Premier Nikita Khrushchev went on television and announced that Russian troops were gathering to terminate Allied-occupation rights in West Berlin. Later that week, construction of the Berlin Wall began.

The only good news that day was on the pop-culture scene: on 8/8/61 a new magazine called *Fantastic Four* hit the newsstands. Its impact on the comic book world was immediate, titanic and irreversible. From the moment they burst onto the scene—with the sudden fury of a thunderbolt—the FF transformed the entire landscape. It was like the scene in *The Wizard of Oz* where Dorothy opens the door and everything changes from dreary black-and-white to glorious Technicolor. Suddenly everything came alive.

In one throw, that first issue, crudely drawn and undeveloped as it was, laid the foundation for an entirely new complex of ideas. It transfigured all the mediocrity and sameness that had become so endemic to comics. It offered nothing less than a Second Coming.

Fantastic Four #1 launched the concept of realism, a markedly intellectual sense of consciousness and complexity that was previously unfathomable. For the first time, the personality and character of the heroes was the focus—how they related to each other, how they related to society, and how society related to them. The stories evolved on the basis of how these characters, each with a distinct persona, responded to the dramas and dilemmas in which they found themselves. In every way it was a major breakthrough. This was not lost on a twenty-one year old college student from Sullivan Missouri who'd been following comics since the Golden Age. According to Roy Thomas, "It was the start of something really different: no costumes, the monster, the human emotion and things to that end—everything was so much there in that first issue."

Lee and Kirby, early 1960s.

In the early 1960s, DC's idea of a modern teenager was the Justice League's Snapper Carr. Compared to Johnny Storm, Snapper's characterization is downright embarrassing.

The exactness of how the FF came to fruition has long since vanished into the mist of time. The issue of credit is forever blurred due to the poor memories of the creators and their competitiveness for top-billing as the book's main architect. Half a century after the fact, all we can do is dispel some obvious myths and try to draw some fresh conclusions.

...When Liebowitz was carefully setting up for the ninth hole, he remarked that it looked like team superheroes were finally on the rebound. A poker player at heart and savvy to any trend that seemed worthwhile, Goodman might have calmly responded, "Oh? How do you mean?" Liebowitz took the shot and both men quietly followed the ball as it bounced onto the green. Then Liebowitz turned to Goodman with a puzzled look and remarked, "You know Marty—our new comic book 'Justice League of America' is a smash success. Didn't you hear about that?" —From The Art of Jack Kirby by R. Wyman Jr. and C. Hohlfeld.

That's a great story, and the meticulous details about the ball bouncing onto the green of the ninth hole add color if not credibility. In any case, it's entirely false.

The legend of Martin Goodman hearing about *JLA*'s impressive sales on a golf outing with Jack Liebowitz has been floating around since the mid-1970s. It's impossible to determine who fabricated the anecdote. The best guess would be that Stan came up with it. In 2002, Lee was still repeating the story as gospel in his autobiography.

One version of the tale has Martin golfing with DC's top man Harry Donenfeld. Another version has Jack Liebowitz, who was then publisher of DC Comics, as Goodman's golf partner. Either way, both Jack and Harry have denied the entire account. Donenfeld swore he'd never been on a golf course with Martin Goodman in his entire life. Beyond that, the final nail in the coffin for the golf game anecdote came from Goodman himself, who in his later years admitted the entire episode was largely apocryphal. In view of all this, it's rather amazing that the golf game story is still being presented as fact in nearly every history of comics. In recent years some authors have even attached a specific date to the non-event.

DC Production Chief Sol Harrison has stated that Goodman learned of the *JLA's* sales figures during golf with one of the heads of Independent News, the DC-owned distribution outlet. Harrison worked closely with Independent News' top management for many decades, and he may have gotten the story straight from the horse's mouth. But to obfuscate the truth even further (if that's possible), other DC insiders claim that Goodman had paid informants working at Independent News, and that he received the *Justice League*'s sales figures through them.

A recent interview with Stan strongly indicates that the "paid informants" scenario might be the correct one. According to Stan, "Martin Goodman, who was the Publisher, called me in and said, you know Stan, I think the superheroes are coming back. I was looking at the sales figures for DC's *Justice League*. Why don't we do a team of superheroes?"

Note that in this version of the story there's no mention of any golf game. Martin said he'd been "looking at the sales figures" as if he had a sales report in front of him. One is more likely to obtain a confidential sales sheet from a paid informant than from a business rival at a golf outing.

Here's the odd thing: despite Goodman's fixation with obtaining distribution figures by any means necessary, Sol Brodsky, Stan's Production Assistant, was often surprised at how quick Goodman could be to cancel a title, even before the numbers came in. Martin axed *Two-Gun Kid* right after Kirby took over the book, then later discovered sales had shot way up. Ironically, Goodman was considering replacing *Fantastic Four* with another western title until the sales figures came back.

At any rate, the details of how it all fell into place are of little significance compared to the events that would soon be set into motion. The important thing is that Goodman heard of *JLA*'s success and ordered Stan to whip-up a team of comic book superheroes. Ergo, Stan and Jack were acting on a mandate from their boss when they launched *Fantastic Four.* This much we know.

Beyond that, the extent of Lee and Kirby's individual contributions to *Fantastic Four* #1 has long been a subject of acrimonious debate. In the 1980s Kirby was taking credit for the entire concept. He claimed the Justice League's popularity had nothing to do with it. Kirby maintained that he conceived the four characters and their origin story completely by himself. And then, after he had it all worked out, he presented it to Stan.

In answer to Kirby's allegations, Lee pointed to the original plot synopsis for *Fantastic Four* #1, which resurfaced in 1983. It was a two-page outline detailing the quartet's first adventure. The outline describes the four main characters by name and lays out the basic storyline. According to Stan, "After I had nailed down the concept for the Fantastic Four and selected Jack as the illustrator, I didn't have time to write a detailed script for him because I was burdened by a myriad of other duties. But, knowing that Jack had a great knack for visual storytelling, I decided to merely give him a brief written outline containing the plot points that had to be covered. He'd be free to illustrate them in any way he chose, so long as he adhered to the original premise. Then, when he delivered the penciled pages, I'd add the dialogue and captions. I told him the plan. He agreed. I gave him the outline. He drew the strip. I checked the strip and wrote the copy. It went fast. It was good. It worked."

It may have worked as far as Stan was concerned, but in other circles Lee's *FF* #1 plot outline raised as many questions as it answered. Roy Thomas vouches for its authenticity, but only in the sense that he first saw it in the late 1960s. *(Note: Lee reveals more about the FF #1 outline in the "AFTERWORD" section of this book.)*

In a 1989 interview, Kirby called Stan's *FF* #1 plot synopsis "an outright lie" and Roz Kirby swore she'd never seen it. It's not the intent of this publication to defend either side of the "who did what" conflict, but with all due respect to the Kirbys, Stan's controversial *FF* #1 plot outline is most likely genuine. Analysis has concluded that it was typed on the same dilapidated Remington typewriter that Stan used to type all his other Marvel scripts from the early 1960s. Still, between Lee's unbending assertion of the document's authenticity and Kirby's adamant claim that it's fake, the *FF* #1 plot outline really settles nothing.

But what is there to settle? The point is, in terms of fundamental uniqueness, the early Marvel superheroes didn't even begin. Does it really matter whose idea it was to update Russell Stamm's Invisible Scarlet O'Neil and call her Sue Storm? And what difference does it make who decided to revamp Carl Burgos' Human Torch or recast the Golden Age Plastic Man as Reed Richards?

The more you study comic books, the more you'll reach the inescapable conclusion that most of the early Marvel superheroes were merely recycled past. Almost all of them can be traced back to

SYNOPSES: THE FANTASTIC FOUR   JULY '61 SCHEDULE   (F1)

STORY #1. INTRODUCTION. "MEET THE FANTASTIC FOUR"

This story is told in 2 chapters. Chapter one is 6 pages long. Chapter 2 is 5 pages.

There are four main characters: 1) REED RICHARDS. (Mr. Fantastic) He is young, handsome scientist. Leader of the four. Invents a space ship to go to Mars. Hopes to be first man to reach Mars.
2) SUSAN STORM. (Invisible Girl) She is Reed's girl friend. She's an actress. Beautiful, glamorous.
3) BEN GRIMM. (The Thing) Ben is very husky, brutish guy. He's a pilot. He falls for Susan also.
4) JOHNNY STORM. (Human Torch) He is Susan's kid brother. A teen-ager. 17 years old. High school star athlete.

Story might open up with a meeting of Fantastic Four. As meeting starts, caption tells reader that we will go back a few weeks to see how it all began....

Reed Richards tells Susan and her brother Johnny that his space ship is finally completed. He hopes to be first man to Mars. But he needs a pilot. They hire Ben Grimm. Ben is huge, surly unpleasant guy who doesn't want any part of project until he sees Susan. He falls for Susan, and she manages to coax him into piloting ship. Ben is crackerjack pilot, ex-war hero, best pilot available.

As the four are about to begin flight, they are warned against it by authorities. Told that no one yet knows what effect cosmic rays will have on human bodies so far out in space. But they decide to go anyway. They fear that if they don't go, Reds may beat us to it.

(NOTE: At the rate the Communists are progressing in space, maybe we better make this a flight to the STARS, instead of just to Mars, because by the time this mag goes on sale, the Russians may have already MADE a flight to Mars!)

So, without clearance from the authorities, in the dead of night, they take off for the nearest star-- very dramatically.

In space, on the way to the stars, FOOOF! They are bombarded by cosmic rays which penetrate the ship and which affect all four of the occupants. They can't continue the trip-- have to turn back-- are lucky to land alive. But they are all different now-- they sense it-- although they don't yet quite know HOW they've changed.

Suddenly, they can't see Susan! But they know she's there! They can HEAR her. They realize she has become invisible. She can not become visible again. Later, she will buy a mask with a face like the one she had and she will have to wear that mask in order to be seen. Her clothes of course can be seen, so it is only her flesh that is invisible. When she takes her clothes off, she's completely invisible. (I hope this won't seem too sexy in art work. Better talk to me about it, Jack-- maybe we'll change this gimmick somewhat).

As for Johnny, Susan's brother, whenever he gets excited, he bursts into flame. Becomes a Human Torch, and can fly, as his body gets lighter than air. BUT doesn't last for more than 5 minutes. At end of five minutes, his flame goes out and he becomes normal again, until he gets excited again. But can't flame on for at least 5 minutes after he's gotten back to normal. Comics Association told me he may never turn anyone with flame, he may only burn ropes, doors, etc.--never people. And, he cannot toss fireballs as the old Human Torch could. His biggest asset is that he can fly.

more--

First page of Lee's FF #1 synopsis; the second page is on "the next page following," as they said in the comics.

older comic book characters, comic strips, pulp fiction, movies, television, old radio serials or classic literature.

Once you get past that, the rest is easy to dope out. The real innovation wasn't the Marvel superheroes themselves. It was their verisimilitude, their solid connection to reality; their flaws, their romantic dilemmas, their pathos, their humor, their introspection, their snappy dialogue and their ironic take on life as a superhero. Stan Lee contributed that. All of those elements are found in Lee's pre-*FF* writing and scripting. They are not found in Jack Kirby's pre-Marvel superhero comics. None of Jack's pre-1961 superheroes were neurotic, tormented or self-analytical. As Gil Kane observed, "It wasn't until Marvel started the superhero stuff that sales started to improve. Stan had a lot to do with the characterization which was appropriate for the time; it was fresh and filled with mock irreverence. And that's not Jack, that was Stan."

What Kirby did is more obvious. He took those hackneyed, recycled action heroes and made them come alive in panel after panel of rapid-fire action rolling at breakneck speed. His dramatic, energetic figures and his never-a-dull-moment *Citizen Kane* camera angles electrified the pages; it was like nothing the comics had ever seen.

And from the beginning, right up until the end, both men had input on the book's storyline. So who created *Fantastic Four*? Stan Lee and Jack Kirby—or, if you like, Jack Kirby and Stan Lee—that's it and that's all. Neither man could have done it without the other.

Undoubtedly, many specific details surrounding the *FF*'s creation will remain forever shrouded in mystery and conflict. But behind the mythification, what we *can* ascertain are Lee and Kirby's motivations as the series was launched.

Lee, who was thirty-eight at the time, desperately wanted out of comics. He'd been in the medium since he was eighteen and was totally burned out. At this point Stan was a hack writer who worked for a bottom-feeding publisher. Lee was hopelessly mired in crank-it-out mediocrity. He was forever copying other companies' successful books, always the first to be second.

He was anxious to move on to other types of writing; anything other than comics. By the early 1960s he'd already made a few forays into the field of writing humor. Stan was buying photos from the UPI wire service, and writing his own amusing captions. For example, in a book called *Golfers Anonymous,* Stan took a photo of two golfers and a dog approaching a green, and added this non-sequitur: *It wasn't bad enough giving him his own full membership! NOW he's got the lowest handicap in the club!* In this way, Lee was learning to manipulate his audience to a desired reaction by adding dialogue to a wordless image—an image that someone else created. This is how he honed the skills which he'd soon incorporate in his "Marvel Method" of writing comics.

Stan would later say his pre-Marvel humor books were a welcome diversion from his comic book vocation, which by 1961 he was ready to abandon. Lee claims he was going to give Martin Goodman his resignation the very same day that Martin issued his "give me a super-team" directive. If that claim sounds somewhat less than authentic, remember what Stan has often said: "You can't expect a guy who lives in a world of superheroes, mutants and monsters to be overly concerned with total authenticity."

So, in the gospel according to Stan, he forestalled his resignation and accepted the assignment. That night, his wife Joan convinced him to give this final comic everything he had—to do it his way. What did he have to lose?

To be brutally honest, if Lee had resigned from Goodman's tattered, bottom-rung comic book line before *Fantastic Four* was created, his legacy would have barely amounted to a footnote in someone's book on the history of comics. By contrast, Jack Kirby's pre-*FF* career had been everything Stan Lee's had not. At this point in his life Kirby had already revolutionized the comics industry twice. With

They think Reed Richards, the pilot, is unaffected by cosmic rays, as he seems normal—UNTIL he tries to reach for something. Then they realize his arm has STRETCHED toward the thing he reached for. After awhile they realize Reed's body has become like RUBBER. He can get skinny, elongated, anything that you can do with rubber. He can squeeze thru key-holes, etc. Of course, the more stretched-out he gets, the weaker he gets— but the point remains that he can twist and stretch his body into almost any shape. (He can even alter the appearance of his face to make himself look like someone else) BUT it is quite painful to do all this, so he can only maintain the strange shapes for a very short period of time until the pain gets to be unbearable.

Finally, Ben Grimm steps out of the shadows. They all gasp— his body has changed in the most grotesque way of all. He's sort of shapeless— he's become a THING. And, he's grown more fantastically powerful than any other living thing. He is stronger than an elephant. BUT, he is so heavy that he moves very slowly— he's very ponderous, and these slow, ponderous movements should make him look very dramatic. He cannot alter his appearance as the others can, so he must wear a coat with turned-up collar, sunglasses, slouch hat, and gloves when he goes out in public. But when he takes 'em off, he is a THING!

So much for who they are and how they got that way. Now, here's a gimmick I think we might play up to advantage: Let's make The Thing the heavy- in other words, he's not really a good guy. He's part of the Fantastic Four because they all got that way together and they decide to remain a team, and also because he has a crush on Susan— but actually, he is jealous of Mr. Fantastic and dislikes Human Torch because Torch always sides with Fantastic. Let's treat him so that reader is always afraid he will sabotage the Fantastic Four's efforts at whatever they are doing— he isn't interested in helping mankind the way the other three are— he is more interested in winning Susan away from Mr. Fantastic. (We might indicate that he feels he may return to his normal self at any time, because none of them know how long their strange powers will last- or whether or not the effect of the cosmic rays will one day wear off them).

Anyway, the four of them decide to form a unit— they think it is an act of Fate which made them as they are and they think they owe it to fate to use their powers to help mankind. So they adopt their new names: HUMAN TORCH, MR. FANTASTIC, INVISIBLE GIRL, and THE THING, and vow to spend their lives fighting all sorts of evil menaces which the normal forces of the world cannot cope with. And, to keep it all from getting too goody-goody, there is always friction between Mr. Fantastic and The Thing, with Human Torch siding with Mr. F. Also, the other three are always afraid of The Thing getting out of their control some day and harming mankind with his amazing strength. Occasionally also, you might have the Thing wanting to do something for personal profit- and the other 3 try to stop him. In other words, the Thing doesn't have the ethics that the other three have, and consequently he will probably be the most interesting one to the reader, because he'll always be unpredictable.

So much for the introduction—— the preceding should have covered exactly 11 pages, consisting of 2 chapters. (Chapter one: 6 pages. Chapter 2: 5 pages)

The next two chapters, in which the Fantastic Four undertakes their first case, will also be chapters for a total of 10 pages— (3,5,5.)

3   13

Captain America he showed every artist in the field how to draw action heroes. Later, when superheroes became a dead end for everyone but DC, Kirby and Joe Simon revitalized the industry by creating the Romance comic genre.

Unlike Lee, Kirby didn't view comics as someplace you worked your way up from. It was what he did. Period. While *Fantastic Four* was to be Stan's swan-song to comic books, Kirby, now forty-four, was battling with desperate velocity to save his chosen field from extinction. As Kirby remarked, "It was a losing field, but working on comics was the only profession I knew. I was a married man and I had to make a living."

Jack Kirby's desperation would prove to be the crux of *Fantastic Four*. In 1961 Kirby was in his absolute prime, ready to tackle the new series with more vigor and veracity than anyone could imagine. It was just what the magazine needed; someone with tremendous resources of energy and vision, someone with enough force and hunger to recreate the entire context in which superheroes function.

Over the years Kirby would cite the contributing factors that influenced his input on the Fantastic Four. Jack said the idea of the FF being bombarded with cosmic rays came from something that he'd read about the early space program. "They were worried about what effect the Van Allen Belt radiation might have on astronauts" said Kirby. "It turns out that the radiation was easily shielded, but it had everybody worried for awhile."

The King also said he was thinking about the monsters that he and Stan had been churning out since 1958. Shortly before he died, Kirby's final statement on the creation of the Fantastic Four went like this: "The early monsters were precursors to the 1960s superheroes. Even the concept of the Fantastic Four was derived from the monster period. While flying about the planet in their spaceship, the crew was pelted by cosmic rays. Reed Richards mutated into a stretching figure; a monster with human attributes. Johnny Storm transformed into a flaming creature, while Sue storm became invisible, like a supernatural ghost. Ben Grimm changed into a rock creature, the Thing! Now there's a monster if I ever saw a monster, a direct derivative from the early monster books."

When evaluating Kirby's above statement, one should consider that those remarks were written for *Monster Madness* #2 (Jan. 1994), a Marvel monster-comic anthology. The King may have been slightly overstating the Fantastic Four's monster roots for the sake of the assignment.

As for Stan, it was subsequently revealed that his mindset during the creation of the FF was influenced by two contributing factors: the events of April 12, 1961, and an old pulp fiction hero. According to Stan, "Doc Savage and his oddly assorted team might be considered the progenitors of today's Fantastic Four and many other teams of super-heroes."

During his boyhood, Lee was an avid reader of the pulps. *Doc Savage* was one of his favorites, as was *The Spider*. In one of Stan's versions of how he created Spider-Man, he sighted the old pulp

fiction Spider as an inspiration. All things considered, there appears to be a solid connection between the FF and the Doc Savage saga.

To begin with, Reed Richard's similarities to Doc Savage are unarguable. Savage was a 1930s science-detective who led a team of often-quarreling heroes. Doc's headquarters occupied the top floor of a New York skyscraper. The building had a private elevator and a built-in hanger full of exotic vehicles and specialized aircraft. Savage funded his enterprises with patents from his many inventions, and one of his foes lived beneath the Earth's surface. Does that sound familiar?

Now let's go back to the controversial *FF* #1 plot outline that Roy Thomas first saw at the end of the 1960s. On reading it, one will find this rather curious statement: *NOTE: At the rate the Communists are progressing in space, maybe we better make this a flight to the STARS, instead of just to Mars, because by the time this mag goes on sale, the Russians may have already MADE a flight to Mars.*

As absurd as that afterthought now sounds, it may be the key to the document's authenticity. In 2006, a comic book historian named Will Murray started digging, and by cross-referencing some early Marvel job numbers with the work records of inker Dick Ayers, he determined that *FF* #1 was probably drawn in May 1961, and conceived the previous month in April 1961.

April 12, 1961 was the day that Yuri Gagarin, the Soviet Union's first cosmonaut, was launched into space. This event undoubtedly had a profound effect on Stan, who was decidedly anti-Communist at the time. When Murray reminded Lee of Gagarin's trip to space, it triggered a long dormant memory. Stan told Murray it was "a very safe bet" that Yuri's trip to the cosmos was the inspiration to send the FF into space. Said Stan, "It all fits too neatly to be just coincidental."

On the whole, the best scenario we have at this point is that Kirby was thinking about radiation and monsters when creating the Fantastic Four. Lee on the other hand, was thinking about Russians in space and Doc Savage. The two men met*, tossed around their ideas for the series, then Lee typed out a two-page outline for the first issue. And so, in this colorful milieu, America's first family of superheroes came to life. (*Note: Over the years Stan has backpedaled on whether or not he conferred with Kirby before he typed the FF #1 outline: He's told some interviewers that he "may have

spoken with Jack about it first." Interestingly, Stan told us "I did not discuss it with Jack first." But he knew from the start that "Kirby would be the best artist to draw it.")

Fantastic Four had roots in other elements as well. Lee's humor books spawned the FF's irreverent dialogue. Kirby's romance comics gave the series its emotional nuance and the Golden Age superheroes provided templates for Reed, Sue and Johnny's powers. This rich blending of ingredients from multiple genres was an improbable stew, a bizarre and chaotic marriage; but from it would spawn a whole new order.

Goodman's mandate that Lee and Kirby create a *team* of superheroes, as opposed to a single main character, was the key to the book's success. By putting a variety of superheroes in the new series Goodman avoided gambling on the popularity of a single character to sell the book. Obviously, at this time solo comic book stars were hit and miss propositions for Jack and Stan. Dr. Droom was proof of that. On the other hand, a team of heroes would be more conducive to characterization. In the beginning, the way the Fantastic Four interacted among themselves was the driving force of the storyline.

Once the "team concept" had been decided on, Jack and Stan's first problem was to determine how many characters would be on the team. Because they wanted a female in the group, they needed at least three male partners to balance her. According to Stan, "Having only one male partner could easily have turned the series into a love affair, while two male partners could have made it an all-too-predictable love triangle. Five or more characters might have been too many for the readers to keep track of, particularly in a brand-new series. But once the number four was fixed at, everything fell into place, including the alliterative name Fantastic Four."

It's been said that Stan originally called the quartet the "Fabulous Four," but Goodman changed it. Martin claimed there were certain words that subliminally induced kids to buy comics; "fantastic" was one of them. So "Fantastic Four" it was.

Who were they? Reed Richards was the group's academician and levelheaded leader. On a minor note, he was the first superhero with graying hair. This early injection of reality must have been Jack's idea, because it contradicted Stan's plot synopsis which described Reed as "a young handsome scientist."

Like four comic book characters before him—Flexo the Rubber Man, Plastic Man, the Elongated Man and Elastic Lad—Mr. Fantastic could stretch his limbs to infinity and transmogrify his body into any shape he desired. In Stan's original plot synopsis, Reed was to be in acute pain every time he stretched his flexible frame. Kirby ignored this idea, but it shows that Lee was

Many pre-FF comic book characters had the ability to stretch—by 1961, Reed's power was old hat.

conceptualizing the idea of less-than-super superheroes from the beginning.

Back in 1965 Lee told Roy Thomas he always felt Reed's elasticity was too humorous and that he never wanted Richards to become another Plastic Man. Stan needn't have worried; Kirby's ideas were far too dark and offbeat to let that happen. As it turned out, Mr. Fantastic's scientific prowess would win more battles for the FF than his stretching ability ever did. In this way, Reed was like Lester Dent's pulp-fiction hero Doc Savage.

Sue Storm was more than a knockoff of Invisible Scarlet O'Neil from the 1940s comic strip. Unlike the typical comic book girlfriend who didn't know the hero's true identity, Sue fought alongside her man, willingly and uncomplainingly sharing the dangers with him. Her presence gave the group's chemistry a perfect shade of melodrama that would be lacking in an all-male team.

Invisible Scarlet O'Neil—Sue Storm's progenitor.

Sue's beauty made her the matrix for romantic triangles, the first of which involved Ben and Reed; an idea from Stan's plot outline which was dropped after the third issue. After that, Sue actually encouraged and reciprocated the advances of Sub-Mariner, sparking a rivalry between Reed and Namor that would take years to resolve. This forbidden love between a heroine and an arch-villain had no parallel in the history of comic books. Stan claims he also considered making Susan the object of Dr. Doom's desire, which would have legitimized Victor's obsession with destroying Mr. Fantastic. For better or worse, he never got around to it.

From the beginning, the Invisible Girl's role as the group's integrator was far more important than her ability to dematerialize. As the Torch's sister and Reed's future bride, she linked the FF together to a degree that was almost incestuous (an idea the writers would take even further with the Inhumans). Sue gave the quartet a bond that was unprecedented. Because of her, the Fantastic Four became a family; this was her main contribution. Other than that, she was always a bit marginal.

On the other hand, her kid brother was anything but marginal. Like Reed and Sue, Johnny Storm was cloned from a previously established superhero, Timely's Golden Age Human Torch. According to Stan, this was a compromise to placate Martin Goodman, who originally suggested that Timely's "Big Three" be part of the new team. This modern Human Torch, however, was cast in an entirely new light.

Original art for the house ad in Incredible Hulk #1 (May 1962).

Until 1961, most teenagers in superhero comics were monumentally lame "kid-sidekicks" whose main function was to keep the adult hero from talking to himself. On the other side you had DC's Legion of Super Heroes; the most pathetically unhip group of teens who ever gathered under one roof. The Silver Age Human Torch was the only one who didn't fit the "boy wonder" mold. The big difference was that Johnny Storm was cool. Even his name sounded like a 1960s teen idol. Johnny's radically modernized juvenile slant made him the first truly convincing teenager ever seen in a superhero comic. Brash, rebellious and occasionally obnoxious, he was a hothead and a showoff who was never above using his flame to impress the guys or win the girls.

Of all the astounding innovations that Roy Thomas would find in the FF's debut, one concept towered above all else. The introduction of the Thing, the only truly original character in the book, was a masterstroke. The hideously disfigured Ben Grimm was, in numerous ways, a detonator who would set off a constellation of changes— changes that would expand

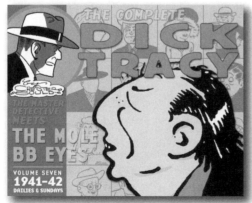

Historian Will Murray feels that "without a doubt" the Mole Man from FF #1 *was based on "The Mole" from* Dick Tracy.

and complexify the notion of comic book heroes fundamentally and forever. Joe Sinnott has described the Thing as "Jack Kirby's greatest creation."

According to Jack Kirby, "When I first drew the Thing, I tried to give him skin that was a dinosaur's hide. I wanted to give the suggestion that he was as strong as a prehistoric beast. People often comment that the Thing is a lot like me, smoking cigars, kind of rough around the edges. I didn't plan it that way, but I guess it's true."

The 1961 Thing looked like nothing on Earth. He had craggy orange flesh and was cast as a bitter malcontent. He rampaged through the streets of New York like a wounded mastodon, smashing everything in his path. The deep self-loathing his deformity had wrought would often invert itself, and seek surrogate victims like the Torch. This element of anguish in Ben's persona elevated him from a mere Atlas monster retread to comic's first truly tragic figure.

The idea that having super powers could bring misery and disconnect a man from his society was unheard of. Ben's prodigious strength couldn't compensate for the loss of his humanity. This paradox gave the early Thing a depth and darkness that was entirely new—an almost Greek sense of tragedy. In the beginning he struggled with self-hatred and self-pity harder than he struggled with any villain.

At last, the tortured superhero was born.

Almost as a matter of course, the FF's imperfections were the crucible from which the entire series was forged. Their super-powers were derivative; almost a sideline. It was their flaws and foibles that made them startling and splendid. They were defined by their weaknesses more than their strengths.

Stan's original plot synopsis was firm that power struggles, romantic triangles and character flaws should be the main thrust of the magazine; not action or mystery. In this way, the early *Fantastic Four* gave the concept of superheroes wholly new dimensions. They were easily the most original thing comics had ever coughed up, and once the series hit the ground running it hardly ever faltered for nine years.

CONTINUED AFTER NEXT PAGE...

Original art from Fantastic Four #15 (June 1963), showing uninked Kirby pencils of the Thing. At this stage, Dick Ayer's soft ink line wasn't accurately capturing the chiseled look Kirby was giving the character.

5

In *Fantastic Four* #1 (Nov. 1961), revelations flew off the pages right from the start. "*Look! In the sky— what in blazes does it mean?*" "*I dunno, but the crowds are gettin' panicky! Rumors are flyin' about an alien invasion!*" Kids never read dialogue like that in the squeaky-clean DC comics. The speech patterns were colorful, the spelling was arbitrary and even a casual declarative sentence might end in three exclamation marks. It was the most jarring, visceral and gut-level writing the industry had ever seen. With no corporate editor to make him script the "right" way, Stan Lee was unleashed.

Another breakthrough: in the initial stories, the team fought monsters and aliens in their street clothes and never even considered concealing their true identities. Being superheroes was their only profession. The quartet's lack of "secret identities" gave them a high public profile that was totally unique. It led the general populace to be both suspicious and in awe of them, and the FF often found their celebrity status to be a mixed blessing. Invariably, the group didn't even act like superheroes. DC action heroes were never seen quarreling, but these four were constantly bickering and belittling each other.

Another divergence from the norm was the writer's use of the entire book for one storyline. This was something that Kirby had done in *Challengers of the Unknown*, but in *Fantastic Four*, sometimes even 23 pages weren't enough. With the Lee/Kirby *FF*, a new era of epic-length comic book adventures began.

Even the look of the magazine was weird. The early issues had no conception of quality whatsoever. The production values seemed crude and heavy-handed. The coloring was dreary with too many grays. The word-balloons on the covers had garishly thick borders that distracted from the artwork. In fact, the entire magazine seemed totally devoid of corporate craftsmanship.

But whatever else it lacked, *Fantastic Four* had a raw vitality that had been missing from comics for years. It seemed dark and downright subversive; the perfect antidote to the sterile, sprayed-with-antiseptic *Superman* books. It was, in every way, the anti-*Justice League*.

These were exciting times for comic book fans. With each subsequent issue this strange new comic would produce something totally unique, something wilder than anything that had gone before. The book's lack of prettiness only added to its strange allure. One issue would turn almost any uncommitted reader into an instant loyalist, a *True Believer*. Roy Thomas, sufficiently intoxicated after the first three issues, was ready to pony-up for a two-year subscription as he stated in one of the magazine's earliest letters. The revolution had begun.

It must be said that Kirby's artwork in the FF's origin issue and in *FF* #2 (Jan. 1962) had been slow off the mark. Over-pressured and overworked as always, the King's initial penciling looked sparse and hurried. And it wasn't bolstered much by the craggy brushwork of Timely Comics vet George Klein, who inked the first two issues unaccredited. Jack's art on *Challengers of the Unknown* and *Sky Masters* had been markedly superior. However, by *FF* #3 (March

One of the earliest original FF pages known, from issue #3 (March 1962).

Joe Sinnott dropped FF #6 *after inking a few panels, to do a higher-paying assignment for Treasure Chest. Check out Sue's "Sinnott face" from page 2 above.*

1962), Kirby's vitality had returned.

FF #3 brought more advancements. In a totally unexpected closing moment, an embittered Human Torch quit the group and blazed off into the sky. It was another shocking revelation, something that never happened in other super-team comics. Also in this issue, the FF began wearing their utilitarian blue uniforms. Kirby said they were based on his no-frills Challengers of the Unknown jumpsuits.

A couple of books have reported that when Kirby first designed the FF's uniforms they were totally plain, and that Lee took a pencil to Jack's concept-drawing, and added a circle with a number "4" on their chests. In an exclusive interview for this book, Stan denied this. According to Lee, "I don't remember that happening. I think it's more likely that Jack and I discussed it and mutually decided to have the number 4 in a circle on their chests."

On many occasions Stan has claimed the FF's costumes were a bow to reader demands, but there's no evidence of this in the early letter-pages. In the beginning there were so few *Fantastic Four* fan letters that Stan wrote some himself and had Sol Brodsky and colorist Stan Goldberg add others. If the fans were writing letters to request uniforms (or anything else for that matter), Lee surely would have printed them.

Comics historian Greg Theakston has an alternative theory about the FF's costumes. In 1961 Goodman's comic books were being distributed by Independent News, which was owned by National Publications. DC had a lock on superhero comics, and they might have considered Marvel's new action heroes a conflict of interest. If this had irritated them, they could have refused to renew Goodman's contract once it expired. Theakston believes that Lee and Kirby may have been trying to sneak *Fantastic Four* under DC's radar by making it look more like a monster/sci-fi title than a superhero comic. Only when National failed to complain did the writers turn *Fantastic Four* into a full-fledged super-hero series. Such was DC's power in those days.

And speaking of DC, there's an often-reported misconception that surrounds the birth of *Fantastic Four:* Various books have stated that *FF* #1 was the ninth title in Goodman's eight-books-a-month deal with Independent News, and that Martin snuck it into the line-up in an unauthorized distribution slot. In an exclusive interview, Stan dispelled this myth. According to Lee, by 1961 IND. had loosened its restrictions, allowing Goodman to publish 9 to 12 titles a month. "There's no way we could have snuck it in," said Stan. "The people at DC were way too smart to let something like that happen."

Meanwhile, a few blocks north of the DC offices at 655 Madison Avenue, Martin Goodman's cousin-in-law was feeling his oats. Stan Lee and modesty had never been an easy fit. Indeed, Stan was constitutionally incapable of understatement. Preposterously, on the cover of *FF* #3, Lee had the audacity to write "*THE GREAT-EST COMIC MAGAZINE IN THE WORLD!!*" That slogan, slightly altered, would become a fixture of the book's cover, but to make that claim after only three issues, no matter how groundbreaking, was ludicrous.

In just two years the slogan would be entirely justified.

Fantastic Four seemed a perfect place to rekindle the faded glory of the Golden Age Timely superheroes. In *FF* #4 (May 1962), Johnny finds a bearded amnesiac in a Bowery flop house who turns out to be Bill Everett's aquatic anti-hero, the Sub-Mariner. Subsequently Namor becomes enamored with the beautiful (and apparently fickle)

Stan Lee and "J. Kirby" remove the Thing's uniform for good in Fantastic Four #3.

Invisible Girl, which sets off a mutual infatuation that wouldn't be resolved until *FF* #27 (June 1964). How many radical ideas could the writers cram into one story? *FF* #4 was a model of ceaseless innovation.

More changes: Beginning with *FF* #4, the storyline's locality changed from the fictional "Central City" to New York, an idea that Stan probably got from the Doc Savage stories. Into the breach created by the FF, there would soon surge a battalion of new Lee/Kirby superheroes. All of them would reside in The Big Apple except the Hulk, and even he would come to visit.

Almost immediately, New York City became a vital element in the adventures of the Fantastic Four. The city's tangible presence became almost as important to the storyline as the FF themselves. Ordinary men in suits (all with Bronx accents) and women in pillbox hats gawked from street level at all the heroes and villains flying, fighting and stretching up in the sky. Kirby, a lifelong native, obviously had a great feeling for the town. The Big Apple, seen from all angles as Kirbyized cityscapes, kept the entire storyline rooted in reality.

Ultimately, there was Doctor Doom.

FF #5 (July 1962), introduced the vicious, vainglorious Victor Von Doom; wreaker of cataclysms, the man in the iron mask. He was the nastiest piece of work imaginable. His mind seemed a labyrinth of dark, twisted corridors. He was the FF's first antagonist who was able to balance an atmospheric creepiness with a true sense of majesty. Throughout the series the megalomaniacal Dr. Doom would keep coming back, totally obsessed with defeating the FF, and Mr. Fantastic in particular. It was as if the idea had crawled into his brain and set up housekeeping. He appeared in the magazine no less than seventeen times before Kirby left the book, and to this day he's still Marvel's premier villain.

FF #8 (Nov. 1962) introduced Alicia Masters, a blind girl who immediately became Ben's love interest. It was a brilliant plot twist, right out of a Simon/Kirby romance comic. Only the innocent and sightless Alicia accepted the Thing for the basic goodness and decency of his character, indifferent to what the rest of the world saw. Bathed in Alicia's refracted light, Ben's persona slowly began to shift. He softened. It was a significant turning point in the Thing's characterization.

More milestones: In *FF* #8, Sue called the Thing "Ben" for the first time since his transformation by cosmic rays. Previously, his teammates had referred to him exclusively as "the Thing." In a year's time they would be addressing him by his Christian (or in his case, Jewish) name only. Little by little, the man within the monster was beginning to emerge.

In *FF* #9 (Dec. 1962), our heroes get evicted from the Baxter Building due to financial woes. This story has been praised time and again for its unusual premise. However, some claim this idea had been done earlier by DC in *Strange Adventures* #114 (March 1960). In this story, 21st century detective Star Hawkins couldn't make the rent and had to pawn his beloved robot-secretary Ilda for some quick cash. *FF* #9 also saw the first inker/letterer credits (Stan and Jack had been singing their names on the book's splash-page since *FF* #1).

In FF *#8, Sue called the Thing "Ben" for the first time since his transformation. Slowly, the man within the monster was beginning to emerge.*

FF #11 (Feb. 1963) was the debut of Willy Lumpkin, the FF's exasperated, overworked mailman. There's a backstory to Willy: In the days before Silver Age superheroes held the limelight, many comic book creators were moonlighting, trying for success with syndicated newspaper comic strips. Stan, along with Timely artist Dan DeCarlo, managed to get a strip published in 1960 about a small town mailman named Willy Lumpkin. The strip flopped after fourteen months, but Lee recycled the character later in *Fantastic Four*. (DeCarlo didn't exactly starve after the cancellation of *Willy Lumpkin* either. He went on to Archie Comics where he eventually created *Josie and the Pussycats* and *Sabrina the Teen-Age Witch*.)

FF #12 (March 1963) was the book's first-ever crossover, featuring the brutish Hulk. It should have been a blockbuster, but except for the mesmerizing Kirby cover, it was pure anticlimax. In a rare and egregious case of the writers dragging the storyline, the action didn't get underway until page seventeen. The end result was a lackluster three-page battle. Lee and Kirby would make up for this in spades the next time the two monsters met.

In *FF* #13 (April 1963), the team met a moon-based cosmic sage called the Watcher. An obelisk of bland passivity, he stood huge and still, stoic and Sphinx-like, surveying apocalyptic upheavals in which he could take no part. He was the FF's first supporting character, and Kirby's first "space god."

Beginning with *FF* #14 (May 1963), a colorful little box appeared in the upper left of the magazine's cover, bearing the faces of the FF, the price of the book and the company's new name. This distinctive "Marvel Comics" logo was reportedly Steve Ditko's brainchild. With this turn of events Martin Goodman's comic book line finally had an identity after being nameless since 1957. Ironically, Stan Lee, whose own name would eventually become synonymous with "Marvel" wanted to re-launch the old Atlas name for Goodman's 1960s comic book division. But Martin insisted otherwise. Goodman had instructed his staff to conduct a survey of common words that appeared in the titles of his better-selling publications. "Marvel" was one of the words that Goodman claimed sold magazines along with "astonish," "suspense," "uncanny" and "incredible."

Now that the comics company had a name, Stan could begin to promote it. Ever since 1939, Goodman's comic book division had suffered from a lack of distinctiveness. That was all about to change; Stan would see to that. And Lee's efforts to push the new Marvel brand would be greatly assisted by his new secretary.

Flo Steinberg was another bright and dynamic personality whose star crossed with Marvel Comics in the early 1960s at a pivotal point in the company's career. Flo, a cabdriver's daughter, hailed from Boston where she'd graduated from the University of Massachusetts and had campaigned for both Teddy and Bobby Kennedy.

In March 1963, when Flo knocked on the doors of Magazine Management Company looking for a job, she was living at the YWCA as many freewheeling young career girls did at the time. Upon hiring Steinberg, Stan told her she'd be required to answer the mail, which was delivered to the floor above the Marvel office, and to take turns with all the other magazine divisions one day a week, covering the switchboard when the regular operator took her lunch break.

In 2010, Flo remembered the 1963 Marvel headquarters like this: "655 Madison Avenue was at 60th Street. It was a big building with a drugstore at street level. This was before the big drugstore chains. The name was "Boyd Chemists" and it's still there! When I first started there weren't many letters and most of them were to *Millie the Model* and *Patsy Walker*. Later, due to the FF, Spidey and all the other superheroes, the mail increased to 20 letters a day, then 30, then 40, and by 1968 we had mailbags full. I mostly thought of it as a wonderful first job in New York. Hindsight tells me I should

have kept a diary or notations. I'm sorry I didn't!"

Contrary to popular legend, there never was an early 1960s "Marvel Bullpen" as envisioned within Marvel's letter-pages and "Bullpen Bulletins"—a mythologized clubhouse in which the likes of Lee, Jack Kirby, Steve Ditko, Don Heck and others could be found kibitzing. That was a fable propagated by Stan (probably in a fit of nostalgia for the old Timely Bullpen), to give his small stable of creators a cohesive identity. In truth, the first Marvel office was merely a small cog in a much larger apparatus.

In 1963, if one rode the elevator to the second-story of 655 Madison Avenue, they would find themselves on a huge floor of offices that housed the many parts of Goodman's magazine operation; an operation which published Marvel Comics along with nearly thirty conventional non-comic magazines. The main division, Magazine Management Company, produced men's magazines. Another division called Humorama published digest-sized books featuring girlie cartoons, and another branch called Lion Books handled paperback novels.

The office decor was insurance-company dull: Grayish white walls and foam tile ceilings, overhead fluorescent fixtures and gray metal desks. Except for the executive offices, which faced Madison Avenue and had carpets and windows, the space was divided into jerrybuilt cubicles with head-high partitions. Editors got a glassed-in area in each cubicle.

Stan's tiny two-room office, which was located in a small back corner of Magazine Management, was totally unpretentious. It was the same working quarters that Lee had toiled in since the fall of Atlas. The only thing that distinguished it from any other Editor's office on the second floor was a tall magazine rack which was stocked with newly published Marvel comics. Stan distributed these comics as complimentary issues to the freelancers who had worked on them. The artists weren't supposed to take any books other than their own, but that never stopped Steve Ditko. He would take the comics which he considered inferior and throw them in the wastebasket right in front of Stan.

Lee had a manual typewriter parked in front of his desk on the right side, which had its own portable metal stand. This was the iconic typewriter that Stan Lee used to co-plot the greatest comics of the 20th Century. Stan described it to us as "an old Remington with a bad ribbon." In the days before he began writing at home, Stan could be seen in his cubbyhole furiously typing

Joe Sinnott's inks made FF #5 a superior-looking issue to its predecessors—just in time for the debut of Dr. Doom.

A Marvel milestone: The Thing first shouts his signature line in FF #22.

away. He would pile his finished scripts on his desk, alternating them vertically then horizontally to keep them separated. When an artist came into Lee's office, he would take his script from the pile.

But not all of Stan's freelance artists needed a detailed plot outline. Lee's top illustrator, Jack Kirby, could draw an entire book after just a brief story conference or phone call. Stan described the process like this: "I realized there was really no need for me to labor over a fully developed script if Jack was to be the illustrator. All that was necessary was to discuss the basic plot with him, turn him loose, and wait until he brought me the penciled drawings. I'd occupy myself elsewhere till he returned with the drawings done. After I received the penciled pages, it was then my task to write the dialogue and captions. After writing the copy, I'd give the pages to a letterer, who'd then letter all the captions and balloons in the areas I had indicated. Next, the pages would be taken by the inker who would go over the penciled drawings with a pen or brush applying black India ink to all the indicated areas. At this point the artwork would be returned to me for final editing and, once the colorist had applied the proper colors to photostats of each and every page, the completed strip would be sent off to the engraver—and what happened then I never knew."

According to "Fabulous Flo" (a title that Lee would soon bestow on her), "Most of Stan's inkers and letterers loved to come to the Marvel office for their pages. It gave them a break from their at-home work routines. But if a deadline was close, the original art would sometimes be sent by Special Delivery messenger service. This was possible because all the Marvel freelancers lived in the Tri-State area. In the days before U.P.S. or Fed-Ex, the U.S. Postal Service would often be used to send out the pages." Dick Ayers has stated that he received nearly all of his 1960s Marvel inking assignments via the U.S. mail.

Stan and Flo worked in close proximity with their cubbyholes separated by a head-high partition. Lee and Steinberg were the only full-time staffers Marvel had in 1963. The rest of the work was handled freelance. Part-time production manager and occasional inker Sol Brodsky would sporadically stop in and set up an extra little drawing board where he would do the paste-ups and mechanicals for the ads. He also did lettering on some of the character logos that remained in use for decades. It was Sol who created the original cover masthead for *Fantastic Four,* using the same font that he used for the *Amazing Fantasy* cover logo.

When Brodsky was a young man he wanted a career in comics so bad that at age 17 he accepted a job sweeping floors at Archie Comics. In 1942, he began a rather unspectacular career as an artist at Timely Comics. By 1954, he decided he'd rather be the company's production manager, working as the right hand of Stan Lee. When Atlas collapsed in 1957, Sol became the founding editor of *Cracked,* a

Mad Magazine knockoff. Sol left *Cracked* in 1964, and came back to work production for Stan, who was grateful to have him back.

Everybody, without exception, liked Sol.

Dorothy Gallagher, a 1960s Magazine Management employee, described the scene like this: "At Magazine Management, magazines were produced the way Detroit produced cars. I worked on the fan magazine line. On the other side of a five-foot partition was the romance magazine line. And across the corridor were the financial staples of the organization, the men's magazines—*Stag, For Men Only,* and *Male*—for which, at one time or another Mario Puzo, Bruce Jay Friedman, David Markson, Mickey Spillane and Martin Cruz Smith wrote, until they became too exalted and rich to do it anymore. I'm almost forgetting the comic book line, where Stan Lee co-created Spider-Man and other classic comics!"

This insider's view of the 1960s Marvel Comics operation is something of a shock to baby-boomers who grew up believing there was a real Marvel Bullpen. Invariably, the True Believers who used to visit 655 Madison Avenue for a glimpse of the Bullpen were doomed to disillusionment. According to Flo, "They always wanted to have tours of the office, so I'd go out and they'd have to be satisfied with me. There was just nothing back there to see." Some of the fans didn't believe this, and would try to bulldoze their way past Steinberg, who soon became adept at throwing body-blocks.

Flo was only answering a handful of letters a day in 1963, but amazingly many of them were from college students and even adults.

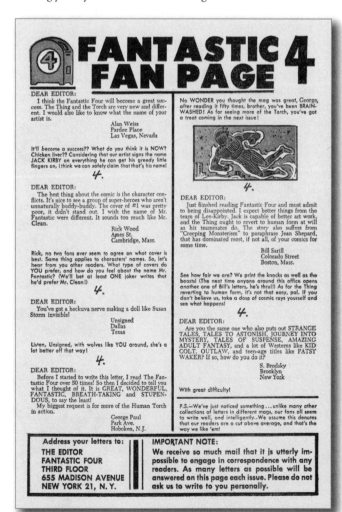

"S. Brodsky" penned one of the fan letters from this FF #3 letters' page. And "Unsigned" uses the term "heckuva"—just like Stan often did. It's curious they had to use fake letters, considering the "Important Note" about receiving so much mail.

Not the ten-year olds who wrote to DC to tell them about a "boo-boo" they found in *Lois Lane.* The "Fantastic Four Fan Page" soon became a crossroad where scholars and housewives, GIs and peaceniks were linked by a common devotion to the Thing or Prince Namor.

Suddenly, for the first time in his career, Stan began setting trends instead of following them. In *FF* #10, he decided to loosen things up and promote a sense of casual camaraderie between himself and his readers: "Look—enough of that 'Dear Editor' jazz from now on!" Lee exclaimed. He instructed the fans to change the salutations to "Dear Stan and Jack." This immediately made the DC letter-pages seem stodgy and impersonal.

As much as Lee blew his own horn and bragged about Marvel, he could be equally humble and self-effacing when readers wrote in about mistakes they found in his comics. Unlike the stuffy DC letter-pages where nameless editors would try to worm their way out of every goof with an implausible explanation, Stan would own up, and express so much humility that the fans cut him considerable slack.

Taking the whole thing a step further, Lee began awarding a "no-prize" to every reader who discovered an oversight. At first the no-prize was conceptual, but at some point kids began to receive envelopes with a headshot of the Hulk stating: "Congratulations! This envelope contains a genuine Marvel Comics NO-PRIZE which you have just won!" In the latest fashion of 1960s conceptual art, the envelope was empty.

Using an ingenious idea that originated in the letter-pages of the 1930s sci-fi pulps, Stan not only listed the names of the correspondents but their entire address as well, so they could contact one another directly. And they did. In the early 1960s comic fandom was growing, finding its own complex identity and coalescing around Marvel comics, *Fantastic Four* in particular. The True Believers sensed they were a part of something entirely new, something that mattered.

By the end of *Fantastic Four's* formative months, the magazine's radical innovations were getting noticed by fans and pros alike. Against all probabilities, the series had survived the substandard production, sparse art and second-rate inking of its early issues to leave every other superhero comic in the dust. It became a barometer of what superhero stories could aspire to in the hands of an ambitious writer and artist.

It's just about impossible to overestimate how big an impact the early *FF* had on the comics industry. The magazine sparked a renaissance in the comic book field via new, relevant characters with humanistic traits, presented in a fresh, highly literate writing style. Initially, the management at DC loathed these four outrageously modern

comic book stars because they threatened the existing structure. But before long, *Fantastic Four* spurred the entire medium into a radical reassessment of superheroes.

Picking up the gauntlet flung by Marvel, DC began producing their own offbeat characters like the Doom Patrol and the Metal Men. It would soon become obligatory for action heroes to have backstories, distinctive personalities and character-delineating speech patterns. In this way, *Fantastic Four's* catalytic effect shifted the axis of emphasis from science-fiction to characterization, and in the process it opened the gates to real innovation.

CONTINUED AFTER NEXT PAGES...

Namor and the Thing duke it out in FF #9 (Dec. 1962). Inks by Dick Ayers.

The Age of Innovation

AT A GLANCE *FF* #1 (Nov. 1961)
Ayers-cover inks
   "The Fantastic Four" 13p Klein-
inks
   *"The Fantastic Four Meet The
Mole Man"* 12p Klein-inks

The entire comic book medium was about to be forever altered.

In one pass, this startling debut issue managed to utterly demolish DC's straight-jacketed ideas of superheroism with a sense of anarchy and recklessness that was previously unfathomable. *FF* #1 shattered limitations of every kind. It immediately forced a stagnant comics industry to reevaluate its unenlightened and outmoded notions of the superhero genre. It was as fast, and simple, and complete as that. Readers knew immediately that *Fantastic Four* was going to shape up to something big.

On the first page we see a strange man—who is somehow *more* than just a man—holding a still-smoking flare gun that he used to signal the most unique superhero team comics had ever seen. Once the quartet has gathered, the story flashes back to the FF's origin—the unauthorized flight to the stars, the bombardment of cosmic rays, the crash and the amazing discovery; they had all gained superhuman powers. *And so was born "the Fantastic Four!!" and from that moment on, the world would never again be the same.*

The sweeping action begins on page 14 as the FF discover the subterranean grottoes of the grotesque Mole Man—a tragic, unwanted soul who would rather face the underground's darkness than the scorn of those who breathe in the light of day. The FF managed to polish him off in a mere three pages, but not for good. He would return many times to make scattered appearances throughout the series, right up to Kirby's final months on the book.

That a comic book like this could have come to exist at all is extraordinary; but that it came from a nowhere outfit like Martin Goodman's was a complete shock. This radically dark-edged anti-superhero story changed everything. It ushered in an unforgettable era of hope, upheaval and

achievement. It was like a window opened to let some bad air out.

The enormity of *FF* #1's impact is incalculable. It was the comic book medium's ultimate declaration of change; a decisive goodbye to everything that came before it. In terms of historic significance, this revolutionary origin issue is second only to *Action Comics* #1, which featured the first appearance of Superman.

The Marvel Universe, the greatest fictional playground ever created, has officially begun.

AT A GLANCE *FF* #2 (Jan. 1962)
Ayers-cover inks
   *"The Fantastic Four Meet The
Skrulls from Outer- Space!"* 24p
Klein-inks/*Thing* 1p Klein-inks

This sophomore issue achieved the same impact as its predecessor: the promise of new possibilities presenting themselves, of a great new breadth and sophistication, of a whole new style made possible.

Has any *Fantastic Four* comic ever resembled an Atlas alien tale more than *FF* #2? All the elements of Jack and Stan's "take me to your leader" stories are found in this issue: Earth's impending doom at the hands of space-invaders and the intruder's inevitable defeat—not by might, but by an ingenious use of human wit. There's even a *Tales to Astonish* type ending where the Skrulls turn themselves into contented cows.

And in this issue we find seeds of the Universe to come.

Previously, in both Atlas and DC comics alike, alien invaders hailed from various planets and endless galaxies, no two alike. After being defeated at the story's end they were never seen again. But in an unprecedented move, the Skrulls would return to *Fantastic Four* time and again, adding another consis-

tent element to the ever-expanding Marvel Universe.

Reed vanquishes the Skrulls by convincing them that monsters from *Strange Tales* and *Journey into Mystery* actually roam the Earth. Stan's penchant for hyperbolic salesmanship was already rearing its head, and *Fantastic Four* was only in its second installment.

Here's the odd thing: The artwork that Kirby was producing for many of Goodman's other titles at this time seems superior to the underdeveloped art in *FF* #1 and 2. Take for example Kirby's "Sserpo" tale from *Amazing Adventures* #6 (Nov. 1961). The King's art in *AA* #6 is noticeably more labor-intensive compared to the sparse backgrounds, simple layouts and lack of detail seen in the early issues of *Fantastic Four*. Obviously, the King had a staggering workload at this point, but why wasn't he giving these all-important first issues his best stuff? Unfortunately, the answer is unknowable.

Seen in the warm nostalgic glow of hindsight, Kirby's sparse, raw-edged vitality in *FF* #1 and 2 harks back to something older, something more archaic, something that had been missing from comics for years.

In fact, these thrilling, crudely-drawn early *Fantastic Four* stories seem like a throwback to the dark, fearsome, pre-Comics Code aesthetic of the 1940s Timely superheroes. And in that light, *FF* #2 shines brightest.

AT A GLANCE *FF* #3 (Mar. 1962)
Ayers-cover inks
   *"The Menace Of The Miracle
Man"* 23 p Brodsky-inks/*Human
Torch* 1p Brodsky-inks

To have come out of such a vacuum and wreak such changes at such speed, with such totality—even now, it's hard to conceive the

daring and self-belief it must have taken from Lee and Kirby.

Astonishingly, it took only three issues for Jack and Stan to get *Fantastic Four* stabilized. The foundations they established in *FF* #3 would be the magazine's template for the next fifty years and undoubtedly longer.

"The Menace of the Miracle Man" is a prime example of the writers shifting boldly into new terrain. The costumes, the Doc Savage-style skyscraper headquarters and the original bathtub-like Fantasticar all make their debuts.

Emotional nuance is introduced on page 16, when the Thing once again acknowledges his attraction to the Invisible Girl, just as he did in *FF* #1.

The introduction of another Atlas-type monster in *FF* #3, the second in a mere three issues, displayed an uncharacteristic caution on the part of the creators who seemed reckless in every other regard. Perhaps at this point Martin Goodman was hedging his bets on a full-blown superhero revival.

Another development in this issue was the first "Fantastic Four Fan Page" with a letter from Sol Brodsky and an unsigned correspondence that was undoubtedly written by Stan. This wouldn't be the last time Lee would slip a letter into the *FF* Fan Page. At this point the letters all began with "Dear Editor" in the age-old DC tradition.

The key to this issue's immortality is its totally unexpected twist ending. The flaming mad Human Torch, sick of the Thing's haranguing, quits the team in disgust and blazes off into the sky. Superheroes simply did not act like this in 1962. It was spellbinding.

Now the stage is set, now all the necessary elements are at hand.

Now the long upward climb begins.

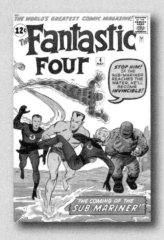  

AT A GLANCE *FF* #4 (May 1962)
Brodsky-cover inks
"The Coming Of The Sub-Mariner" 23 p Brodsky-inks/*Mr. Fantastic* 1p Brodsky-inks

In its fourth installment *Fantastic Four* simply explodes.

This is one of the few comic books from the early 1960s that fifty years later still retains all the freshness and originality that was instantly apparent on the day it was released. At this point *Fantastic Four's* Age of Innovation was in full bloom, and it would soon spur a total revitalization of the action hero genre.

Because *Fantastic Four* made it the norm, it's easy to forget that in 1962 very few superhero comics used the entire book to tell a single story. And even at this early stage, 23 pages weren't always enough. Johnny's cliff-hanger resignation in the previous issue ensured that this tale would pick up right where *FF* #3 left off, with a search for the Torch.

The very idea of a teenage superhero wandering the Bowery and seeking shelter in a rundown flophouse makes for one of the strangest comic book stories ever told; but Jack and Stan were just getting warmed up.

The main reason for *FF* #4's splendor was the return of the Sub-Mariner, who hadn't been seen since 1954. Lee and Kirby shrewdly revived Bill Everett's anti-social aquanaut with the same sleek, post-modern aesthetic that DC used to revive the Flash. Under Lee and Kirby, Namor would never again be heard muttering expressions like "Sufferin' Shad."

Two significant components of the Marvel Universe were established in this groundbreaking tale. First, the generic "Central City," the group's original locality, is dropped in favor of New York. The Big

Apple would become the hub of all the Marvel superheroes except the Hulk. It was inevitable that they would run into each other while flying above the Statue of Liberty or hurtling over the Brooklyn Bridge. Having the same hometown made their never-ending crossovers thoroughly plausible.

And second, when Prince Namor became part of the same time-continuum as Marvel's Silver Age heroes, it added yet another element to the Marvel Universe; Timely's Golden Age history. Marvel's past and present had been linked by the Sub-Mariner, and it paved the way for other Timely superheroes to follow in his wake.

Very few comic books will ever come close to this one. With clear hindsight, one can see that *FF* #4 is a staggering achievement from every point of view.

AT A GLANCE *FF* #5 (July 1962)
Sinnott-cover inks
"Prisoners Of Doctor Doom" 23p Sinnott-inks

Fantastic Four #5 made it thrillingly clear that a new Renaissance in superhero comics was fully—and irreversibly—under way.

The magazine's fifth installment was a landmark *par excellence*. It introduced Victor Von Doom, Jack and Stan's evildoer extraordinaire. Doctor Doom instantly became Marvel's premier villain; a position he still holds to this day.

In these pages we get a tantalizing taste of what the early *Fantastic Four* would have looked like if Joe Sinnott had signed on as the book's inker from the beginning. Sinnott's masterful control of the Winsor-Newton brush makes this story easily the best-looking *FF* tale to date.

Lee had never received fan let-

ters praising a comic book's inking as far as he could remember. But after *FF* #5, he was getting mail saying how great the inks on the Dr. Doom story looked. Stan never forgot that. He knew Joe Sinnott would be the perfect inker for his flagship magazine, and he wouldn't give up until he got him. Unfortunately "the Prince of Pen and Ink" as Lee called him, was too busy working for Treasure Chest and Archie Comics. And at this point, Martin Goodman wasn't paying enough to lure Sinnott away.

When asked what he remembered about inking this milestone masterwork, Sinnott recalled how complete Kirby's pencils were, and that he received $10 a page for the job. Obviously, Goodman got his money's worth.

This period of unbridled wonderment was *Fantastic Four's* Age of Innovation; the months when the foundations were being laid. And now that the FF had an opponent worthy of their mettle, the magazine's success was cemented. With each new issue *Fantastic Four* was moving relentlessly forward, exposing the mediocrity and insignificance of everything that preceded it.

AT A GLANCE *FF* #6 (Sept. 1962)
Ayers-cover inks
"Captives Of The Deadly Duo" 24p Ayers/Sinnott -inks

The seeds planted in *FF* #4 come to full fruition in *FF* #6, as Sue Storm and Prince Namor's mutual infatuation shocks Sue's teammates and comic book readers everywhere.

The idea of Mr. Fantastic's girlfriend falling for the arrogant, sociopathic Sub-Mariner was a masterstroke, an out-of-the-park grand slam. It was light years ahead of any other superhero

comic in terms of emotional nuance, and a brilliant synthesis of Lee and Kirby's romance-comics skills.

Any other comic book writers would have resolved this *ménage a trois* in one issue. Sue would have "come to her senses" then tearfully embraced Reed in the last panel. Instead, Jack and Stan milked the melodrama for years before the unpredictable Invisible Girl finally chose Reed over Namor. It was this type of gradually unfolding narrative that gave *Fantastic Four* its guts, its focus, its inseparable bond with reality. And it made the fans ecstatic.

Retrospection illumes a near-subliminal offshoot of the Sue/Reed/Namor triangle. The dynamic between Ben and the Invisible Girl changed significantly after this issue. The adoration that Ben felt for Sue, which was established in *FF* #1 and reinstated in *FF* #3, was a road that Lee and Kirby now deemed a dead end. So they cleverly laid it to rest in this story as Ben bitterly exclaimed, *"Bah! I knew it—all a gal wants is a good-lookin' guy—it doesn't matter if he's the most dangerous creep on Earth!"* The Thing would never again mention any amorous feelings for his beautiful teammate. After this issue, the chemistry between the Thing and the Invisible Girl slowly evolved to where "Suzie" was like a kid sister to Ben.

Dick Ayers reported that Joe Sinnott inked some of the drawings of the Invisible Girl in this story. Sinnott corroborated this claim, explaining that after inking a few panels he dropped *FF* #6 to do a higher-paying assignment for *Treasure Chest*. Check out Sue's "Sinnott face" on the fifth panel of page 2.

Up to this point *Fantastic Four* had been on a bi-monthly publishing schedule. After this issue, the Lee/Ditko sci-fi anthology *Amazing Fantasy* would be given the heave-ho, and the adventures of the FF would appear monthly.

The Ayers Age

AT A GLANCE FF #7 (Oct. 1962)
Kirby-cover inks
    "Prisoners Of Kurrgo, Master Of
Planet X" 24p Ayers-inks

At this point it seemed the magazine's intensity had diffused.

The first six issues of *Fantastic Four* had been tightly compressed with both daring and innovation. Stan Lee was modernizing superhero comics with an against-the-grain aggressiveness that only a man with nothing to lose would have dared to attempt. Indeed, at this time Lee practically had his bags packed, ready to move on from comics at any given moment. And his partner Jack Kirby, who'd been a rebel from day one, was always willing to match Stan's sense of anarchy tit-for-tat. But after the first flush of systematically groundbreaking neophyte issues, one comes to *FF* #7 and the winning streak stops here.

One of the few things worth mentioning about this unremarkable story is Will Murray's observation regarding the cover. Reed's face on the front of *FF* #7 is a self-portrait of Jack Kirby. Moreover, in a rare break with tradition, Kirby inked the cover himself; so the resemblance can't be attributed to another illustrator imposing his own style of art on the drawing.

The self-portrait and the self-inking are intriguing. Were they related? Such questions now have only an academic poignancy because the answers are lost forever.

As for the ridiculous looking Kurrgo, he was just another Atlas throwback right down to the unnecessary double-consonant in his name.

Doubtless, stories like this would allow readers an easier transition between the Marvel alien tales and the Marvel superhero stories. But coming on the heels of *FF* #1-6, which were virtual object lessons in originality, this issue seems like a celebration of mediocrity—a major step backwards.

Very little in this story commends itself. The daring, force and invention that the series demonstrated in the Age of Innovation will be, to some extent, noticeably subdued during the forthcoming months.

AT A GLANCE FF #8 (Nov. 1962)
Ayers-cover inks
    "Prisoners Of The Puppet
Master" 23 p Ayers-inks/*Human
Torch* (facts page) 1p

Ayers-inks

The first page of Stan's plot synopsis for *FF* #8 has survived in reprinted form because Lee mailed the original copy to *Alter Ego* co-founder Jerry Bails in late 1963. This partial synopsis covers the first 13 pages of *FF* #8, and unlike the 1961 *FF* #1 story outline, which Jack and Roz Kirby called a fraud, the authenticity of this plot synopsis has never been challenged.

What does it prove? To begin with, if one compares *FF* #8 to Stan's synopsis, there's only one conclusion to be drawn: Kirby followed Lee's directions exactly as written, right down to the number of pages that Lee recommended for each set of events.

In light of this, even the most rabid pro-Kirby pundits would have to concede that Jack's later statements—claiming that Stan never wrote anything—were utter nonsense.

Question: Does Stan's *FF* #8 plot outline indicate that Lee single-handedly conceived the entire story where Ben meets Alicia? Answer: Not necessarily. Stan might have conferred with Kirby about the storyline first, and then typed the synopsis afterwards.

AT A GLANCE FF #9 (Dec. 1962)
Ayers-cover inks
    "The End Of The Fantastic Four"
23p Ayers-inks/"*How The Human
Torch Flies*" 1p
    Ayers-inks

In the 1950s the sunny optimism of the Superman comics made them hugely successful. In the 1960s it made them something to rebel against.

In *FF* #9 our heroes are evicted from the Baxter Building due to financial problems. You'd never see the JLA getting ejected from

their "secret sanctuary" or Batman hitchhiking because the Batmobile got repossessed. In 1962, the creators of *Fantastic Four* were innovating with a zeal that at times felt almost reckless.

Given all this, it's clear that the *real* recklessness of *FF* #9 was the idea of Sue Storm and the Sub-Mariner out on the town together; dining in a swank Hollywood nightclub with Sue dressed to the nines and Prince Namor looking as debonair as James Bond. It was riveting. Wasn't this chick supposed to be Reed's girlfriend?

Kirby geeks are adamant that a Kirby-written *Fighting American* story called "Roman Scoundrels" had the same storyline as *FF* #9, where the heroes are enlisted to make a movie—but the film studio is owned by the villain, and the on-camera stunts that the heroes perform are very real hazards. "Roman Scoundrels" was written in 1955, but didn't see print until 1966, when Harvey Comics put it out in a giant-size Harvey one-shot.

Most of history's great visionaries had a Nostradamus-like ability to see into the future and Kirby was no exception. He predicted Hollywood's current infatuation with comic book heroes decades before the fact. The last panel of *FF* #9, where the Fantastic Four walk the red carpet at their movie premier, can easily be seen as a glimpse into the distant future when the FF's adventures hit the big screen.

AT A GLANCE FF #10 (Jan. 1963)
Ayers-cover inks
    "The Return Of Doctor Doom"
23p Ayers-inks/*Invisible Girl* 1p
Ayers-inks

At this point the magazine's storyline took a sharp turn toward the peculiar.

FF #10 is an extrapolation on the ending of *FF* #2, where Reed tricks the Skrulls with some Marty Goodman monster comics. Once the first breach had been made, the cracks were bound to get wider. The concept of Lee/Kirby comics co-existing in the world of the Fantastic Four is taken a step further in this story as the readers meet Stan Lee and Jack Kirby themselves.

It's not the intention of this book to straddle either side of the "who contributed what" debate. With that said, it might be safe to speculate that this issue's plot was founded on a Jack Kirby premise. *Boy Commandos* #1 has a segment that depicts Simon and Kirby plotting a *Boy Commandos* story at the DC offices. As the Simon/Kirby sequence unfolds, the Sandman walks into their office and interacts with them. In this tale, as Lee and Kirby are plotting a *Fantastic Four* story at the Marvel offices, the demonic Dr. Doom walks in on them.

There was an uncanny similarity between the Simon/Kirby appearance in *Boy Commandos* #1 and the Lee/Kirby appearance in *FF* #10. In both cases it was a rather shameless way to generate some self-publicity for the magazine's creators.

Jack and Stan were even featured on the cover.

AT A GLANCE FF #11 (Feb. 1963)
Roussos-cover inks
    "A Visit With The Fantastic
Four" 11p Ayers-inks/"*The
Impossible Man*" 11p
    Ayers-inks/*Sub-Mariner* 1p
Ayers-inks

Lee and Kirby were totally different than any other comic book creators of their era in their desire to play with the superhero genre; to shake it up, restructure it and

 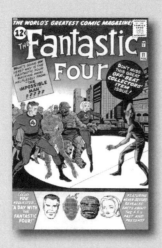  

stretch its boundaries to fit their creative needs. *FF* #11 is a perfect example of this experimentation.

The first feature in this issue, "A Visit With the Fantastic Four" is the last serious attempt at a concept that simply wasn't working. *FF* #2 established the premise that the Fantastic Four were real people living in the same world that we do: a world where Stan's monster comics existed. *FF* #10 revealed that Stan and Jack co-existed in the same world as the Fantastic Four; and that Lee and Kirby produced a comic book based on the quartet's adventures.

This story takes the idea a step further by having the FF "break the fourth wall" and speak directly to the readers of *Fantastic Four*—addressing issues that were normally tackled in the letters-page.

This over-the-top attempt to blur fantasy and reality apparently received a lukewarm response. And with good reason; this magazine was supposed to be about Reed, Ben, Sue and the Torch, not the *Fantastic Four* comic book—and not about Stan Lee and Jack Kirby, as much as they liked to think otherwise.

After *FF* #11, everything went back to normal. There'd be no more intersection of Fantastic Four the group and *Fantastic Four* the comic, save for an insignificant breach in *FF* #34. All future breaking of the fourth wall would be done through Stan's captions and footnotes.

Likewise, there'd be no further Lee/Kirby appearances in the pages of *Fantastic Four* save for one last humorous cameo in *FF Annual* #3, where Nick Fury ejects them from Reed and Sue's wedding (and the satirical "This Is a Plot?" in *Annual* #5).

Regarding this issue's second tale, the impossibly lame Impossible Man had a downright

odd love/hate relationship with his creators.

The way Roy Thomas tells it, in the 1970s when he told Stan he wanted to bring the alien back, Lee groaned and said they received more negative mail about the Impossible Man than any other character.

As far as Jack Kirby was concerned, he told a reporter the Impossible Man was the worst idea he ever worked on at Marvel.

And yet…Stan reprinted the Impossible Man tale in *FF Annual* #3, and Jack immortalized him in his legendary 1970s sketchbook; a book that featured only 134 of Kirby's countless characters. Johnny Storm didn't even make the cut.

Besides *FF* #1, this was the only *Fantastic Four* comic in the entire Lee/Kirby canon that utilized DC's then-standard two stories per issue format.

AT A GLANCE *FF* #12 (Mar. 1963)
Ayers-cover inks
"*The Incredible Hulk*" 23p
Ayers-inks

When analyzed from a historical perspective, *FF* #12 has not worn well.

Anytime Stan thought one of the Marvel superheroes needed a boost, he would give the character a cameo in Marvel's flagship magazine.

At this point, *The Incredible Hulk* was limping to an early discontinuation. Distributors were returning unsold *Hulk* comics by the truckload, and Stan hoped a last-minute change of artists (from Kirby to Ditko) plus this crossover in *Fantastic Four* might save the oblivion-bound *Hulk* series at the eleventh hour.

Hindsight reveals the Hulk's appearance in this issue may have done him more harm than good.

Seldom has a book's cover promised so much and its story delivered so little. The tale loses a great deal of momentum due to its drawn-out beginning. The Green Goliath and the FF don't square off until page 17. By page 20, it was all over.

Net result: short weight.

The True Believers turned the final page with an inescapable sense of anticlimax; and the needle of the reader's personal Ecstatograph pointed sullenly to zero.

AT A GLANCE *FF* #13 (Apr. 1963)
Roussos-cover inks
"*The Fantastic Four Versus The Red Ghost And His Indescribable Super-Apes*"
22p Ditko-inks

Harry Donenfeld, founder of DC comics, led a life that was almost legendary. But DC editorial director Irwin Donenfeld, Harry's son, just wasn't the man his father was. Harry was constantly browbeating the kid in front of the DC staff, and Irwin claims that DC's co-founder Jack Liebowitz, who always befriended him, seemed more like a father than his real dad.

That has nothing to do with *FF* #13, but this does: One of Irwin's more questionable editorial decisions was that *apes sell comics*. Apparently, back in 1951, an issue of *Strange Adventures* that featured a gorilla on the cover sold well, so Irwin decided there must be a simian sub-current running through comic fandom. "We're gonna do more apes!" he announced.

Soon, Superman was battling a Super Gorilla called Titano, and Superboy had a pet called Super Monkey. There were DC back-up strips starring "Congorilla" and "Bobo the Detective Chimp." And in 1958 there was even a Bat Ape.

Inevitably, they decided the gorilla-cover's success was a fluke.

Someone should have told Stan.

The idea of combining an evil commie cosmonaut with a trio of super-monkeys is one of the lesser ideas that graced the pages of *Fantastic Four*, which goes to show: You are who you steal from.

The wondrous Watcher was another matter entirely. With his *FF* #13 debut readers were introduced to the first "cosmic" element in the book's storyline. He was also the FF's first pro-social supporting character (i.e., a recurring character, but not a villain, who would make sporadic appearances in the series).

The Watcher, in hindsight, was a tantalizing glimpse into the magazine's cosmic future. He was Kirby's first "space god," and a precursor to *Fantastic Four's* flirtations with space-age mythology; a concept which eventually spawned the Silver Surfer, Galactus and the Kree.

Fantastic Footnote: This was the first *FF* story inked by the enigmatic Steve Ditko. The second (and last) Ditko-delineated *Fantastic Four* tale appeared in *FF Annual* #1. Oddly enough, Stan always claimed that Sturdy Steve was his favorite Jack Kirby inker.

AT A GLANCE *FF* #14 (May 1963)
Ditko-cover inks
"*The Merciless Puppet Master*"
22p Ayers-inks/Advertisement:
(Thor/Spiderman/
Iron Man/Ant-Man/Human Torch) 1p Brodsky-inks

After Steve Ditko's unmistakable inking on *FF* #13, and on the cover of this issue, Dick Ayers is back for the interior pages and the consistency of the book's art has returned. Prince Namor has also returned: *FF* #14 marks the Sub-Mariner's 5th appearance in the

pages of *Fantastic Four*.

The adventure begins with Reed walking in on Sue as she scans the depths of the ocean with a "roving-eye" apparatus, searching for the Sub-Mariner. Sue's internal conflict over Prince Namor is far from resolved at this stage. Namor had motivations that she could sympathize with, and faults she could identify with. The magazine's regular readers were constantly intrigued by the strange hold Sub-Mariner seemed to have on the emotionally conflicted Invisible Girl.

Alicia Master's stepfather, the androgynous Puppet Master, is back for the second time and he brainwashes Namor into kidnapping Sue to lure her teammates into a trap. The Puppet Master's scheme is foiled by a giant octopus, and Namor allows the Fantastic Four to leave his undersea domain in peace after the Puppet Master's spell subsides.

The odd element in the tale is Alicia, Ben's love interest. The Thing brings her along for the ride, even though her presence in the storyline serves no narrative purpose whatsoever.

With this bottom-of-the-sea adventure, *Fantastic Four* seems to be treading water.

AT A GLANCE *FF* #15 (June 1963) Ayers-cover inks
"*The Mad Thinker And His Awesome Android*" 20p Ayers-inks/*Fantastic Four* 1p Ayers-inks

It's tempting to speculate that the Mad Thinker was probably Stan's idea, and that the Awesome Android was probably Jack's.

The idea of a villain who sits inert like Rodin's statue, making complex calculations, doesn't seem like something the most action-oriented artist on Earth thought up.

On the other hand, the huge grey blockhead with no facial features other than a large mouth seems pure Kirby. It was the exact type of freakishness that upset the pansy DC editors who were put-off by the King's disturbing energy.

While many early issues of *Fantastic Four* suffered from the malady of Monsterism, the "Awesome Android" is so twisted that he works like mad.

Fantastic factoid: After this issue the cover-title dropped its *The* and became simply *Fantastic Four*.

AT A GLANCE *FF* #16 (July 1963) Ayers-cover inks
"*The Micro-World Of Doctor Doom*" 22p Ayers-inks/*Mr. Fantastic* 1p Ayers-inks

The biggest turkey on the Lee/Kirby farm had always been the Ant-Man.

In 1962, with *The Amazing Spider-Man* shaping up to be a critical and commercial success, Stan probably figured that another insect-hero with a hyphenated name would give the company another hit.

In this case the second time wasn't a charm. Not even the King's powerful art, matched by his best inker of the period, Dick Ayers, could make such an absurd character palatable.

Kirby biographer Mark Evanier reported that Jack was always asking if Henry Pym's adventures could be assigned to someone else. In hindsight, Steve Ditko might have done a better job on the quirky Ant-Man than the King.

Ant-Man's guest appearance in *FF* #16 wasn't mere happenstance. At this point the initial sales figures for Ant-Man's slot in *Tales to Astonish* were coming in, and the news wasn't good. Jack and Stan were now using their flagship magazine to boost the disappointing

sales of *Tales To Astonish*.

In addition to his crossover in *FF* #16, Ant-Man's flirtatious female sidekick, the wonderful Wasp, appeared around this same time in *Tales To Astonish* #44. Stan was hoping this two-pronged redevelopment strategy would give the tiny hero a much-needed shot in the arm.

Lee's plan fell on barren ground and failed to take root. The ditzy, hypersexual Janet Van Dyne (Marvel's answer to Tinker Bell) was just as ineffective as the Ant-Man himself. Bringing her in to save the series was akin to throwing a drowning man an anvil.

In this second *FF* crossover tale, Dr. Doom has become the ruler of a Micro-World. Previously, in *FF* #10, he'd been shrunk by Reed and now he's wreaking havoc from below. The quartet uses Pym's shrinking serum to locate Doom and defeat him.

Oddly, just as they did in *FF* #12, the writers decelerated the storyline and Ant-Man doesn't get in on the action until page 19. By page 22 the entire skirmish was over, which made the FF's encounter with Ant-Man Ant-iclimactic.

As for Kirby, he finally got his wish. After *Tales To Astonish* #40, he was pulled off *TTA* and the penciling chores were handed over to Don Heck.

As it turned out, Kirby's departure from the series would shrink the Ant-Man's prospects infinitely more than any amount of reducing serum.

AT A GLANCE *FF* #17 (Aug. 1963) Ayers-cover inks
"*Defeated By Doctor Doom*" 22p Ayers-inks

On this issue's exciting cover Stan announced that "The Marvel Age of Comics" had begun. And who besides DC would argue with

that? At the time it seemed like the dawn of a glorious new Renaissance in superhero comics. It felt like everything was just beginning, that everything lay ahead and the possibilities were infinite.

The diabolical Doctor Doom is back for his fifth appearance in the series. The True Believers loved him, and since the writers couldn't come up with another villain who was half as good, here he is again, folks.

AT A GLANCE *FF* #18 (Sept. 1963) Roussos-cover inks
"*A Skrull Walks Among Us*" 21p Ayers-inks

With this issue the readers get their first taste of George Roussos' *FF* inking on the cover of the book. Actually, the Thing looks superb, but regrettably this would not be the norm.

In this story the Skrulls from *FF* #2 return, and they've created a Super Skrull to defeat our heroes.

Suspension of disbelief, that unspoken pact between the comic book reader and the comic book writer, is sorely tested at this point. First, why is this Skrull "super" just because he can morph into any member of the Fantastic Four? Any Skrull could do that, and in fact they did in *FF* #2.

Next, the Super-Skrull has the FF's powers, but there's one of him and four of them, so it seemed like a shutout from the beginning.

As you might expect, such academic questions are antithetical to the very nature of comics. One is better off to cast aside the jaded skepticism that comes with age and rediscover their misplaced sense of wonder.

With that done, note how impossibly cool the Super-Skull looks when he adopts the head of a battering-ram and uses Reed's

powers to stretch his neck on page 14.

That's something you don't see everyday.

AT A GLANCE *FF Annual* #1 (1963) Ayers-cover inks

"Sub-Mariner Versus The Human Race" 37p Ayers-inks/*Mole Man/Skrulls/Miracle Man/Sub-Mariner* 4p Brodsky-inks/ *"Questions And Answers About The Fantastic Four"* 2p Ayers-inks/ *"Inside The Baxter Building"* 1p Kirby-inks/*Doctor Doom/Kurrgo/ Puppet Master* 3p Brodsky-inks *"The Fabulous Fantastic Four Meet Spider-Man"* 6p Ditko-inks/ *Impossible Man/Hulk/Red Ghost* 3p Brodsky-inks/*Mad Thinker*-1p Ayers-inks (reprint *FF* #1) "Origin Of The Fantastic Four" 13p (Torch re-drawn by Brodsky)

Propelled by a seemingly inexhaustible supply of daring and innovation, the early *Fantastic Four* swept through the stagnant world of superhero comics like a crossfire hurricane; mowing down all the life-diminishing boredom and mediocrity that stood in its unstoppable path. By dawn's light there was nothing left but a luminous trail of freshness and vitality that was previously undreamed of.

That, and *Fantastic Four Annual* #1.

Has any four-color stapled-in-the-middle masterpiece ever given a reader more value for their money than this Holy Grail of all Annuals? Anyone who owns an original copy, no matter how low-grade, can simply hold it in their hands and feel the magnificence dripping from every story-page, every pin-up page and every special-features page.

At the time of its publication, it was easily the most impressive American comic book ever seen. Just at a point when the series

seemed like it had leveled off, Lee and Kirby stood up and showed the world what *Fantastic Four* was all about.

With the benefit of hindsight it becomes clear that *FF Annual* #1 was the glorious grand finale to the early Lee/Kirby *Fantastic Four.* After this never-to-be surpassed Annual, many new phases and changes would begin.

Obviously, the introduction of Lady Dorma would further complicate the emotional drama between Namor and the Invisible Girl. And Sub-Mariner's reclaiming of his lost kingdom would eliminate his main source of rage, thereby removing Sue's primary motivation to sympathize with him.

This masterful *magnum opus* not only contained a 37-page FF epic, it also had a 6-page Spider-Man crossover plus 14 pages of pin-ups and special features. Nobody cared more about blowing the reader's minds than Jack and Stan at the dawn of the Marvel Age.

Fantastic Four Annual #1 shines with epic majesty. This was the best 25 cents a comic book fan ever spent.

AT A GLANCE *FF* #19 (Oct. 1963) Roussos-cover inks

"Prisoners Of The Pharaoh" 22p Ayers-inks

Who was Rama Tut? Even the writers seemed unsure.

In *FF* #5, Dr. Doom's time machine was introduced as the FF went back to the days of Blackbeard. The machine is exploited again in this story where our heroes meet an enigmatic "time looter" from 3000 AD.

This trans-temporal tyrant had used Dr. Doom's time-displacer to travel back to ancient Egypt where he was ruling as Pharaoh Rama Tut. The story ends with Rama Tut

escaping to another time-continuum as Reed theorizes that Rama Tut might be Doom himself.

He was right. While en route to the year 3000, Pharaoh Tut meets Dr. Doom in the 20th Century and the two decide they may be the same man whose lives have intersected either in the future or the past. Perplexingly, they can't resolve how they're both able to co-exist at the same moment in the present.

Let the confusion begin.

Before it was over, the enigmatic "Doom/Tut" would be reincarnated as Kang the Conqueror in *Avengers* #8, then as Immortus in *Avengers* #10, and later as the Scarlet Centurion in *Avengers Annual* #2. It was suggested that this time-displacing demon may have assumed further identities during various other travels through eternity.

The situation soon became staggeringly convoluted and one needed an Einsteinian grasp of relativity to understand it all. But it added yet another dimension to the ever-expanding Marvel Universe—the Future.

As for the *immediate* future, readers got a taste of the despoilment to come with the second consecutive FF cover inked by "George Bell."

AT A GLANCE *FF* #20 (Nov. 1963) Roussos-cover inks

"The Mysterious Molecule Man" 22p Ayers-inks (page 17, panel 3 by Ditko)

Fantastic Four #20 marked the end of a very memorable era.

After the first flurry of progression in issues #1-6, there was a stillness, almost as though the storm had blown itself out. In the pages of *Fantastic Four* #7-20, there would be no new villains equal to Dr. Doom, and no big events. Just

a few scatterings; a few isolated innovations like the Watcher.

This is not to imply that the Dick Ayers era was barren, or even a holding pattern. It does however seem like the writers had pushed the envelope as far as they dared (for the time being) and then felt the need to consolidate; to stabilize the series by offering some solid, unwavering craftsmanship. The deployment of a dependable long-term inker helped to achieve this.

Hence, *Fantastic Four* acquired a newfound consistency; but this isn't to imply that the Ayers Age was stagnant or formulary. Given hindsight, it was an era of subtle changes, constant motion and growth, as typified by Ben's gradual change of temperament after he met Alicia.

It would be most appropriate to think of *FF* #7-20 as a period of settling in. A bit of a lull perhaps, but the lull was only the calm before the storm of *FF Annual* #1, the most magnificent comic book anyone had ever seen.

In this tale another totally forgettable villain called the Molecule Man is introduced; one of Kirby's most ridiculous looking characters ever. His absurdity is somewhat offset by the return of the wondrous Watcher, but coming on the heels of *FF Annual* #1, this story seemed a rather tedious effort.

Given detailed analysis, the fairest way to assess the now-concluding second phase of *Fantastic Four* is in juxtaposition to what was happening at DC and other comic book companies at the time. In that context, the Ayers-era *FF* was a lush oasis in a dry desert of dross.

Nowadays any *Fantastic Four* story inked by Dick Ayers will trigger fits of nostalgia in first-generation fans. It was an era of hope and promise—a preamble of the wonders to come.

THE SUB-MARINER

FIRST APPEARANCE: FF #4

JACK KIRBY SEEMED TO HAVE THE SAME EMPATHY FOR PRINCE NAMOR AS HE DID FOR HIS OWN ORIGINAL CHARACTERS. THE KING DREW TWO MAGNIFICENT FULL-PAGE PORTRAITS OF THE SUB-MARINER IN FF #102 AND CAPTAIN AMERICA #112. HE ALSO RENDERED THREE PIN-UPS OF SUB-MARINER IN THE PAGES OF FANTASTIC FOUR (SEE FF #11, ANNUAL #1 AND FF #33). IN FACT, FANTASTIC FOUR'S FIRST-EVER TWO-PAGE SPREAD DIDN'T EVEN FEATURE THE QUARTET. FF ANNUAL #1'S MAJESTIC DOUBLE-PAGE PANORAMA DEPICTED NAMOR'S TRIUMPHANT RETURN TO HIS UNDER-SEA KINGDOM.

JACK'S AFFINITY FOR THE PRINCE OF ATLANTIS MAY HAVE STEMMED FROM HIS CLOSE FRIENDSHIP WITH THE SUB-MARINER'S CREATOR BILL EVERETT, AN ARTIST THAT KIRBY LOVED AND ADMIRED. IN THE EARLY DAYS OF COMICS KIRBY AND EVERETT WERE BOTH EMPLOYED BY THE VICTOR FOX STUDIO. THEY STAYED IN TOUCH FOR YEARS AFTER THAT.

IN THE LATE 1960S, KIRBY WAS REPORTEDLY AMAZED WHEN HE HEARD THAT EVERETT HAD BEEN INKING HIS PENCILS IN THOR. THE KING FELT THAT EVERETT SHOULD BE DRAWING HIS OWN BOOKS INSTEAD OF FINISHING ARTWORK DONE BY SOMEONE ELSE.

KIRBY WAS RIGHT. BUT IN FACT NO ONE, NOT EVEN THE INCOMPARABLE BILL EVERETT, EVER IMBUED THE PRINCE OF ATLANTIS WITH THE UNRIVALED SENSE OF POWER, DIGNITY AND GRACE THAT KIRBY GAVE HIM. AS SEEN ON THE PIN-UP PAGE FROM FF #33 (SHOWN AT RIGHT), NAMOR STANDS REGAL, MAJESTIC, AND NEAR-GODLIKE IN HIS AWESOME AQUATIC SPLENDOR.

A GALLERY OF THE FANTASTIC FOUR'S MOST FAMOUS FOES!

PRINCE NAMOR, THE SENSATIONAL SUB-MARINER

FIRST APPEARED IN F.F. #4 MAY

SUB-MARINER! RULER OF THE SEAS! ROYAL PRINCE-OF-THE-BLOOD OF A MIGHTY, ALMOST LEGENDARY RACE! HIS STRENGTH IS THE STRENGTH OF MANY SURFACE-MEN, AND HIS FIGHTING HEART AND RAW COURAGE MAKE HIM AN INDOMITABLE FOE! ABLE TO BREATHE UNDER WATER, TO WITHSTAND THE CRUSHING PRESSURE OF THE OCEAN'S DEPTHS... ABLE TO FLY FOR SHORT DISTANCES AIDED BY HIS WINGED FEET... POSSESSING THE INCREDIBLE POWER OF ALL THE UNDERSEA CREATURES, PRINCE NAMOR, THE SUB-MARINER, IS THE MOST TALKED-ABOUT, MOST COLORFUL HERO-VILLAIN IN ALL OF COMICDOM TODAY!

CONTINUED AFTER NEXT PAGES...

A MARVEL MASTERWORK PIN-UP

PRINCE NAMOR

REGAL NAMOR THE FIRST!
* PRINCE OF ATLANTIS
* EMPEROR OF THE DEEP
* LORD OF THE SEVEN SEAS AND
* SUPREME COMMANDER OF THE UNDERSEA LEGIONS

THE SUB-MARINER

DOCTOR DOOM

**FIRST APPEARANCE:
FF #5**

THE MORE ONE STUDIES THE LEE/KIRBY *FANTASTIC FOUR*, THE MORE IT BECOMES CLEAR THAT JACK AND STAN'S STRONG SUIT WAS CREATING NOBLE, DIGNIFIED HEROES. SO NOBLE IN FACT THAT THEY OFTEN BORDERED ON MESSIANIC, IN THE VEIN OF BLACK BOLT AND THE SILVER SURFER. LIKEWISE, THE DUO'S GREATEST FAILING WAS THEIR INABILITY TO CONCOCT THE ANTITHESIS OF THESE HEROES—MENACING VILLAINS, EVIL-DOERS, AND BAD GUYS.

DURING THE FF'S COSMIC ERA, THE BOOK'S MOST SIGNIFICANT PERIOD, IT'S NOTEWORTHY THAT THE QUARTET OFTEN FOUND THEMSELVES BATTLING CHARACTERS WHO WERE BASICALLY HEROES LIKE THE INHUMANS, THE SILVER SURFER AND THE BLACK PANTHER. THIS TENDED TO AMPLIFY THE WRITER'S STRENGTHS AND CAMOUFLAGE THEIR WEAKNESSES.

JACK KIRBY'S FANTASTIC FOUR HAD THREE INCOMPARABLE ADVERSARIES: SUB-MARINER, DR. DOOM AND GALACTUS. GALACTUS WAS A DOUBLE-EDGED SWORD BECAUSE HE WAS SIMPLY TOO POWERFUL, TOO OMNIPOTENT TO BE CONVINCING AS A REOCCURRING CHAR-ACTER. THE WRITERS KNEW THE MORE HE WAS EMPLOYED THE LESS EFFECTIVE HE WOULD BECOME. AS FOR NAMOR, AS SOON AS HE GOT HIS OWN SERIES HE BECAME TOO BUSY TO SQUARE-OFF WITH THE FF. ALMOST BY DEFAULT DR. DOOM BECAME FANTASTIC FOUR'S EVILDOER EXTRAORDINAIRE; THE VILLAIN TO BEAT.

AND SELDOM HAS A COMIC BOOK ANTAGONIST EVER BEEN GIVEN SUCH DEPTH AND DIMENSION. *FF ANNUAL #2* CONVINCINGLY ESTABLISHED THE ROOT OF HIS EVIL, AND DEEPER INSIGHTS INTO HIS DARK, TWISTED PERSONA WOULD BE REVEALED WITH EACH SUBSEQUENT APPEARANCE.

UNSURPRISINGLY, THE OFTEN-AT-ODDS LEE AND KIRBY DISAGREED STRONGLY ON WHAT LAY BENEATH DOOM'S HIDEOUS METAL MASK. LEE CLAIMED THAT VICTOR'S FACE WAS HORRIBLY DISFIGURED FROM A COLLEGE LAB ACCIDENT, WHEREAS KIRBY INSISTED THAT DOOM ONLY RETAINED A SMALL SCAR FROM THE MISHAP. THE KING FELT THAT VON DOOM'S OBSESSIVE VANITY CAUSED HIM TO HIDE HIS VISAGE FOREVER BECAUSE OF THE TINY FLAW.

THE WATCHER

FIRST APPEARANCE:
FF #13

AND WHAT A TREMENDOUS CHARACTER HE WAS. A BENIGN DEMIGOD OF BOUNDLESS WISDOM, HIS EXISTENCE WAS DEVOTED SOLELY TO OBSERVATION AND SOLITUDE. HE SEEMED UTTERLY DETACHED, PASSIVE IN EVERYTHING. HE STOOD LIKE STONEHENGE, MASSIVE AND MOTIONLESS, SILENTLY SCRUTINIZING ALL THE EVENTS OF THE UNIVERSE WHILE ALLOWING HIMSELF TO TAKE NO PART IN THEM.

BEGINNING WITH *TALES OF SUSPENSE* #49 (JAN. 1964), THE WATCHER WAS FEATURED IN HIS OWN BACK-UP SERIES, COHABITATING IN A SPLIT-BOOK WITH IRON MAN. THESE SHORT STORIES WERE DRAWN AND SCRIPTED BY STAN'S BROTHER, LARRY LIEBER. FOR THE MOST PART, THE *TALES OF SUSPENSE* BACK-UP TALES WEREN'T ABOUT THE WATCHER. THEY WERE THE TYPE OF INTERPLANETARY MORALITY STORIES THAT ATLAS HAD CRANKED OUT FOR YEARS. BUT IN *TALES OF SUSPENSE* THE WATCHER INTRODUCED AND CONCLUDED THE EPISODES LIKE A COSMIC ROD SERLING. AFTER THAT, THE WATCHER WAS GIVEN A 10-PAGE BACK-UP STRIP IN THE LEE/BUSCEMA *SILVER SURFER*, SCRIPTED BY STAN AND EVOCATIVELY RENDERED BY GENE COLAN.

AS IT TURNED OUT, THIS INTERGALACTIC OBSERVER BROKE HIS CONSECRATED VOW OF NON-INTERFERENCE MORE THAN ONCE TO HELP THE FF. BUT DESPITE THIS PARADOX, FEW OTHER CHARACTERS IN FANTASTIC FOUR EVOKED THE SAME SENSE OF UNBRIDLED AWE AS THE WONDROUS WATCHER.

FANTASTIC FOUR #17-9

The recurring menace of Dr. Doom—their first truly great villain—kept readers coming back for more. Original art from FF #17.

46

MOMENTUS

Fantastic Four drifted along, erratically and on occasion brilliantly.

The magazine's swift popularity meant a shift away from scattershot innovation and a move toward calculated refinement. The writers seemed to have stumbled onto the right formula. Now they could get down to the business of fine-tuning.

After the prodigious innovations in the first six issues the series cooled off and began to gather steam slowly, almost imperceptibly. This period was a bit of a lull, a leveling-off. On the plus side, the book finally had a consistent look due to the dedicated and dependable inking of Dick Ayers. Ayers may not have been the best in the business but his warm, unassuming brushstrokes gave the series a visual signature that will nowadays trigger fits of nostalgia in any first-generation *Fantastic Four* fan.

Throughout this period the big stumbling block was the book's antagonists. Many of them were thoroughly third-rate; boring, ludicrous and one-dimensional. In particular, Kurrgo, the Impossible Man and the Red Ghost were total losers.

When you compare the FF's early villains to the rich array of evildoers that Stan and Steve Ditko created for *Spider-Man*, Lee and Kirby's shortcomings become clear: bad guys were their Achilles' heel. This is probably why the book's two most potent adversaries, Dr. Doom and Prince Namor, kept returning again and again almost to the point of over-saturation.

Fantastic Four's most consistent strength during this era was its rich character depictions and scripting. The Thing, over time, developed a wisecracking Brooklynesque dialect that counterbalanced his angst. Ben's speech was peppered with remarks like "what a revoltin' development," William Bendix's catchphrase from the 1930s radio sitcom *The Life of Riley*. Ben called Reed "Stretcho" as if Richards was the lost Marx Brother. There were arcane references to a mysterious Aunt Petunia, and curses for the despicable Yancy Street Gang. Unquestionably, the colloquialism that towered above all else in

Ben's vocabulary was his iconic battle-cry "It's clobberin' time!" From the moment he first shouted it in *FF* #22 (Jan. 1964), it became his immortal hook.

Lee's characterization shone brightest on the emotional triangle between Sue, Reed and Sub-Mariner. Readers were astonished to see Namor and Storm dating in *FF* #9. In 1962, the idea of a fickle super-heroine being infatuated with a villain was unheard of. You wouldn't see Lois Lane doing the town with Brainiac. But unlike the psychologically unsophisticated Lois, Sue Storm was wracked with complex

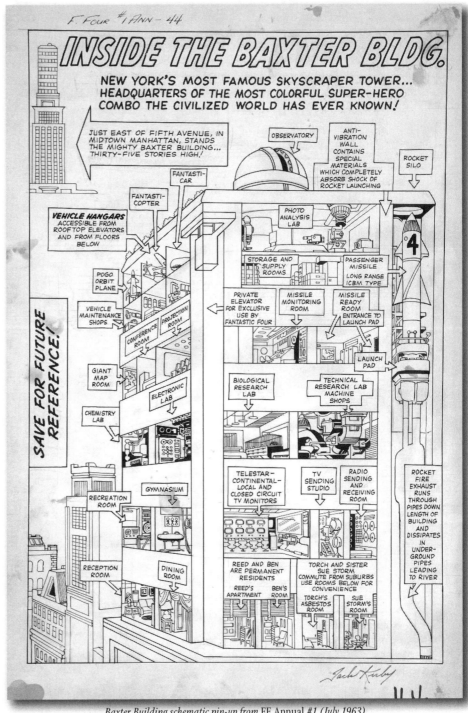

Baxter Building schematic pin-up from FF Annual #1 *(July 1963).*

emotions. She was tormented by self-doubt and conflicted about who she wanted to be.

No doubt about it, these characters acted impossibly real. They were moody and unpredictable. They worried and got depressed. They showed their dark sides and wore their neuroses like a badge. They were every bit as flawed as we are, which made them irresistible. It was impossible not to feel involved with them.

Fantastic Four's most spectacular issue during this period was *FF Annual* #1, which went on sale in July 1963. The True Believers had been howling for a *Fantastic Four Annual* like the 25-cent "80 Page Giants" that DC had been successful with. But there was a problem. The DC Annuals featured reprints from decades past, while *Fantastic Four* only went back eighteen issues. Even Martin Goodman wasn't dodgy enough to re-sell comics that were barely two years old.

In an uncharacteristic gesture of goodwill, Goodman gave Lee and Kirby the green light to whip-up a blockbuster summer Annual with a whopping 57 pages of new stories, pin-ups and special features. In the lead story Sub-Mariner finds his lost race and declares war on the surface world.

The ensuing marathon-length clash was a larger-than-life spectacle with a cast of thousands; the comic book equivalent of a Cecil B. DeMille big-screen apocalypse. Kirby pulled out all the stops, creating remarkably epic battle scenes and treating the True Believers to the book's first double-page spread. It was a dazzling consummation to *Fantastic Four's* first golden era, the most auspicious beginning any superhero series could have hoped for. Could all this really have happened in just two years?

The era after the first *FF Annual* brought more changes. The Invisible Girl's infatuation with Namor was finally winding down. Sub-Mariner's reunion with his lost race removed Sue's principal reason to pity him. In *FF* #22 (Jan. 1964), Susan was endowed with expanded powers including a maternal, womb-like force field that immediately became her greatest asset. This was done to placate a number of fans who claimed the Invisible Girl didn't contribute enough to the team.

Ben and Johnny's room-wrecking brawls in the Baxter Building became a staple of the series during this period, as did Ben's highly amusing war with the Yancy Street Gang. These ingredients added an exuberant light-hearted sense of fun which was notably lacking in most superhero comics.

Reed's ceaseless attempts to revert the Thing to human form became another recurring theme occasionally found in the neglected corners of the series. Inevitably, the readers who thought Ben's misery would eventually end were in for a rude surprise. He would, from time to time, change back to a human being, but never for any significant length of time—just long enough to have his hopes for a normal life dashed once more. The psychological cruelty of these brief returns to human form intensified Ben's malignant fate, and it made for heartfelt reading.

Another early *FF* trademark seen throughout this period was Stan's hucksterism. Hype is short for hyperbole. It means to promote by hustle, by pressure or by any means necessary. The idea is that you leave nothing to chance. Hype was an integral part of Lee's approach to *Fantastic Four* and other Marvel titles in this period. Stan hustled like mad; a tireless self-publicist, he came on crass and utterly bombastic like a barker at a strip-show. His huge, ubiquitous blurbs promising "*pulse-pounding thrills!*" and "*enough fantasy to*

When Chic Stone became Kirby's main inker, Jack's margin notes become faintly visible on the original art...

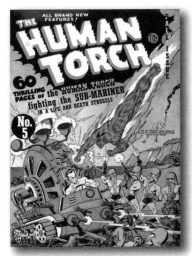

fill three magazines!" were pasted all over the *FF*'s early covers. They were cheap and tawdry but they were also endless, and cumulatively, they worked. It was almost as if Lee was a modern-day P.T. Barnum and Kirby's creations were his Museum of Wonders. And Jack made sure that the contents of those comics lived up to Stan's hype on the covers.

From one angle, a setback occurred at this point. Dick Ayers was pulled off *Fantastic Four* to pencil other Marvel books and the inking chores were handed over to George Roussos, a former Simon and Kirby employee who was then using the sobriquet George Bell. "Inky" Roussos, as Kirby called him, had a style that the readers found unappealing. His harsh and choppy inking sent the magazine's visual template back to the Dark Ages. This wouldn't be the last time Stan would give Marvel's hottest book to the wrong inker.

It didn't matter. What happened next was a *FF* story so grand and apocalyptic that no inker, no matter how mediocre, could ruin it.

First some background: sometime in the summer of 1941, Timely's Carl Burgos and Bill Everett threw a marathon party at Everett's apartment. It lasted three days, and nobody left except to procure more food and liquor. But it wasn't all frivolity. The assembled faction of five writers and six artists had gathered to create an epic sixty-page story with a short deadline. The end result, *Human Torch* #5 (Fall 1941, shown above), was a world-shattering slugfest between the Torch and the Sub-Mariner that ended with the duo destroying New York. The very idea of two superheroes battling each other was highly unique; something that never occurred in the 1940s DC comics. Stan Lee called this epic saga "the pinnacle of the Golden Age."

Human Torch #5 may have been Stan's seminal influence for the titanic double-length struggle between the Hulk and the Thing in *FF* #25 and 26 (April-May 1964). After the first insubstantial Hulk crossover in *FF* #12, the writers stumbled onto an ingenious solution. The key to a successful FF/Hulk encounter would be to eliminate Reed, Sue and Johnny, and let the two misunderstood monsters have at it.

And they did. Pounding, smashing and annihilating everything in their path, Ben and the Hulk ripped through brick walls like wet tissue-paper. Concrete shattered, skyscrapers toppled and entire city blocks came tumbling down. Chaos, catastrophe, wreckage and rage reigned supreme in a clash so monumental New York itself was shaken to its very core.

The Hulk's fury was uncontrollable as he pounded the Thing senseless. At the end of *FF* #25 Ben was bested. He staggered like a Chicago drunk, but stubbornly refused to yield. He seemed more heroic in defeat than he ever had in victory.

The subplots were just as intoxicating as the battle scenes. Reed was ill and Johnny was injured but they heroically refused to succumb to their infirmities. They regrouped, bandaged and half-delirious, just when Ben needed them most. In the second installment of this milestone masterpiece, the Avengers entered the fray and all hell broke loose. It was a triumphant *tour de force*, a stunning achievement; easily the best *Fantastic Four* tale to date.

FF #25 and 26 was the magazine's first two-part thriller. It proved that the superhero genre and its audience were capable of concepts far more ambitious than the publishers at DC and Marvel had previously thought. By breaking the bonds of the single-issue story, the Hulk/Thing battle introduced an epic scale; a foretaste of

...with the earliest examples being FF Annual #2 *(previous page),* FF #28 *(above), and* Avengers #6. *Were earlier inkers like Ayers and Reinman simply erasing them, while Stone didn't?*

In the last panel of FF #22, there's an overabundance of text telling us what happened—an instance where Kirby thought he had one more page to draw, and Stan had to fake an ending.

grander, more ambitious storylines to come.

In *FF* #25-29 (April-Aug. 1964), there was an extended run of crossovers which at times seemed almost excessive. The Hulk, the Avengers, Namor, Dr. Strange, the X-Men and the Watcher all invaded the series for five issues running. As it turned out, there was a point to all this seemingly gratuitous guest-starring. Jack and Stan's latest revelation was a consistent, ever-evolving fictional cosmos sustained by an undulating web of interconnections where everything impinged on everything else.

The world of Marvel Comics was becoming a codified, continuity-conscious Universe.

Almost from the start, Lee and Kirby had established that all their characters coexisted in the same world, and that the Golden Age Timely superheroes had existed in that same world 20 years earlier. But the exact pivotal point where the writers (quite consciously) consolidated their dazzling new Universe was *Avengers* #4, *FF* #25, *FF* #26 and *Avengers* #5. The apocalyptic Hulk/Thing battle in *FF* #25 had its actual beginning in the last panel of *Avengers* #4, and the storyline of *FF* #26 finally concluded in the first two pages of *Avengers* #5.

It was unprecedented; it was brilliant. By tying all his superheroes together, Stan could sell the entire Marvel line as one inseparable unit. In this way, the unification of the Marvel Universe was Stan Lee's crowning achievement. In due course it would change the face of comics permanently and prodigiously.

A significant improvement: The look of the magazine received a major facelift in *FF* #28 (July 1964), when Chic Stone became *Fantastic Four's* second long-term inker. Stone was probably the first Marvel inker to bring out the unadulterated power of the King's artwork. His forceful brushwork and boldly tapered holding-lines gave Kirby's superheroes an in-your-face three-dimensionality that few have approximated since. Just as Dick Ayers was the ideal early-period *FF* inker, Chic Stone would be the perfect delineator for Kirby's mid-period *Fantastic Four*.

Notable change: "It Started on Yancy Street" *FF* #29 (Aug. 1964). This issue had a Kirby/Stone cover so spellbinding that Lee published it totally unmolested by the usual hard-sell blurbs. This was a first. By issue #43, the cover blurbs would be gone entirely.

Milestone issue: *FF Annual* #2 (Summer 1964). The similarities between this remarkable Dr. Doom story and the Sub-Mariner epic from *FF Annual* #1 were uncanny. In *Annual* #1, the True Believers were introduced to Atlantis, Namor's empire, and in *Annual* #2, Marvelites discovered Latveria, Victor Von Doom's kingdom. Hence, the FF's two most popular adversaries were given very similar backstories. As the monarchs of their respective realms, they both acquired multilayered personalities and emotional depth. No longer one-dimensional villains, the human side of both men was beginning to emerge.

And still Kirby's energies were volcanic. By this time the King's storytelling instincts were improving with each subsequent issue. Many of *Fantastic Four's* early tales had begun with a traditional "symbolic" splash page which typically (and prematurely) depicted the heroes in the clutches of the bad guy. But now, more often than not, Kirby was forcing himself to find a riveting visual moment to begin each story; a beginning that would grab the reader's attention and keep it in a stranglehold.

The opening page of *FF* #25 is a classic example of this; the Thing is literally climbing the walls in a desperate attempt to thwart Reed's latest effort to revert him to normal. The drama and energy of that scene draws you in compulsively and holds you captive until the story's final page. In many cases, Jack's opening splash-page would be more appealing than the book's cover.

At this juncture there wasn't a single aspect of sequential storytelling that Kirby hadn't mastered. Nothing on a Kirby page was inserted casually or arbitrarily. Every panel was intelligently arranged for a specific narrative purpose. In many interviews Jack acknowledged that he designed his pages to be (quote) "easy on the eyes."

Manipulating a reader's field of vision across a comic book grid was a trick that Kirby knew better than anyone. Using ingenious layouts, he would arrange a panel's human figures and background objects in specific formations to create lines, semicircles and other geometric patterns. He would then use these patterns as subliminal roadmaps; directing the reader's attention to the most important parts of the panel, while absorbing the background details on a more subconscious level.

At will, he could bring the viewer's gaze to a pause or an abrupt halt—or send it hurtling in another direction, by bouncing it off a secondary element in the panel which the reader's eye will reject as a landing-point and pull away from. But after that detour, and maybe a couple more, the onlooker will inevitably lock onto Kirby's intended focal-point. Every time. In this way, the King had a genius-level understanding of sequential art. All these techniques, which were accumulated from a lifetime of drawing comics, produced crystal-clear storytelling.

Kirby's penciling in this phase displayed a film-director's intellectuality and a narrative drive that propelled the action from panel to panel with cinematic clarity. His page-designs depicted the story so vividly you could tell what was happening without reading a word of dialogue. His artwork during this "I'm drawing as fast as I can" period was far from what it would later become, but it still evoked a great natural vitality despite its hurried execution and occasional crudeness.

At this stage, with ever-growing regularity, Kirby began incorporating photo-realistic montage scenes into his stories. The King would laboriously cut pictures from *Life*, *Look* and *The Saturday Evening Post* and glue them onto his Marvel art boards. These labor-intensive paste-ups were sur-realistic post-Dada mosaics; space-age visions of *noir* insanity and, despite their post-printing loss of quality, they were really quite ambitious.

Throughout this period, what Lee brought to the table was his talent for presenting humor through dialogue, his ability to effectively script character-driven romance stories and his knack for natural sounding speech. Once these talents were blended into the *FF's* superhero framework, it provided much of what was extraordinary and unique about the early *Fantastic Four*.

For decades, DC Comics had been churning out bland superhero stories which were unpunctuated by either passion or rage. Because DC's scripts were so painfully placid, even the slightest Stan Lee innovation seemed like a radical progression; as if Stan was rewriting the rules of superhero storytelling with each new issue of *Fantastic Four*.

Indeed, a whole new Stan Lee was now coming into focus. The burnt-out hack whose career in comics had once seemed like a prison sentence was gone. In his place was "Stan the Man" who had risen like a phoenix from the ashes of Atlas and obscurity to take on the world.

Lee's attitude of having one foot out the door of the comics industry led him to throw caution to the wind, churning out flawed, neurotic super-heroes with little hope that they'd ever catch on, and not giving a damn either way. This altered his writing, which had once been purely mechanical, into a flippant, devil-may-care voice that could flirt and cajole with the reader one minute, shift to adolescent angst the next, or suddenly turn

into hyperbolic self-aggrandizing.

No one in history ever promoted a comic book line so effectively. Stan ballyhooed his magazines with more energy than anyone was used to. Lee preached for Marvel with the zeal of a Southern Evangelist, testifying that the "Marvel Age of Comics" was now upon us. His contagious, esoteric catchphrases like "Nuff Said" became his trademarks. Another Marvel slogan was "Face Front" which was derived from Stan's stint in the Signal Corps. Lee's most renowned watchword, "Excelsior," was the New York State motto meaning "ever upward."

Like everyone else in the comics industry, Stan had been envious of Bill Gaines' 1950s E.C. comics line. E.C. produced books of such high quality and had such a good rapport with its readers that many of E.C.'s fans were one-brand consumers. Now Stan was employing

Kirby/Stone original art for Fantastic Four #37 *(April 1965).*

the lessons he'd learned from Gaines and his "usual gang of idiots," such as the importance of catering to fans on a personal level, giving greater creative freedom to his top artists, and loosening up the letter-pages.

Suddenly, from out of nowhere, Lee began to display an uncanny ability to connect with his readers that was entirely lacking during his Timely/Atlas years. In welcome contrast to the staid, serious

approach of DC's editorial staff, Stan injected an element of irreverent fun into his comics. He developed pet names for all his superheroes like "Subby" and "Match-Head" (for Namor and the Torch),

and he devised in-jokes for his readers like Irving Forbush, Marvel's fictional mascot whose face was never seen. Lee went to great lengths to forge a sense of intimacy between Marvel's creators and Marvel's readers, assigning snappy nicknames to all his artists, inkers and letterers. Even Fabulous Flo Steinberg (above) had her own fans.

In the late spring of 1964, Stan did some checking and reported that there were over 200 Fantastic Four Fan Clubs worldwide; an estimate which he may have (typically) exaggerated. Nevertheless, it was around this time that Lee decided the True Believers should have an official fan club.

Beginning with Marvel comics dated November 1964, the initials "M.M.M.S." started to appear in Goodman's comics with no indication of what the letters stood for. Fans from across the globe wrote in, hoping to be the first in line to crack the code. Stan introduced the company's fan club, "the Merry Marvel Marching Society" in *Fantastic Four* #33 (Dec. 1964). It was Stan's one-up version of E.C.'s "Fan-Addict Club" which had been the first comic book fan club.

The M.M.M.S. offered the True Believers a $1 membership kit that included a welcoming letter along with a scratch pad, a pinback button, a certificate, a membership card and a one-sided vinyl LP called "The Voices of Marvel." The vinyl record was totally Stan's brainchild. He and other Marvel luminaries like Kirby and Fabulous Flo held court, bantering back and forth from a script of Stan's that was filled with corny gags. True to form, the intensely private Steve Ditko, a camera-shy and uncommunicative loner, refused to participate. "Nobody expected the fan-club to be so big," said Flo Steinberg. "There were thousands of letters and dollar bills flying around all over the place. We were throwing them at each other."

The early 1960s Marvel Comics Group seemed to exude a breezy "anything goes" attitude that the collective consciousness of comic fandom swallowed hook, line and sinker. Marvel's first-generation fans were almost religious adherents. Nothing like this had ever happened before. The readers were beyond impressed; they were utterly demolished, and they lined up in droves.

By mid-1964 Marvel was successful enough that Martin Goodman was able to move Magazine Management to a more lavish setting. The new location was at 625 Madison Avenue near 58th Street; a large building in a business district that was crowded with shops and restaurants. Marvel's sector of Goodman's operation consisted of three offices and a room which would eventually be used by Marvel's freelance artists. Stan had a comfortable corner office next to another office shared by Flo and Sol, who in 1964 became a full-time member of the Marvel staff. And in July 1965, a young man who wrote the first-ever review of *FF* #1 would join Steinberg and Brodsky in that office. Roy Thomas had moved to New York to write comic books.

Stan's desk at 625 Madison Avenue was located in front of a big window which overlooked the street several stories down. It was adorned by a small twin-picture frame that contained two black-and-white headshots of Stan's beautiful British wife. To the left of Lee's desk was his drawing and proofreading board. The wall behind his desk was decorated with Stan's favorite Marvel comic book covers, and below the Marvel covers there was a couch—a couch very similar to Martin Goodman's, which Stan once claimed was a sign of indolence.

Across the hall from Lee's office there was a reception area and a room with drawing tables that could hold up to three of Stan's freelance artists. Flo Steinberg called the new 625 address the first "real" Marvel Bullpen where a roomful of artists at drawing boards making corrections and preparing art for printing was established.

The fan club, the new location and the media attention that Marvel Comics was enjoying were all testimonials to the nonstop work Stan had been doing to promote the Marvel brand.

Around this time Martin Goodman became worried about Stan's popularity and

The most sinister seductress of the Silver Age, Madam Medusa looked intimidating, even in repose.

the monolithic control that Lee exerted over the Marvel line. Leon Lazarus, who wrote the Giant-Man tale in *Tales To Astonish* #64 (Feb. 1965), remembered it like this: "Goodman started pressuring Stan to have other writers do some of the stories. Martin wasn't sold on the Marvel Method of doing stories in which writers would supply artists with a plot synopsis, rather than a full script. He became concerned that Stan would have too much leverage over him, and he worried about what would happen if Stan ever decided to leave the company. Goodman wanted other writers as a back-up in case he needed them, so he ordered Stan to use other writers. Goodman told Stan to 'Have Leon write some stories.' Stan called me up and asked if I was willing to come in and work there again. I didn't want to say 'no' because I was working for Goodman's men's magazines, and didn't want to lose the account. I only did one story, because I wasn't comfortable with the way Stan wanted writers to work with the artists, though I see now how right he was."

Major development: In *FF* #35 (Feb. 1965), Sue finally accepted Reed's marriage proposal after resolving her confusion over Sub-Mariner eight months earlier. This was the type of milestone the writers usually saved for the *FF* Annuals. Events such as these gave the series a veneer of realism, development, change and progression. Beyond this, it cemented the quartet's internal consolidation. Now more than ever, the Fantastic Four were the closest-knit group of superheroes on Earth.

Iconic new character: Madam Medusa. The Frightful Four, who first appeared in *FF* #36 (March 1965), were classic examples of how Kirby's boundless imagination could turn the mundane into the monumental. They were a couple of *Strange Tales* also-rans and a lawbreaker-on-loan from Steve Ditko. Only one of them had true intensity.

The malevolent mistress with the mentally-manipulated mane was the only female character in the Marvel Age that Kirby rendered with real eroticism. She was seductive, irresistible, and had no redeeming qualities whatsoever. Had she stayed evil, and not ended up as Black Bolt's worshipful girlfriend, Medusa could have gone on to become a female Doctor Doom; nothing less. It was such a waste—one of Lee and Kirby's major miscalculations.

Either way, Medusa was the essential link between Jack and Stan's mid-period *Fantastic Four* and the book's "cosmic" era. She was the nexus, the intermediary to many irrevocably altering events. The coming of the Inhumans, Crystal's role as Johnny's soul-mate and the three-pronged storyline which the series would eventually acquire all connect back to the ravishing redhead from *FF* #36.

Fantastic Four rolled on. Before the Chic Stone era the book's progress had been erratic. Now it was on a steady upward spiral. The magazine began to increase in popularity on word of mouth and its own continuous improvement. At this crucial crossroad there was definitely something in the air. Readers sensed that something big could happen at any minute, something great. No one however, could have predicted the epic cosmic sagas that were about to unfold. No one could have foreseen them because these apocalyptic spectacles were beyond mortal comprehension. They existed solely in the mind of Jack Kirby.

Greater glories were just up ahead.

CONTINUED AFTER NEXT PAGES...

Final page of FF #36, *which Mark Evanier says (like the last page of #22) was an example where Kirby miscounted his pages—hence the abrupt ending, and dialogue describing events not seen in the panels.*

THE ROUSSOS PERIOD

AT A GLANCE *FF* #21 (Dec. 1963)
Roussos-cover inks
"The Hate-Monger" 22p
Roussos-inks

Now the barren months begin. George Roussos' inking on *FF* #21-27 was crude, choppy and unattractive. It was rushed-looking at best. At its worst it was amateurish. This was a huge pitfall for the look of the magazine. For purposes of identification, the era that begins with *FF* #21 will be called the Roussos Period; the age of Bad Art.

This major step backwards wasn't entirely the fault of Roussos' inadequate inking, although it certainly was the biggest contributing factor. Kirby was simply too loaded down at this point to produce great work. Marvel was launching their "team" books (*Sgt. Fury, the X-Men* and the *Avengers*) which the King was drawing along with *Thor, Fantastic Four* and a host of Marvel covers every month. It was a workload that was tantamount to legalized murder.

In this story Nick Fury, now a Colonel in the C.I.A., returns to enlist the aid of the FF to defeat a rabble-rousing Klansman-type called the Hate Monger.

Many comic book writers have commented on how trite the conclusion of this story is. They miss the point. When the Hate Monger is unmasked at the end, the writers didn't mean he was *literally* Adolph Hitler. It was a metaphor. Whenever the ugly specter of intolerance, racism or xenophobia rears its head, the Third Reich lives again.

In this context, *FF* #21 is a fairly formidable morality tale.

AT A GLANCE *FF* #22 (Jan. 1964)
Ayers-cover inks
"The Return Of The Mole Man" 22p Roussos-inks

The splash page of this story is classic. Reed is conducting experiments on Sue to tap into her previously unexploited invisibility powers. The lissome, long-legged society girl stands with her back arched, arms swept elegantly above her head with her long nimble fingers gently caressing the complex Kirbytech apparatus that's fitted onto her platinum blond hair. Only the gracefully gorgeous Invisible Girl could make Reed's cold metal apparatus look like a fashionable Jackie Kennedy pillbox hat.

In the story's closing moments, there's definitely something off-center.

In the last panel there's no sign of the Mole Man's isle blowing up and sinking beneath the surface—just an overabundance of text telling us that it happened. This seems to be an instance where Kirby thought he had one more page to draw, and then realized he had miscounted. Subsequently, Stan had to fake an ending in the dialogue, which resulted in Kirby's final panel being almost obliterated by Lee's verbiage.

Fantastic factoid: Dick Ayers inked the cover of this issue. Other than the Sub-Mariner pin-up in issue #33, this would be his last-ever inking of *Fantastic Four.*

AT A GLANCE *FF* #23 (Feb. 1964)
Roussos-cover inks
"The Master Plan Of Doctor Doom" 23p Roussos-inks

In this issue Dr. Doom returns once again, and he's assembled a team of three villains with distinctive abilities: Bull Brogin, "Handsome Harry" Phillips and Yogi Dakor.

The plot of *FF* #23 seemed to have a lot in common with the Lee/Ditko "Enforcers" tale from *The Amazing Spider-Man* #10 (March 1964). Both storylines featured a trio of troublemakers with diverse talents who had a nefarious leader manipulating them from behind the scenes.

Since these two stories were drawn about the same time, and since the Enforcers tale had a Kirby cover, it's tempting to speculate that Kirby got the inspiration from Ditko or vice versa.

AT A GLANCE *FF* #24 (Mar. 1964)
Roussos-cover inks
"The Infant Terrible" 23p Roussos-inks (1st collage art: 2 panels)

Meticulous reinvestigation concludes that at this point the series is temporarily drained of all positive inspiration, enthusiasm and direction. George Roussos (a.k.a. George

Bell) had an inking style that the fans didn't like. At this time comic fandom was producing a new breed of critical and discriminating readers—readers who were developing strong opinions about writing and art, and becoming more vocal regarding the aesthetic value of the comics they cared about.

It was clear to the fans that George Roussos' inking was too inept to supply the needed atmosphere to Kirby's pencils. In the letters-page of *FF* #26, Stan explained that "Darlin' Dick Ayers" now had a full schedule of penciling and inking on books like *Strange Tales, Sgt. Fury, Two-Gun Kid and Rawhide Kid.* For this reason, he'd been pulled off *Fantastic Four.* Stan's announcement was obviously a reply to a number of fans who were writing to ask why the magazine's art had become so unattractive.

At this stage Lee didn't have much of a knack for matching the right inker and artist. Paul Reinman wasn't doing any better than Roussos in the pages of the 1964 *Avengers* and *X-Men.* This wasn't all Stan's fault. It's a cinch that he didn't have the industry's top talent beating down his door for the rock-bottom rates Goodman was paying. Thus, Ayers was out and Roussos was in.

This issue features Kirby's first cut-and-paste photomontage attempts (see pg. 18, panels 1-2). These collage pages, more often than not, became somewhat compromised in the printing process. Oftentimes when seen in reprints, they don't even make sense. It's been reported that Marvel's production department hated Kirby's paste-ups. So did Joe Sinnott. According to Sinnott, "I thought they were a visual distraction from the story—they'd have looked better if Jack had just drawn it." Kirby obviously thought otherwise.

Despite this story's clever title (derived from the French colloquial-

ism *L'Enfant terrible*), this is a monumentally mediocre offering. Whenever Lee and Kirby couldn't come up with a decent opponent for the FF they fell back on their customary contingency plan, which was to whip-up another Atlas-type monster or alien. By this point the practice was becoming derivative, unadventurous and self-conscious.

FF #24 was another regrettable rearward glance at the Atlas-era alien tales. Unfortunately, it wasn't the last one.

AT A GLANCE *FF* #25 (Apr. 1964)
Roussos-cover inks
"The Hulk Vs. The Thing" 22p Roussos-inks

Mark Evanier has stated that he was, and still is, puzzled by a comment Kirby made to him regarding the assassination of John F. Kennedy (which, by Evanier's estimate, occurred when Jack was drawing *FF* #25-26).

Kirby told Evanier the President's death had a profound effect on him, and had a major impact on his work. Mark examined the stories Kirby drew around the time of the assassination and was unable to find any connection. Evanier asked his readers: "Can you see anything in those stories to suggest one of the creators was deeply moved by the murder of John F. Kennedy?" At the risk of falling on my assumptions, I'm going to try.

As abstract as this may seem, the overall sense of emotion in *FF* #25 runs parallel to the feelings that were rampant in America during the infamous "three days that shook the world." In what sense? Well, for starters, in the sense of chaos on an epic scale.

In *FF* #25 the police and the Army are totally ineffective as the rampaging Hulk destroys everything in his path. Just as the Secret Service and the Dallas police were totally ineffec-

tive as Kennedy and Oswald were gunned down on national television. New York City being torn apart by Ben and the Hulk could be a metaphor for America being torn apart by a tidal wave of grief and despair.

In the story's subplot, Reed, Sue and the Torch are too disabled and weak to do anything except watch in horror as the awesome battle is broadcast by television news crews—just as the country sat glued to their TV sets, watching the death of JFK with the same sense of shock and disbelief.

Parallels between the events of *FF #25* and the events of November 1963 can be drawn from the turmoil, the mass confusion, the sense of momentousness and the enormity of the two events. It's no coincidence that the clash between the Hulk and the Thing was the most powerful and unforgettable story Kirby drew in 1963. It reflected the most powerful and unforgettable story the world would witness in 1963.

Too bad the inking sucked.

AT A GLANCE *FF #26* (May 1964)
Roussos-cover inks
  "The Avengers Take Over" 23p
Roussos-inks

Jack Kirby's relentless storytelling rhythms propelled this *Battle Royal* like a runaway train.

Despite the inadequate inking, despite Stan's temporary memory lapse regarding the name of the Hulk's alter ego, and despite the fact that the proportion on the cover was just downright *off,* this hypnotically compelling slugfest between the FF, the Hulk and The Avengers whisks the reader along with a breathless sense of motion. It encapsulates everything that was mesmerizing about the early 1960s Marvel Comics.

It would have taken any other artist 100 pages to fit all this action in. Not Kirby. On page 9 and 10, in just three widescreen panels, the

unstoppable Hulk manages to tear through the ranks of the Avengers, kidnap Rick Jones, and wreck Tony Stark's mansion with a wall-shattering exit. It was a crash course in superhero storytelling; a lesson in power, speed and economy.

This story was also a lesson in cross-title continuity; it actually spanned four separate comics. *FF #25* picked up precisely where the last panel of *Avengers #4* left off; by answering Rick Jones' question about what the Hulk would do upon learning his confidant had switched allegiances to Captain America. *Fantastic Four #26* would segue directly into the splash-page of *Avengers #5,* with the Avengers surveying the Hulk's damage to their headquarters. This was thematic integration on a scale previously unthinkable. How could a comic book universe that was almost nonexistent just two years earlier support all this connectedness?

And talk about a twist ending. The Wasp is the one most responsible for bringing down the rampaging Hulk; enveloping him in a pestilence of insects until he goes mad and hurls himself into the Hudson River. Only Jack Kirby could find a way for Marvel's weakest character to topple its mightiest one.

This was Marvel's early period at its apogee.

At the story's end, as the undefeatable Fantastic Four stride heroically into the New York night, Sue is holding hands with both Reed and Ben. Imagine how unnatural it would look if Giant-Man, the Wasp and Iron Man did the same.

By way of their long familiarity with each other, the FF had formed a bond stronger than any superhero team had ever known. This was a turning point. From here on, after years of squabbling, jealousy and internal conflict, the Fantastic Four would be an inseparable team and family.

This was their shining hour.

AT A GLANCE *FF #27* (June 1964)
Stone-cover inks
  "The Search For Sub-Mariner"
23p Roussos-inks

This was the third installment in a series of five which seemed specifically designed to consolidate the unification of the Marvel Universe.

More than anything, the year 1964 would be about cross-character pollination in the Marvel Comics line. The idea of superheroes making guest appearances in titles other than their own had proliferated in comics since Day One. But nobody utilized crossovers as casually or continuously as Marvel did between 1963 and 1965.

Previous to *FF #27,* the weird dimensions and eerie enclaves of Dr. Strange had been curiously self-contained. After this impressive crossover tale, the nightmarish netherworlds of Stephen Strange were absorbed into the rapidly evolving topography of the Marvel Universe; a cosmology that was growing in leaps and bounds.

In another significant development, after three long years of fickle indecision, Sue Storm finally chooses Reed over the Sub-Mariner. During Sue's years of uncertainty, Stan, to his credit, kept the melodrama of the Sue/Reed/Namor triangle at economic levels; never sinking to heavy-handed over-the-top emotionalism. By contrast, the soap opera interludes between Jane Foster and Thor in *Journey Into Mystery* often caused the plots to lag.

And at this point *Fantastic Four's* "era of bad art" drew to a close. To be truthful, even the most sentimental Silver Age fan would be hard-pressed to look back on George Roussos' *FF* inking with any deep sense of nostalgia. And yet, despite the undeniably bleak artwork, the Roussos Period was not an unqualified disaster.

The return of Nick Fury in issue

#21 eventually spawned S.H.I.E.L.D., and Sue's big decision in *FF #27* paved the way for the comic book wedding of the century. *FF #25* and *#26* comprised the grandest *Fantastic Four* story to date; even toppling the majesty of *FF Annual #1.*

And it was during the Roussos Period, beginning with *FF #22,* that Kirby mastered the all-important trick of grabbing the reader's attention with the opening splash-page. Sue's scene-stealing moments on the opening pages of *FF #22 and 27,* along with the "riveting moment" splash-pages of *FF #23, 25 and 26* would eventually influence Kirby to discontinue using the traditional "symbolic splash" altogether.

But by now the intolerable inking was wearing thin. The Thing never looked worse than he did in this issue. Fortunately, the "Stone Age" was about to begin, and readers got a taste of it from this issue's magnificent cover, inked by the incomparable Charles Eber Stone.

The Stone Age

AT A GLANCE *FF #28* (July 1964)
Roussos-cover inks
  "We Have To Fight The X-Men"
22p Stone-inks

It seemed logical. Since *Fantastic Four* was burning a hot flame with its group conflicts and romantic triangles, and *The Amazing Spider-Man* was making fans ecstatic with the adventures of an alienated teen-hero, why not combine both premises into one superhero team?

The Uncanny X-Men were teenage mutants who often found it agonizing and awkward to have the ability to fly, freeze, or transmit lethal beams from their eyes. Their adventures were designed to underscore the hardships endured by persecuted minority groups. Their stories attracted young readers who were

grappling with their own adolescent dramas and lifestyle choices. Since the X-Men and the FF both lived in New York, It was just a matter of time before their paths crossed.

The cross-title guest-starring that was prevalent in *Fantastic Four* and other Marvel comics during this period was exciting and unique. It was also something that no other comics company could have pulled off, due to corporate structure if nothing else. Besides being the editor of the entire Marvel line, Stan Lee was the sole writer of all their main titles. Jack Kirby was drawing most of the superhero books and Chic Stone was inking almost all of Kirby's stuff. This meant when the X-Men stepped into the pages of *FF* #28, they looked and spoke exactly like in *X-Men* #6, which ran concurrently with this issue.

No other comic book line had ever shown such consistency. It was extremely satisfying on an aesthetic level, and it was totally beyond the reach of the competition. With DC's large staff, nearly every title had its own editor, writer, artist and inker. And in most cases, each editor ran his stable as if it were an independent company.

FF #28 is blessed by page after page of energetic Jack Kirby battle scenes, as the somewhat outmatched X-Men hold their own against the world's greatest superhero team. The big-panel Kirby/Stone free-for-all on page 18 is a comic-art masterpiece.

These elements alone make this crossover conflict a thoroughly satisfying reading experience.

AT A GLANCE *FF* #29 (Aug. 1964) Stone-cover inks
"*It Started On Yancy Street*" 22p Stone-inks (1 collage page)

In the 1930s Jack Kirby and his Suffolk Street Gang would go to war at the drop of a hat, leaping across the rooftops of New York's Lower

East Side to attack the rival Northfolk Street Gang with fists, rocks and bottles. As Kirby would later recall, "We would fight anywhere we had room enough to swing our fists."

Is it any wonder that the King of comics was so adept at drawing battle scenes?

Since Ben Grimm was a metaphor for Jack Kirby, the Yancy Street Gang was probably based on the Northfolk Street Gang. Oddly enough, the Yancy Streeters were the only "kid gang" that Kirby ever contributed to the Silver Age Marvel Universe; which is surprising in view of how many other kid gangs he produced before and after his Marvel tenure.

The Red Ghost and his Super-Apes appear once again with the Watcher, just as they did in *FF* #13. The DC craze of monkeys in comics and the clichéd "godless commie" villainy of the Red Ghost both seemed like outmoded concepts at the time of this story's publication.

The Watcher's appearance in this tale will be considered a crossover rather than a guest appearance, because at this point the wondrous Watcher had his own back-up strip in *Tales Of Suspense*. This issue was the final installment in a series of five consecutive crossover stories: Five stories that were specifically designed to consolidate a comic book cosmology where everything was interdependent on everything else. In 1964, Stan was using the phrase "The Marvel Galaxy." After countless stories like this, that Galaxy would evolve into a Universe.

FF #29, although somewhat innocuous, was by no means totally inadequate. If nothing else it had the magazine's most impressive cover to date. Kirby would virtually recreate it for *Fantastic Four* #39.

It also had a great title. In 1991 Stan admitted that "It Started On Yancy Street" was his all-time favorite early *FF* title. This is why *FF*

#29 featured the first-ever *Fantastic Four* cover which was totally unadorned by distracting dialogue-balloons or hard-sell hyperbole.

AT A GLANCE *FF* #30 (Sept. 1964) Stone-cover inks
"*The Dreaded Diablo*" 22p Stone-inks

This is a truly lugubrious offering. The way Roy Thomas tells it, Stan and Jack came up with the plot for "The Dreaded Diablo" while stuck in midtown traffic. It's too bad the hold-up didn't last longer. Maybe a stronger storyline would have emerged.

The discriminating reader will note that by page 17 the art begins to look hastily rendered and rough hewn. Many of the panels are devoid of backgrounds, and a lot of headshots that take up the entire panel are employed.

Stan claims that this story had to be drawn and scripted very quickly. He and Jack were behind schedule and the pages were due to go to the engravers in a matter of days. To expedite matters, the King borrowed the name and look of a previous character that he created for *The Double Life of Private Strong* called "Dr. Diablo."

In any case, The Dreaded Diablo was dross, and his legacy didn't last much longer than the traffic jam that spawned him.

AT A GLANCE *FF Annual* #2 (1964) Stone-cover inks
"*The Origin Of Doctor Doom*" 12p Stone-inks/*Super Skrull/Rama Tut/ Molecule Man/Hate Monger/Infant Terrible/Diablo* 6p Stone-inks/(r: *FF* #5) "*Prisoners Of Doctor Doom*" 5p/"*The Final Victory Of Doctor Doom*" 25p Stone-inks/*Human Torch/Invisible Girl/Thing/Alicia/ Mister Fantastic* 5p Stone-inks

This is a sweeping epic of tragedy, madness and destiny.

FF Annual #2 offers a dark and revealing examination of an innocent peasant boy who grows up to be a tragic, tortured tyrant and a dark obsessive genius. Readers discover Victor Von Doom's Gypsy origins, and find the source of his evil in the wrongs suffered by his family in Europe. We then witness his rise to power as he becomes the autocratic monarch of the Balkan Nation of Latveria.

In this majestic second *FF Annual*, Dr. Doom grew from his role of unqualified villainy to a broad humanity. He unfolds as a stern but benevolent dictator who is multifaceted and capable of growth, not just a one-dimensional fiend. In this context Doom became as much of a fully realized character as any of the heroes. He was the first arch villain in comic book history whose persona was explored with such depth.

Readers would find the same wealth of material in *Annual* #2 as in the previous year's Annual: Two new FF stories with a combined total of 37 pages, plus 11 new pin-ups.

The Kirby/Stone splash-page of Doctor Doom on his throne in royal repose is simply staggering; even better than the book's "symbolic" cover, which was the latest in a long line of *FF* covers featuring a sky-scraper-sized Dr. Doom towering over the Fantastic Four like a massive and menacing metallic mountain (see *FF* #5, 16, *Annual* #2, 39, 57 and 86).

Kirby simply couldn't draw a villain of Doom's magnitude normal size.

AT A GLANCE *FF* #31 (Oct. 1964) Stone-cover inks
"*The Mad Menace Of The Macabre Mole Man*" 21p Stone-inks

Despite the disappointing Diablo from the previous issue, the Stone Age, now in full bloom, caught *Fantastic Four* on a strong upswing following the unprecedented bleak-

ness of the George Roussos Period (*FF #25* and *26* notwithstanding). *FF #31* would usher in a string of superlative stories which were unequivocally Lee and Kirby's finest work so far.

The story begins with an adrenalin rush as Kirby employs his most attention-grabbing splash-page to date. The Baxter Building is shaken to its core by a violent earthquake, and our heroes are flung around like rag dolls.

In this issue the menacing Mole Man returns along with the Mighty Avengers for an exciting and well-executed tale that's capped-off by a brilliant shock ending. During the battle with Mole Man, Sue receives a severe head injury and only one surgeon on Earth has the skill to save her. Unfortunately, that surgeon is on the run from the law having recently escaped from prison. The attending physician tells Reed it's not likely this doctor will give himself up to save the Invisible Girl.

But he does. It turns out the fugitive physician is Johnny and Sue's father, Dr. Franklin Richards, who would be featured prominently in the next issue.

AT A GLANCE *FF #32* (Nov. 1964) Stone-cover inks
"*Death Of A Hero*" 21p Stone-inks (1 collage page)

In this drama-drenched tale we get a rare glimpse into Sue and Johnny's past; the car crash that killed their Mother, and the ensuing guilt that ruined their Father's life.

The Super-Skrull, who was last seen in *FF #18*, shifts his shape to impersonate the imprisoned Dr. Storm and deceives the FF into thinking that Franklin Storm has gained their powers via clandestine experiments conducted in the prison lab. The Skrull knows the Fantastic Four won't harm him because they believe he's Sue and Johnny's Father.

In the story's final moments, Dr. Storm is fatally wounded after saving the lives of the FF by smothering a bomb with his body. Through Stan Lee's poignant dialogue we learn that Storm views his demise as a redemption—a reward. He welcomes his heroic death as emancipation from a squandered life.

The theme of self-sacrifice to save another will be revisited in *FF #51*, but with a startlingly different twist.

AT A GLANCE *FF #33* (Dec. 1964) Stone-cover inks (collage)
"*Side-By-Side With Sub-Mariner*" 20p Stone-inks (1 collage page)/*Sub-Mariner* 1p Ayers-inks

According to Jack Kirby, "Collages were another way of finding new avenues of entertainment. I felt that magazine reproduction could handle the challenge. It added an extra dimension to comics. I wanted to see if it could materialize, and it did. I loved doing collages—I made a lot of good ones."

Indeed he did. After his first attempts at photomontage in *FF #24*, the King assembled another collage for *FF #29* and two more for *FF #32*. All three were scenes from outer-space. For the cover of this issue, Kirby assembled a montage that represented the abyss of the briny deep—Prince Namor's Atlantis. This latest Kirby paste-up looked considerably better than the others because it was printed on glossy paper.

Judging from the remarks Kirby made in various interviews regarding his montage pages, the King apparently thought he pioneered the idea. Actually, Will Eisner used photo-collages in his *Spirit* stories way back in the Golden Age.

Apart from that, the "Marvel Masterwork Pin-up" of Sub-Mariner in this issue must be mentioned. It's the best pin-up Kirby would produce until the *FF Annual #5* Inhumans portraits. Against a serene ocean

backdrop, as Namor stands in regal repose, Kirby imbues Bill Everett's greatest character with a nearly sculptural quality; a Grecian grace and nobility that borders on godlike.

Dick Ayers' inking on this majestic full-page portrait is simply magnificent. By this time Ayers had significantly upgraded his inking techniques. He trimmed down the wide, workman-like brushstrokes that typified his early *FF* inking and was now incorporating a refined, streamlined approach which utilized more pen-work and thinner holding-lines.

Unfortunately, fans would only see a few Kirby-drawn stories that featured Ayers' attractive new inking style (see *Sgt. Fury #13*, *Avengers #10*, *Strange Tales #135* and *Tales of Suspense #82* and *83*).

AT A GLANCE *FF #34* (Jan. 1965) Stone-cover inks
"*A House Divided*" 20p Stone-inks/*Fantastic Four On Yancy Street* 1p Stone-inks

The search for a worthy villain continues.

This time the writers launch a new strategy: Instead of a diabolical costumed opponent, the FF battle a ruthless billionaire named Gregory Gideon who turns the team against each other. In the process, Gideon's young son is almost killed.

On page 10 Gideon's boy is seen holding an issue of *Fantastic Four*. This will be the final inference that a comic book about the quartet exists in the Marvel Universe. Thus, the seeds first sown in *FF #2* (where two Goodman comics were featured in the story) are finally laid to rest.

In a widescreen panel on page 14, we see Reed using his legs as wheels to rescue Sue from the Thing and Torch. This is the exact type of Plastic Man comicality that Stan told Roy Thomas he wanted to avoid at all costs.

Despite Gideon's over-the-top repentance in the closing moments,

FF #34 is a refreshing change of pace morality tale that has stood the test of time considerably well.

AT A GLANCE *FF #35* (Feb. 1965) Ayers-cover inks
"*Calamity On The Campus*" 20p Stone-inks

Although the on-campus setting of State University is a welcome change of venue, most of this story is only marginally exciting due to the return of the dreaded (mostly dreadful) Diablo. This time he's in cahoots with Dragon Man, the latest in a long line of Atlas-type monsters which Jack and Stan whipped up whenever they were hard-up for a new *FF* opponent. Stan later said that he and Kirby modeled Dragon Man after both Frankenstein and King Kong.

Marvel Universe continuity-cameos are provided by Professor X, Scott Summers and Peter Parker, all of whom are seen touring the campus.

Fortunately, the unrelenting mediocrity of Diablo is completely swept away by the story's shocking and astounding closing moment. In a perfect romantic setting, standing before the campus "sweetheart tree," Reed takes Sue's hand and offers his unspoken proposal. And Sue accepts. Now the couple's long, eventful journey to the alter begins. The only thing that kept Reed's marriage proposal from being perfect was that it didn't happen in *FF Annual #2*. Major events and big announcements like the Richard's wedding, Sue's pregnancy and Franklin's birth were usually reserved for the *Fantastic Four* Annuals.

Reed and Sue, who'd been the Adam and Eve of the Marvel Universe since the very beginning, were finally going to the chapel. And every True Believer who could pony-up two bits when the summer Annuals came out was invited to attend.

AT A GLANCE *FF* #36 (Mar. 1965) Stone-cover inks

"The Frightful Four" 21p Stone-inks

The coming of Madam Medusa would open the gates to events of cosmic significance; events which no one could have foreseen at the time. And it all started in the pages of *Strange Tales*.

Strange Tales featuring the Human Torch (and later the Thing) was one of the worst series of the entire Silver Age—worse than a lot of the DC stuff that Marvel was supposed to have been an antidote to. There were two outstanding Kirby-drawn issues: *Strange Tales Annual* #2 and *ST* #114, but other than that it was total dross. Mostly, the series limped along on the strength of *Fantastic Four's* success.

Marvel continuity was totally abandoned because the *Strange Tales* Human Torch had a secret identity which was known to the world in *Fantastic Four*. Besides this, in *Fantastic Four* Johnny and Sue lived with Reed and Ben in New York. But in *Strange Tales,* they lived by themselves in "Glenville." It was moronic.

This should be noted: Superman's co-creator Jerry Siegel occasionally wrote scripts for the Torch's *Strange Tales* adventures under the alias "Joe Carter." Many comic book historians claim that "Glenville" was taken from Glenville Ohio, where Jerry Siegel hailed from. Not so. Stan introduced Glenville into the *Human Torch* storyline a year before Siegel signed on. Glenville was the home of Stan's "Willy Lumpkin" comic-strip character.

Segue to *FF* #36: The Wizard, the Trapster and Steve Ditko's Sandman were individually battling the Torch in the pages of *Strange Tales*. At some point the Wizard and the Trapster (who was then the imbecilic "Paste-Pot Pete") united. That's probably why the writers threw the

trio together in the Frightful Four. The evil FF would have been a sorry mess had it not been for Medusa. She was the only bright spot in this otherwise mediocre mélange.

But the Frightful Four would all develop and progress considerably. Kirby would see to that. He made radical improvements on the costumes and gadgets of all three male members over the years.

On the final page of this story Stan uses dialogue to describe events which aren't seen in the panels, and the tale comes to an all-too-abrupt ending. This was probably a result of Jack miscounting his pages.

Despite this, *FF* #36 is a truly splendiferous Marvel Milestone. It introduced the most iconic villainess that Lee and Kirby would ever produce.

With the debut of Madam Medusa, the seeds of a new era were being planted.

AT A GLANCE *FF* #37 (Apr. 1965) Stone-cover inks

"Behold, A Distant Star" 20p Stone-inks (1 collage page)

"Behold a Distant Star" holds an unenviable position. The introduction of Madam Medusa came before it, and the story cycle that would eventually launch the Cosmic Era followed it. It is by those standards that it must be judged.

The tale certainly begins impressively enough. Striking a dynamic Kirby pose (is there any other kind?) the Torch leaps off the floor having just burst into flame involuntarily. By now Kirby had the "riveting opening moment" down pat. In the process of flaming on, Johnny incinerates the tuxedo he's wearing and decides he needs an asbestos tux.

A tux?

The previous issue (*FF* #36) opened with a throng of overexcited paparazzi scrambling to snap pictures as Sue and Reed announced

their engagement. And in this issue it's wedding rehearsal time as Lee and Kirby play up the superhero Marriage of the Decade for all it's worth. These were exciting times for the magazine's regular readers. Even second and third generation *FF* fans can sense the anticipation these stories must have generated in 1965.

Sue's capricious nature in the Silver Age was riveting. You never knew what she'd do next; fall for a villain, get married, get pregnant, or leave the group for months on end. She was emotionally volatile and unpredictable, and in this story we see a previously unseen facet of her persona. Sue wants revenge for her father's death at the hands of the Skrulls, and she talks Reed into attacking an entire planet to get it.

Subsequently, the quartet takes a short cut to the Skrull-planet via "sub-space," a space-time warp that was discovered by Mr. Fantastic. (This is not the same region as the Negative Zone, an anti-matter universe that Stan mistakenly called Sub-Space in issue #51.) The FF eventually find the Skrull who was responsible for the death of Franklin Richards, and in the ensuing melee he's gunned down by his own people.

There's one hitch: the bad guy, "Morrat" has a beautiful girlfriend "Anelle" who is innocent and pure of heart. Morrat's death leaves Anelle devastated.

The irony isn't lost on Susan; she's planning a wedding while the Skrull girl, who's about her age, is planning a funeral. This is what Sue's thirst for vengeance has wrought, and she concludes that revenge isn't so sweet after all.

When viewed as a tightly plotted well-paced morality tale, *FF* #37 works just fine. When viewed in contrast to the stories that came before and after, it's a bit light-weight—but only a bit.

AT A GLANCE *FF* #38 (May 1965)

Stone-cover inks (Thing by Powell)

"Defeated By The Frightful Four" 20p Stone-inks

This electrifying issue would signal the end of the Stone Age and usher in a period that was simply relentless in its creativity. The defeat of the Fantastic Four by the Frightful Four would set off a mesmerizing story arc that wouldn't end until *FF* #43.

This is the most extraordinary *Fantastic Four* adventure of the entire Chic Stone period. It's a fittingly majestic sendoff to the inker who greatly aided the magazine's return to preeminence with his vastly attractive brushwork. Charles Eber Stone pulled the series out of the doldrums of the Roussos Period and embellished Jack Kirby's art with the sense of power it deserved.

The Fantastic Four's defeat at the finale was an unexpected upset. But the biggest shock came with the next issue. In *FF* #39, everyone expected Reed and his partners to regroup and demolish Medusa and her thugs. It never happened. In this tale our heroes are beaten thoroughly and decisively by the bad guys. Period.

One wonders how Stan got this story past the Comics Code Authority. Since day one the agency's staunchest rule was that good triumphs over evil every time. No exceptions. Obviously, Lee and Kirby's daring was beginning to loosen things up.

This well-plotted adventure is a superlative combination of energetic art and first rate writing which is epitomized by Lee's caption in the closing moments: *Buffeted by the shock waves, dazed by the noise and force of impact, the unconscious quartet is nevertheless safe, protected by the fantastic power of one girl… a girl whose will to survive is so strong that her force field remains even though she is unconscious…*

This was Sue Storm's finest hour.

MADAM MEDUSA

FIRST APPEARANCE: FF #36

PERPLEXINGLY, ALL THROUGHOUT THE 1960S KIRBY'S TAKE ON FEMALE CHARACTERS WAS FUNDAMENTALLY ASEXUAL. GRANTED, ASGARD'S ENCHANTRESS WAS A BLOND BOMBSHELL, BUT FOR THE MOST PART SUE STORM, BETTY ROSS, JANE FOSTER AND EVEN THE BOY-CRAZY JANET VAN DYNE SEEMED MORE LIKE YOUR BIG SISTER THAN AN OBJECT OF CARNAL DESIRE.

THE ODD THING IS THIS: KIRBY WAS ENTIRELY CAPABLE OF RENDERING THE FEMALE FORM WITH TRUE EROTICISM. HE DID IT HABITUALLY IN THE SIMON/KIRBY ROMANCE COMICS. THE BRAZEN TEMPTRESS WHO SEDUCES HER KID SISTER'S FIANCEE IN *YOUNG ROMANCE* #1 (SEPT. 1947) IS EVERY BIT AS RAVISHING AS THE TO-DIE-FOR BABES THAT WALLY WOOD DEPICTED IN THE GLORY DAYS OF E.C. COMICS. LIKEWISE, "THE GIRL WHO TEMPTED ME" FROM *YOUNG ROMANCE* #5 (JAN. 1950) FEATURES AN EVIL SEDUCTRESS WHO'S VIRTUALLY DRIPPING WITH SENSUALITY—NOT THAT VIRTUE HAD ANYTHING TO DO WITH HER APPEAL. SO THERE'S THE PARADOX: KIRBY COULD DRAW STUNNINGLY BEAUTIFUL FEMALES. HE SIMPLY CHOSE NOT TO. MADAM MEDUSA WAS THE EROTIC EXCEPTION.

EVEN HER BLACK MASK COULDN'T DIMINISH THE ALLURE OF HER GLACIALLY BEAUTIFUL FACE—A FACE ENGULFED BY A HUGE WATERFALL OF RADIANT RED HAIR THAT THUNDERED DOWN LIKE AN AVALANCHE, DOWN PAST HER SKY-SCRAPER LEGS AND ONTO THE FLOOR AROUND HER TINY BOOTED FEET. SHE HAD A BUILT-IN CHARISMATIC SELF-CERTAINTY AND AN ARISTOCRATIC ARRO-GANCE THAT MADE HER, HANDS DOWN, THE MOST INTOXICATING FEMME FATALE THAT LEE AND KIRBY EVER CAME UP WITH.

REGRETTABLY, AFTER SHE LEFT THE FRIGHTFUL FOUR AND RETURNED TO THE INHUMANS, HER ALLURE BEGAN TO WANE. SHE WASN'T NEARLY AS INTOXICATING AFTER SHE BECAME BLACK BOLT'S SERVILE AND SYCOPHANTIC LOVE INTEREST. BUT IN THE CONTEXT OF THE FRIGHTFUL FOUR, SHE WAS THE UNDISPUTED EVIL AND EROTIC QUEEN OF THE MARVEL UNIVERSE.

GORGON

FIRST APPEARANCE:
FF #44

MEDUSA'S PURSUER IN *FF #44* WAS A BEARDED, BEADY-EYED MYSTERY MAN WITH A SPIKED CROWN AND POINTED PAN-LIKE EARS. HIS MASSIVELY MUSCLED LEGS HAD A DEVASTATING KICK THAT SENT SEISMOGRAPHIC SHOCKWAVES STREAMING THROUGH THE STRATOSPHERE. SULLEN, BROODING AND MENACINGLY DRAMATIC, HE RESEMBLED A MYTHICAL SATYR ON STEROIDS.

THE GENTLEMAN'S NAME WAS GORGON.

STOIC AND SEDATE, GORGON'S LACK OF EMOTIONALITY WAS AN INTELLIGENT CHOICE OF CHARACTERIZATION. HAD THE WRITERS PORTRAYED THE LUMBERING INHUMAN AS AN EXTROVERTED, PLEASURE-SEEKING HEDONIST (I.E. A STEREOTYPICAL SATYR), IT WOULD HAVE BEEN AN ALL-TOO-OBVIOUS MOVE.

THE CONSIDERABLE PROMISE THAT GORGON DISPLAYED IN HIS *FF #44* DEBUT WAS SHORT-LIVED. THIS MASKED MISANTHROPE AND HIS THUNDEROUS STOMP PROVED TO HAVE LIMITED POTENTIAL, AND HE QUICKLY FADED INTO THE ROYAL FAMILY BACKGROUND.

UNLIKE MEDUSA, WHOSE MENTALLY-MANIPULATED HAIR HAD INFINITE POSSIBILITIES, GORGON WAS ESSENTIALLY A ONE-KICK-PONY. GRANTED, HIS POWERHOUSE PUNT COULD ACCOMPLISH FEATS OF MAGNIFICENT DESTRUCTION. BUT HOW MUCH COULD EVEN JACK KIRBY DO WITH THAT?

CRYSTAL

FIRST APPEARANCE: FF #45

— ALSO —
LOCKJAW - THE FOURTH DIMENSIONAL BULLDOG

SHE WAS MOTHER NATURE PERSONIFIED AS A TEMPESTUOUS TEENAGE VIXEN.

ELFIN, ETHEREAL AND EFFERVESCENT, THE BEAUTIFUL CRYSTAL DISPLAYED MORE HUMAN TRAITS THAN ANY OTHER MEMBER OF THE ROYAL FAMILY. DISSIMILAR FROM THE REST OF HER CLAN, THIS SIREN-LIKE SEDUCTRESS DIDN'T HAVE AN EXOTIC NAME AND KIRBY DIDN'T GIVE HER A COSTUME FOR OVER A YEAR AFTER HER DEBUT.

SHE WAS EASILY THE MOST PRO-SOCIAL ATTILAN IN REGARD TO MANKIND. PERHAPS DUE TO YOUTHFUL NAIVETE, CRYSTAL DIDN'T SHARE HER FAMILY'S PARANOIAC DISTRUST OF THE HUMAN RACE. THIS LACK OF WARINESS FOSTERED HER FORBIDDEN LOVE FOR THE HUMAN TORCH, AND GAVE THEIR SEPARATION A TRAGIC ROMEO AND JULIET TWIST.

AFTER JOHNNY AND CRYSTAL'S REUNION, THE ENCHANTING ELEMENTRESS WAS THE FIRST MARVEL CHARACTER TO BREAK THE BONDS OF THE FF'S EXCLUSIVITY. SHE WOULD SUB FOR SUE WHEN THE INVISIBLE GIRL WENT ON MATERNITY LEAVE.

THE TURBULENT TEENAGED BEAUTY PROVED TO BE AN EMOTIONAL BUT HARD-HEADED HEROINE WHOSE GENERALLY DEMURE NATURE COULD ERUPT INTO TUMULTUOUS RAGE WHEN SOMEONE SHE LOVED WAS IN DANGER.

HELL HATH NO FURY LIKE THIS WOMAN'S STORM!

KARNAK

HE HAD HANDS THAT COULD LAY WASTE TO BRICK WALLS.

THE IDEA OF A DIMINUTIVE INDIVIDUAL WHO CAN OUTFIGHT LARGER OPPONENTS OR MULTIPLE OPPONENTS WAS COMMON-PLACE BY THE TIME OF KARNAK'S DEBUT IN *FF* #45. KID-SIDEKICKS LIKE BUCKY BARNES HAD ALWAYS BEEN ABLE TO TOPPLE TALLER ADVERSARIES, AS COULD STEVE DITKO'S FANCY DAN FROM *THE AMAZING SPIDER-MAN* #10.

BUT IF KARNAK THE SHATTERER HAD A SINGLE DEFINITIVE PROGENITOR, IT WAS PROBABLY KATO, THE GREEN HORNET'S KARATE-CHOPPING CHAUFFER. KIRBY HAD DRAWN THE GREEN HORNET FOR HARVEY COMICS BACK IN THE 1940S, AND HE WAS APPARENTLY THINKING OF KATO'S HOME-LAND, THE ORIENT, WHEN HE DESIGNED KARNAK'S COSTUME. SAID KIRBY, "IT WAS A JUDO-TYPE UNIFORM, ALMOST ORIENTAL AND HALF-EGYPTIAN."

KARNAK'S UNCANNY KNACK FOR FINDING AN OBJECT'S WEAKEST SPOT WENT HAND-IN-HAND WITH HIS ABILITY TO SHATTER THAT OBJECT AT ITS BREAKING POINT. KARNAK WAS BLACK BOLT'S PERSONAL BODYGUARD, AND HE WAS SELDOM SEEN STANDING AT EASE IN A RELAXED POSE. KIRBY ALWAYS DREW THE DIMINUTIVE DYNAMO IN AN EDGY COMBAT STANCE. TENSE AND COILED IN READINESS, HE ALWAYS SEEMED POISED TO THROW OR DOGE A SUDDEN BLOW.

FIRST APPEARANCE: FF #45

TRITON

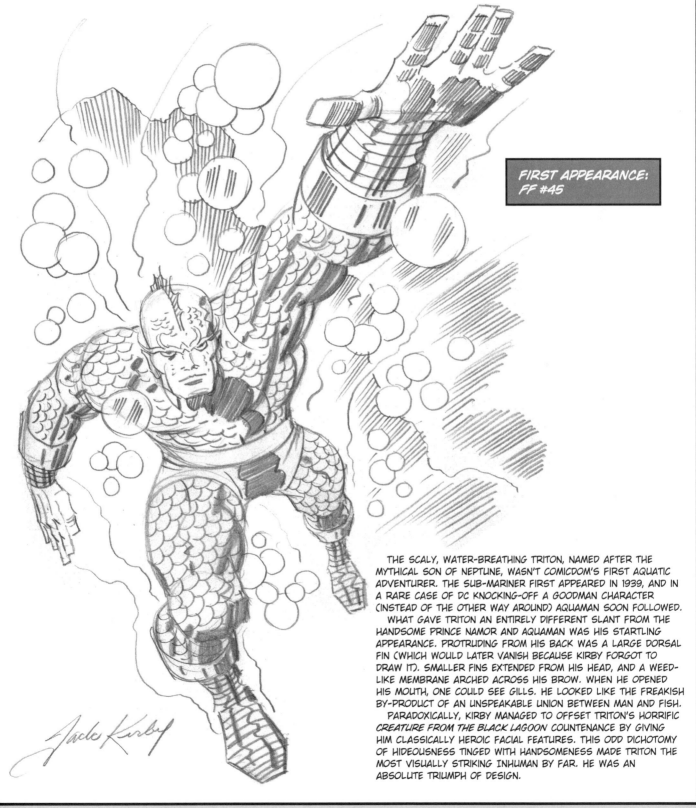

FIRST APPEARANCE: FF #45

Jack Kirby

THE SCALY, WATER-BREATHING TRITON, NAMED AFTER THE MYTHICAL SON OF NEPTUNE, WASN'T COMICDOM'S FIRST AQUATIC ADVENTURER. THE SUB-MARINER FIRST APPEARED IN 1939, AND IN A RARE CASE OF DC KNOCKING-OFF A GOODMAN CHARACTER (INSTEAD OF THE OTHER WAY AROUND) AQUAMAN SOON FOLLOWED.

WHAT GAVE TRITON AN ENTIRELY DIFFERENT SLANT FROM THE HANDSOME PRINCE NAMOR AND AQUAMAN WAS HIS STARTLING APPEARANCE. PROTRUDING FROM HIS BACK WAS A LARGE DORSAL FIN (WHICH WOULD LATER VANISH BECAUSE KIRBY FORGOT TO DRAW IT). SMALLER FINS EXTENDED FROM HIS HEAD, AND A WEED-LIKE MEMBRANE ARCHED ACROSS HIS BROW. WHEN HE OPENED HIS MOUTH, ONE COULD SEE GILLS. HE LOOKED LIKE THE FREAKISH BY-PRODUCT OF AN UNSPEAKABLE UNION BETWEEN MAN AND FISH.

PARADOXICALLY, KIRBY MANAGED TO OFFSET TRITON'S HORRIFIC *CREATURE FROM THE BLACK LAGOON* COUNTENANCE BY GIVING HIM CLASSICALLY HEROIC FACIAL FEATURES. THIS ODD DICHOTOMY OF HIDEOUSNESS TINGED WITH HANDSOMENESS MADE TRITON THE MOST VISUALLY STRIKING INHUMAN BY FAR. HE WAS AN ABSOLUTE TRIUMPH OF DESIGN.

BLACK BOLT

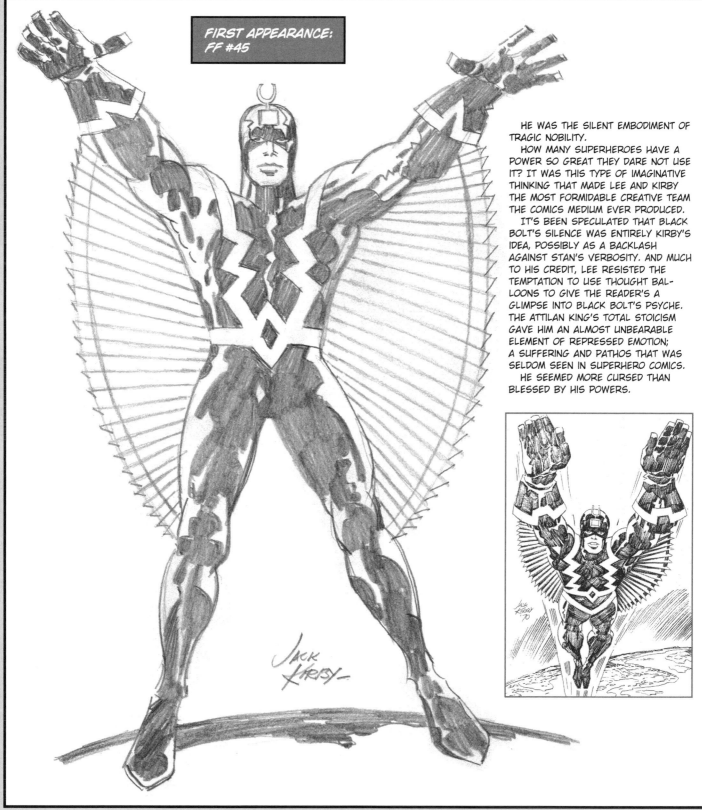

FIRST APPEARANCE:
FF #45

HE WAS THE SILENT EMBODIMENT OF TRAGIC NOBILITY.

HOW MANY SUPERHEROES HAVE A POWER SO GREAT THEY DARE NOT USE IT? IT WAS THIS TYPE OF IMAGINATIVE THINKING THAT MADE LEE AND KIRBY THE MOST FORMIDABLE CREATIVE TEAM THE COMICS MEDIUM EVER PRODUCED.

IT'S BEEN SPECULATED THAT BLACK BOLT'S SILENCE WAS ENTIRELY KIRBY'S IDEA, POSSIBLY AS A BACKLASH AGAINST STAN'S VERBOSITY. AND MUCH TO HIS CREDIT, LEE RESISTED THE TEMPTATION TO USE THOUGHT BAL-LOONS TO GIVE THE READER'S A GLIMPSE INTO BLACK BOLT'S PSYCHE. THE ATTILAN KING'S TOTAL STOICISM GAVE HIM AN ALMOST UNBEARABLE ELEMENT OF REPRESSED EMOTION; A SUFFERING AND PATHOS THAT WAS SELDOM SEEN IN SUPERHERO COMICS.

HE SEEMED MORE CURSED THAN BLESSED BY HIS POWERS.

7 APOTHEOSIS

The cosmos now seemed to shift with each new issue. *Fantastic Four* was about to take on mystical and metaphysical overtones which no one had suspected the comics medium could achieve. The long, interweaving story arcs that typified the magazine's "Cosmic Era" seemed like a colossal payoff; a spectacular reward to the loyal True Believers who had followed the book from its humble beginnings. It was a spellbinding mosaic of futuristic realms, hidden civilizations and god-like beings; a wondrous voyage into uncharted worlds of fantasy that seemed to have no boundaries.

Basically, this is what happened: By 1965, *Fantastic Four's* premise had been defined and fine-tuned like no superhero series before it. By now the quartet's greatest strengths were clarity of image and the way they balanced. There were no loose ends, and it all made for a comforting sense of completeness. By way of long familiarity with their characters, Lee and Kirby were now ready to think big; to become more ambitious, more grandiose with their storylines. Now the book's limitless possibilities hit them like a prophetic vision and they moved fast, racing like mad to see just how far they could bend the envelope.

In this environment, with all the necessary elements at hand, Jack and Stan began to create sweeping sagas that were outside anyone's wildest expectations. It seemed a nonstop fusillade of epic stories and art—an explosion of creativity. Suddenly, everything the magazine had been aspiring to came to full flower. The series was about to begin a two-year hot streak that in all likelihood will never be equaled.

Throughout this period the book's storyline grew to genuinely mythic proportions, relying more and more on a body of sustained character development, multi-issue stories, cliff-hangers and scintillating subplots that occasionally went nowhere. Now only narratives that ran to several issues would be able to contain Lee and Kirby's increasingly complex ideas. At this point *Fantastic Four* became somewhat inaccessible to the casual reader. The dilettantes were soon weeded out, and only the True Believers

remained in the know.

Meanwhile, at the end of *FF* #38 (May 1965), Reed and company were soundly and unequivocally beaten by the Frightful Four. They didn't even regroup in the next issue and defeat the evil FF as you might expect. The idea of this happening in a 1965 DC story is inconceivable. It was a complete shock, a sensational twist ending.

Fantastic Four #38 signaled a dramatic departure from the optimistic 1965 *FF* stories that focused on Reed and Sue's engagement. Comics historian Mike Gartland has opined that after *FF* #38 the

In this page from FF Annual #3 *(1965), note how Dr. Doom is holding his hands in agony—the after effect of the Thing crushing them in* FF #40. *Stan missed this Kirby continuity carry-over in the dialogue.*

plots seem more Kirby-driven with less input from Lee. This was a major turning point. From here on, *Fantastic Four* acquired a darker, more disturbing tone.

After an impressive twelve-issue run, issue #38 would be the last *FF* story inked by Chic Stone. Chic was tired of inking other people's work, and wanted to draw his own comics. Stone claims he practically begged Stan to give him some penciling work, but Lee refused, so he went elsewhere.

Now that Chic was gone Stan had problems. Lee had wanted

Joe Sinnott on *Fantastic Four* ever since issue #5, but at this point he still couldn't lure him away from Treasure Chest and Archie. Frank Giacoia, the next closest inker to Sinnott talent-wise, was Stan's second choice. Frank had aspirations to ink Kirby's work since that day in 1956 when he told Lee he'd bring Jack over to Atlas. Giacoia did a terrific job on *FF* #39 (June 1965), but he missed the deadline and was pulled off *Fantastic Four* after one issue. Before Lee sent Giacoia packing, he had him ink the covers to *FF* #40 and 41 as well.

Just about everybody loved the way Frank Giacoia embellished Kirby's pencils, Joe Sinnott included. Sinnott thought Giacoia (who at the time was going by the *non de plume* "Frank Ray") had a style that was close to his own. Kirby himself admired the way his friend and neighbor kept his energetic figures in fluid motion in the action scenes, which is no small feat. A lively pencil drawing has a way of losing its spontaneity in the inking process.

But Stan needed someone more dependable than Giacoia. Vince Colletta had seen how much work he could get by becoming Kirby's inker and applied for the job, reminding Stan that he'd inked Jack's work in the past on romance comics like *Love Romances*. Still, Stan didn't consider Colletta to be a superhero artist. Lee had pretty much dismissed Vinnie back in '63, at which time he'd decided he didn't even want Colletta on *Millie the Model* or *Patsy Walker*.

Undeterred, Vince asked Sol Brodsky what he could do to get assigned some Marvel superhero books. Sol told Colletta that Lee liked bold blacks and lots of detail. As soon as possible, Vince got some penciled pages from Charlton Comics and inked them in the manner Brodsky had suggested. Then he showed them to Stan. According to Sol, Colletta's Charlton pages didn't look much different than Vinnie's usual stuff, but somehow Lee was swayed.

It was probably good timing on Colletta's part more than the Charlton pages that got his foot in the door at Marvel. At this stage Dick Ayers was busy with his own books and George Roussos had cut back on his Marvel inking for higher paying DC work. Consequently, Vinnie was about the only deadline-dependable freelancer Lee could afford at the time. So almost by default, he became the magazine's new inker.

In a two-part Daredevil crossover

The sparse Colletta inking makes this action-filled page from FF *#40 rather weak, but (next page, top) for one panel from* FF Annual *#3, Colletta's "romance comics" style of inking looked suitable for* Fantastic Four.

(*FF* #39-40, June-July 1965), the series hit its greatest peak yet. The Thing had never seemed so epic, his fury so uncontainable. In a holocaust of volcanic rage, he smashed the arrogant Dr. Doom until he was a busted nothing. He cut him down like chaff, nearly killing him in the process. Now that the main thrust of the storylines was coming from Kirby, *Fantastic Four* acquired a heightened sense of *Sturm und Drang;* a distinctly foreboding undercurrent.

A minor but interesting change began with *FF* #42 (Sept. 1965). Apparently, at this point Marvel was no longer producing comic books. According to their brand-logos, their magazines were now "pop-art productions." It was a concept which would last four months.

If one wants to get technical, Stan had the wrong handle on the idea. Because artist Roy Lichtenstein had been re-contextualizing comic book images in fine art settings, and because his

Fantastic Four #44 *(pencils shown here) was the start of the strip's most fertile creative period.*

work was being labeled "pop-art," Stan assumed comic books were pop-art. But they weren't. Comic books were merely one of the popular mass-culture themes which were incorporated into 1960s pop-art to emphasize the low-brow, banal or kitschy elements of our society. Still, it was a novel idea while it lasted and it showed Marvel's willingness to embrace the changing times; to expand, progress and experiment with the medium.

A sad farewell: Readers saw the last of the electrifying, erotically evil Madam Medusa in *FF* #43 (Oct. 1965). Granted, she'd be back, but never again as the sinister seductress of the Frightful Four, only as Black Bolt's big-haired girlfriend. After that, she was about as carnal as cornflakes. Beyond this point the only thing even remotely interesting about Medusa was the bizarre undercurrent of incest in her relationship with the Inhuman's silent leader. At the end of Kirby's *FF* run, it would be revealed that Black Bolt was Crystal's brother. What was Stan thinking?

Major Event: "Bedlam at the Baxter Building." Although the pressures of saving the world had long been a strain on their relationship, Sue and Reed finally tied the knot in *FF Annual* #3. In the golden summer of 1965, any kid who could cough-up a quarter was treated to Marvel's ultimate crossover. *Annual* #3 was an orgy of fists, weapons and fanciful gadgets with heroes and evildoers merged in a multi-colored mass of madness. Every page was a Jack Kirby apocalypse. It seemed the Ragnarok of the Marvel superheroes, the perfect curtain closer to Lee and Kirby's mid-period *Fantastic Four*. Immediately after *FF Annual* #3, a startling new era would begin—the Cosmic Era.

The wedding of Sue and Reed would prove to be Vince Colletta's final farewell to *Fantastic Four*, and the FF/Colletta mismatch would have an ironic twist. Martin Goodman

page and he went out with a bang.

And still Kirby's drives were inexhaustible. Medusa's slowly unraveling origin in *FF* #44 (Nov. 1965) showcased a significant increase in the range and force of the King's pencils. With each new installment of *Fantastic Four*, Kirby had been steadily working his way toward some kind of breakthrough in his art. Now, with issue #44, he achieved it.

Due to a pay raise, the King was able to cut his workload almost in half, and he began to delve deeper into his craft. At this point Kirby's pages evolved from the conventional standards of superhero art—which Jack had set to begin with—to a style that seemed to transcend the very fabric of space and time itself.

Suddenly, Kirby's panel borders became windows into futuristic otherworlds that were unlike anything comics had ever seen: Worlds with a dark sense of majesty, a strange sense of importance. Celestial realms of space-age splendor, turbulent kingdoms and decadent empires inhabited by powerful Inhuman beings, techno-pop jungle lords and planet-eating gods. This was Jack Kirby's 1966 *Fantastic Four*. This was the stuff of legends.

By this time Kirby's talent had matured to the point where it was capable of expressing in pictures the incredible depth of his visions. The King's pages now became an explosion of line and mass. His subjects gained a newfound symmetry and solidity. They became more dynamic and fluid in their poses, whether in action or repose. Kirby tilted his perspectives and pushed his figures into the foreground, leaping and staggering right into the reader's lap.

The costumes worn by Jack's Cosmic Era gods and heroes became marvelously ostentatious and ornate. Simultaneously, Kirby's backgrounds and cityscapes became increasingly

More pencils from Fantastic Four #44 (Nov. 1965).

was so appalled at the way Vinnie was desecrating Marvel's lead book that he agreed to disburse sufficient funds to lure Joe Sinnott into the fold. In an odd sense, if it hadn't been for Colletta's incompatible inking, Kirby and Sinnott may never have united.

Incredibly, at the end of *FF Annual* #3, when Reed and Sue exchanged the Cosmic Kiss, the romance-book inking of Vince Colletta suddenly looked just right for the first and only time in *Fantastic Four*. It was Vinnie's shining moment. It was his last *FF*

dense. The King's outer-space scenes now evoked a breathtaking sense of wonder, and their vanishing points seemed to recede to infinity. These Kirbyized spacescapes were vast, endless backdrops of streaking comets, craggy planetoids, distant suns, black holes, cosmic debris and meteor heat-trails.

During this period Kirby's machines became wild geometric prodigies, huge and lavishly detailed; so Byzantine and complex that they took on a life of their own. Even his spot blacks and squiggles were suddenly bolstered by a powerful new design sense. Most notably, his battle scenes became so explosive that it now seemed the pages could barely contain them. Free from the shackles of a crippling workload, Jack Kirby's art simply exploded.

This quantum leap in the look of *Fantastic Four* had a lot to do with the inking. In an uncanny stroke of luck and perfect timing, just when Kirby gained the time to improve his art-work, Joe Sinnott became the *FF's* regular inker. Sinnott was a master crafts-man, fiercely proud of the effort and meticulous detail he put into his work. In later years Joe would cite specific pages from *Fantastic Four* that he lost money on due to the amount of labor he put in. The slick, stylized layer of India ink that Sinnott painted over Kirby's pencils finished Jack's work in a way that no other inker ever would. Comic fans had never witnessed art this strange and powerful in its scope and strength.

While on the subject of art, it should be noted that one often-over-looked contribution of Stan's was his role as the company's art director. For someone who didn't draw, Lee had an intrinsic grasp of what made comic art appealing; of what worked and what didn't. Stan's revisions usually made significant improvements to the fin-ished pages.

Lee also had a flair for the super-vision and creation of eye-catching, kid-thrilling covers. He was gifted with a highly developed sense of what would draw a casual browser's hand compulsively to a Marvel title on a comic book rack. According to Stan, "I devoted as much time to each cover as I did to the stories themselves. I still remember Martin Goodman telling me that the cover is the most impor-tant single element of any magazine. It's the cover that first catches the buyer's eye."

FF #45 (Dec. 1965) introduced a fascinating species called the

The visual scale Kirby gave Galactus in FF #49 makes even a powerful character like the Thing seem helpless in comparison.

Inhumans, the most intoxicating group of characters Kirby had pro-duced to date in terms of distinctness and variety. They were almost entirely innovative save for Karnak, who was similar to the Green Hornet's Kato (or Ditko's "Fancy Dan" from *Spider-Man* #10). The water-breathing Triton could almost be compared to Sub-Mariner or Aquaman, but his scaly, piscine appearance gave him a stunning originality. He was Kirby's most inventive design concept to date.

Regrettably, in regard to character-delineation, the Inhumans were Stan's biggest failure. The Royal Attilans, for the most part, all had the same personas and speech patterns. They were proud, humorless outsiders with no individual character-traits. Excluding the speechless Black Bolt, their group discussions sounded like one person having a conversation with himself.

Lee and Kirby, both classic literature buffs, shrewdly rewrote

Shakespeare's *Romeo and Juliet* by casting the FF and the Inhumans as the warring families and Johnny and Crystal as the ill-fated young lovers. The yearnings that the Human Torch felt for the tempestuous Crystal were much deeper than anything he'd ever experienced. Subsequently, Johnny's longtime love interest Dorrie Evans (his "old flame"), was quietly ushered into obscurity.

Meanwhile, from beyond the stars came the great Galactus.

His sole purpose was to suck the life from this planet and swallow it like a python. This was not a negotiable verdict. He was a spectacle terrible to behold. His fury was almost Biblical, his every word like scripture, and all who observed him were thunderstruck.

By now it's become almost impossible to write about the Galactus Trilogy and its effects without sinking neck-deep in cliché. The ground has been covered so often and so thoroughly and the conclusions to be drawn are so clear-cut. One can hardly see a way in which to be original.

Obviously, the Trilogy's basic premise had been done to death. One of the direst clichés of the early 1960s sci-fi comics was the invasion of Earth by aliens who were bent on destroying our planet. Here's what made this one different: More than anything, this is a story about waiting—waiting for the end of the world, totally helpless to do anything about it. The overwhelming element in the tale is tension—tension slowing building, tension so unbearable that all one can do is take a bath (like Ben) or shave (like Reed) and wait for the oncoming apocalypse. And there

FF #49: The Silver Surfer first appeared as pure and undecorated as possible—not even with leg lines showing his "bathing suit."

lies the Trilogy's true splendor: the quiet moments. Kirby's sense of pacing in the tale is uncanny. The calm stillness and shifting perspectives of the interior scenes make the infrequent storms of action outside the Baxter Building that much more impressive.

Above all, Kirby's newly improved art gave the Trilogy a sense of grandeur and monumentality never before witnessed on a comic book page. Galactus was easily the most imposing character readers

had ever seen. He seemed an impossible act to follow.

And that was his undoing. Nothing is ever new twice. Repetition trivializes all greatness, and the great Galactus would seem less godlike, less awe-inspiring with each subsequent appearance. He had nowhere to go but down, and that's exactly what he did. Almost by default, the seemingly emotionless Silver Surfer would be the story's most enduring legacy.

Inevitably, in the end, the Trilogy's major problem was anticlimax. In the story's closing moments, the Watcher sent Johnny through sub-space to procure the necessary weapon. It was the exact same way that *FF Annual* #3 ended, but with Reed as the retriever.

During his Timely/Atlas years, Stan Lee made a career of imitating other people's successes. Now that he had some of his own, he was imitating those.

It's almost mandatory to cap-off any dissertation on the Trilogy with a summation of sorts. Everyone who writes about it signs off with a lot of verbiage about the story's "ultimate significance" or its "final importance." There are a ton of Galactus Trilogy reviews in various books and fanzines, and the shortest summation one can find is about four-hundred words.

Four will suffice: *It enlarged the possible*.

The Inhumans tale that came before the Trilogy and the Black Panther story that followed it have common roots. At the exact time Kirby was drawing the Inhumans story cycle, the entire comic book industry was gearing up like mad to exploit what would undoubtedly be the Next Big Thing.

ABC-TV had long owned the rights to DC's Batman, and the word was out: Instead of turning Batman and Robin's adventures into a cartoon show as originally planned, William Dozier was going to produce a live-action *Batman* TV series. Publishers were downright giddy about the inevitable shot in the arm the comics industry would receive if the show was a hit. As it happened, it was more than a hit. It was a national craze.

Immediately, sales on *Batman* comics soared, hitting levels no comic book had touched in over a decade. Public interest in superheroes suddenly skyrocketed, and the rush was on. At precisely the same time the Inhumans appeared, nearly every comic book publisher in America began pumping out new superheroes like Jiffy-Pop. Archie Comics, Mighty Comics, Harvey Comics, Western/Gold Key, Dell, Charlton and Tower Comics all

scrambled to get in on the action.

Unsurprisingly, Martin Goodman, the biggest bandwagon-jumper in the industry, instructed Stan to come up with some new superheroes to exploit the inevitable *Batman* backlash. Subsequently Lee passed Goodman's instructions on to Kirby. Jack has stated that he created the Inhumans and the Black Panther on the same weekend,

FF #55: Joe Sinnott gave both the Thing and the Surfer their counterbalancing rough and smooth textures like no other inker.

FF #57 (Dec. 1966)—Stan at times follows Jack's margin notes very faithfully in writing the final dialogue.

heroes who emerged during the 1965 *Batman* bonanza.

The King reflected on this furiously competitive "year of the bat" in a 1976 interview. According to Kirby, "I created the Inhumans because the competition was coming up in the field—so I thought I would try a new concept; the family concept. So, when someone came up with one superhero, we would slap them with five. As simple as that."

There was something else: Martin Goodman didn't instruct Lee to create more heroes just to have them languish in the pages of *Fantastic Four*. Goodman had plans for Marvel to expand as far back as 1965. He felt he could convince Jack Liebowitz at DC to distribute more of his titles because Marvel's sales were soaring. Martin was determined to add more superhero titles to his line-up as soon as possible. At several points in 1966 and 1967, Goodman thought he was on the verge of convincing Independent News to expand his line. One week he'd tell Stan it was on, the next week no dice.

This unpredictable situation would eventually change the course of *Fantastic Four* quite significantly. Because the Inhumans were to be the first new characters to receive their own book, it was imperative that Jack and Stan give them high-profiles in the pages of *Fantastic Four* as a lead-in to their upcoming solo series.

Meanwhile, just when the True Believers had grown accustomed to the magazine's sprawling, multi-issue story cycles, Lee and Kirby whipped up a self-contained, single-issue story which many consider to be the high point of the entire series. "This Man, This Monster" (*FF* #51 June 1966) was Marvel's answer to fans who wondered

to stave off the competition. Considering that Black Bolt and the Black Panther from Kirby's unused *FF* #52 cover both look like Marvel versions of the Caped Crusader, there's little doubt that T'Challa and the Inhumans were a response to the new horde of

what *Fantastic Four* could possibly do for an encore after Galactus.

In this flawless, unsurpassed masterpiece, Jack and Stan confound the expectations of the reader. Instead of the obvious conclusion where Ben clobbers his evil twin, they allow the villain to achieve nobility by sacrificing his own life to save Reed. The plot is almost entirely character-driven, with only two panels showing any demonstration of the FF's super-powers. It was a story that introduced unthought-of sophistication, complexities and subtleties. It was a veritable 7" x 10" miracle, stapled in the middle.

Many artists would have considered coasting at this point; resting on their laurels or taking a long, creative rest. Not Jack Kirby. He kept innovating at full steam as if Martin Goodman was paying him by the idea.

The Black Panther came next in *FF* #52 (July 1966), and despite his startling originality as comic's first black superhero, one couldn't help but notice how similar T'Challa's genesis was to Victor Von Doom's origin in *FF Annual* #2. Jack and Stan were beginning to recycle their own ideas with ever-increasing frequency. It was not a good sign.

After *FF* #54 (Sept. 1966), there was a tacit understanding among the True Believers that the Torch had dropped out of Metro College (which he began in issue #50), to pursue Crystal with Wyatt Wingfoot. It was a 1960s cultural cliché—cut school and take a road trip. But in typical Kirby fashion, Johnny and Wyatt would forgo the standard big American car and take the Panther's gyro-cruiser. Instead of driving to Tijuana, they would visit savage, labyrinthic landscapes inhabited by bizarre, otherworldly beings. At any rate, Johnny never went back to college after reuniting with Crys. Who could blame him?

Throughout this stratospheric era of cosmic spectacles and intergalactic space- gods, one might think the series would lose some of its old flavor of being grounded in reality. But that never happened. Issue #54 opened with the FF playing baseball. Ben still had trouble finding a parking space for his jet-cycle. Reed used his scientific genius to develop a dishwasher. Johnny and Wyatt sipped coffee from a thermos while searching for Crystal. And Sue designed a mini-skirted FF uniform to attract the attention of her often-preoccupied husband. These tender moments gave *Fantastic Four* a warmth and humanity that made it both heartfelt and authentic. It was a stunning juxtaposition of the commonplace and the incredible world of superheroes.

What happened next was unprecedented. Lee and Kirby had briefly experimented with a secondary storyline in

Fantastic Four a couple of months earlier, shifting the narrative between events at the Baxter Building and Johnny's affairs at Metro College. Now the writers had wider ambitions. Goodman's attempts to expand his line circa 1966-1967 required that Jack and Stan keep the FF's supporting cast in the public eye; to promote them until they had books of their own. Consequently, the writers began using the Inhumans, the Silver Surfer, the Black Panther, Wyatt Wingfoot and the Watcher in regular supporting roles. Expansive, multiple-cast storylines would now develop which sometimes wouldn't resolve for months.

Suddenly, beginning with issue #54, Lee and Kirby transformed

In FF Annual #4 (1966), *Johnny Storm finally meets Martin Goodman's original Human Torch of the 1940s.*

Fantastic Four into a triangulated saga whose prongs were Reed, Sue and Ben in New York, the Inhumans in the Great Refuge, and Johnny and Wyatt residing wherever Lockjaw, the interdimensional bulldog led them. Johnny and Wyatt's journey into the vast unknown became the unifying element between the residents of the Baxter Building and the inhabitants of the Great Refuge.

Fantastic Four's remarkable triple-storyline was an entirely new approach to comic book writing. Nothing this ambitious had ever been attempted in the medium's history. It was one thing to create all these mesmerizing new characters. It was another thing to develop them, integrate them and have them play key roles in the book's increasingly complex plot-structure. No superhero series had ever been populated by such a rich and colorful supporting cast. By this time *Fantastic Four* was soaring from one astonishing peak to another. The storyline never seemed to run out of steam.

But the bold experiment had its drawbacks. The common complaint was that the FF now seemed like bit players in their own magazine. Apart from this, it was now virtually impossible for a new reader to pick up a single issue of *Fantastic Four* and understand who all these characters were, and what they were trying to accomplish.

On occasion, these hop-scotching narratives tended to overtax the writer's organizational faculties. Stan could never remember if the huge dome that imprisoned the Inhumans was in the Himalayas or the Andes. Sometimes he called it the Great Barrier. Other times he referred to it as the Negative Zone or the Negative Barrier. Kirby was also known to drop a thread here and there (see **AT A GLANCE** *FF* #54). But despite the occasional slip-up, this period of *FF* monumentality—issues #54 through #60—seemed to synthesize all the underlying potential that *Fantastic Four* had been hinting at since day one.

FF #56 (Nov. 1966) was the first issue where the opening credits stated "Produced by Stan Lee and Jack Kirby" as opposed to "Stan Lee writer" and "Jack Kirby illustrator." This was done at Jack's prompting. He wanted it known that he had a hand in the writing process. Inexplicably, Stan still refused to give Kirby a full writing credit even though he'd given that perk to *S.H.I.E.L.D.* illustrator Jim Steranko after only four months with the company.

A puzzling disappointment: "The Torch That Was" from *FF Annual* #4 (Nov. 1966) proved to be a superb story with Kirby/Sinnott art at its zenith. But it only weighed-in at nineteen pages. With no milestone events

or Kirby pin-ups, it seemed more like "*FF* #56 *and* " than a bona fide *Fantastic Four Annual*.

The period between *FF Annual* #3 and *FF Annual* #4 had solidified the quartet's personalities once and for all. They had all mellowed with age. Reed and Sue's early squabbling gave way to a deep love and commitment now that they were man and wife. There would be no more tempestuous moments between them. The days of Reed calling the Invisible Girl "scatterbrained and emotional" (and Sue's inevitable rejoinder, *"Go polish a test-tube!"*) had vanished into the haze of 1963. Like many married couples they were becoming a bit dull. It was yet another dose of reality.

Ben's mood swings, ranging from morose depression to explosive rage, were all but over. He seemed to have finally come to terms with being the Thing. He now played the lovable cutup, giving the series an element of comic relief. But sometimes a sense of tragedy showed through the comedy.

Johnny too had changed significantly. He was becoming an

From Kirby's files, a remnant of a photocopy of his pencil art from FF Annual #5 *(1967), showing some basic outline inking, presumably by Frank Giacoia.*

adult. By now Stan seldom let him lose his temper and Kirby began to fill him out, no longer portraying him as a skinny teenager. Most notably, as soon as Crystal and the Torch reunited, Crystal became a full-time resident of the Baxter Building. Crystal's sleeping arrangements remained ambiguous, and this eyebrow-raising situation made Johnny seem decidedly more mature than he'd ever been in *Strange Tales*. Whatever else, by 1966 the FF had settled into the personas that they would retain for the rest of Kirby's run.

Fantastic Four #57 (Dec. 1966) began a four-part story that was so riveting it challenged the Galactus Trilogy's unparalleled sense of cosmic grandeur. Until now, the single vital element that had been missing from *Fantastic Four's* illustrious "Cosmic Era" was the sinister presence of the Lord of Latveria.

Suddenly, Doctor Doom was back with a vengeance.

In this multi-issue masterpiece, the Silver Surfer's cosmic power is purloined by the FF's greatest rival. Unschooled in the ways of human treachery, the silver-skinned skyrider is easily deceived and vanquished by the vicious Victor Von Doom. Kirby's mesmerizing full-page drawing on page 15 depicts Doom looming over the helpless alien like the embodiment of Evil Itself, the personification of human nature at its most vile and corrupt.

Meanwhile, back in the real world (as if anyone would call the Marvel offices the "real world"), Stan Lee was riding the crest of a wave. Because of Lee and Kirby's belief that the comic book medium had boundless potential, their post-1964 stories had done much to eradicate comics' built-in inferiority complex. From the very beginning, comic books had been deemed sub-literary junk; desperately unfashionable and definitely non-chic. Outside its cultish following, the medium was seen mainly as a joke.

Not anymore. Since 1965 the mass-media had been heaping unmitigated praise on Stan's new breed of flawed, neurotic superheroes. Lee was suddenly a critical and commercial smash. Against all odds, Stan's deepest, wildest fantasy was now coming true: Intelligent adults were reading his comic books and calling them brilliant. Newspapers and magazines were asking him for interviews, and he'd been fielding offers from the worlds of TV, movies and publishing. Noted artists and celebrities like director Federico Fellini and rock star Peter Asher were visiting his office claiming to be major fans, and Stan suddenly found himself basking in the adoration of university students everywhere. Before long Lee was working the college lecture circuit like a second job, and by 1966 the Dow-Jones reported that Marvel was selling 33 million comics a year.

That career Stan wanted as a "serious" writer would have to wait awhile.

By this time Stan Lee was the most entertaining dialogue man in comics by a wide margin. His scripting was as good as the art his best illustrators could produce. In his

most innovative move yet, Stan began to take an approach that no comic book writer before him had dared. With ever-increasing frequency, Lee would use his boxed-in captions to break the "fourth wall" and speak directly to his readers; humorously pointing out various absurdities in the *FF's* storyline, and charming his audience with his tongue-in-cheek self-mocking tone. It was the same tone he used in his letter-pages and his "Bullpen Bulletins" column; the voice of an easy going "with-it" adult who was totally in sync with the latest trends and hang-ups of the younger generation. Lee now began to use his comics as a platform; a podium from which to espouse his philosophies to the masses. He did this in his "Stan's Soapbox" column, and through the dialogue of his more astute characters like Reed Richards, Thor and Captain America.

Joe Sinnott was now hitting his stride as well. He took enormous pride in his work, sometimes spending an entire day on a single page if necessary. When he initially became the book's inker he altered Jack's faces; imposing his own style of art, and obliterating some of the True Kirby. By this time he'd made a conscious decision to let more of the King's original pencils come through.

The result was the apogee of the Kirby/Sinnott collaboration: awe-inspiring superhero art that staked-out a perfect middle-ground between realism and cartooning. Sinnott's inking at this point was such a powerful force that it began to influence the way Kirby drew. Certain visual aspects of *Fantastic Four*, such as the shading of the Thing's rocky epidermis and Kirby's "crackles" (i.e., round black dots of energy) were now being penciled the way Kirby had seen Joe ink them.

Sinnott's intuitive understanding of Jack's panel compositions allowed him to add depth and dimension, separating Kirby's planes by varying the thickness of his figure-lines and background work. Kirby's pencils had never been finished with such pristine polish. Sinnott's slick control of the pen and brush smoothed-out Jack's rougher edges

No inker in the 1960s captured the "cosmic" feel of Jack's work better than Joe Sinnott, shown here in his 1960s home studio.

without diminishing one granule of the King's latent power.

And still Kirby's ambitions were infinite. At forty-nine, an age when most artists would have been content to coast into retirement, to settle in for the long decline, Kirby's drives were still phenomenal. His range, his speed, his sweep of vision, his will—no one in comics had ever moved faster, or been more gifted, or had a more ferocious sense of his own potential. He would now use the second half of his life to delve deeper into his art, using the lessons he'd learned in the first half as building blocks.

Kirby's sense of a panel's emotional moment was spellbinding. He varied his camera angles wildly to create the most dramatic viewpoint for his drawings. He had long ago mastered the infinitely expandable and contractible fragments of time that exist between the borders of a comic book grid. He was now distorting and exaggerating his perspective with a mathematical precision that no artist to this day has equaled.

More than anything, it was the energy of his compositions that distinguished his work from any of his contemporaries. His desire to give the impression of vigorous movement in his panels meant avoiding monotonous page-designs at any cost. He could draw heroic figures of monumental power from whatever angle the action demanded. "I would always tip the perspective of a room to make it less static," he said.

Jack was tearing the envelope to shreds, changing the way every superhero artist in the business would approach their craft. He was developing impossibly innovative techniques which over time would become clichés, but only because everyone copied them. Kirby's cosmic-era heroes and gods were all about mass, density and forward thrust—pushing the action so far into the reader's face that the pages became a 3-D experience without the glasses.

Meanwhile, just when the True Believers were convinced the World's Greatest Comic Magazine couldn't possibly hit another crest, something strange happened. It did.

On page 11 of *FF* #59 (Feb. 1967), Black Bolt, the noble, dignified King of the Inhumans stood at the edge of the Great Barrier, braced his feet and spewed forth a mad, anguished shriek; an end-of-the-world scream, a Godzilla roar. It was cataclysmic, torrential, deafening. Readers found themselves rolling with the impact. This apocalyptical howl instantly reduced the seemingly impenetrable Great Barrier to nothing. All that remained was rubble. Kirby's Black Bolt seemed an epic "figure, poignantly shielding his mad brother from debris beneath his gilded membrane.

Finally, the secret of the Attilan King's speechlessness was revealed. It was one of the most climactic events ever witnessed on a comic book page; something that only Jack

Kirby could have done right.

After the Doom/Surfer story cycle there would be many more mesmerizing issues, and the Kirby/Sinnott synergy would produce many more visually stunning images. But Kirby's verve and vitality in *Fantastic Four* would never shine quite this blindingly bright again. After an unfathomable series of peaks, this was the final dazzling apex; the last stunning apotheosis. Whatever Lee and Kirby would do with the series from here on was largely immaterial. This was it. They had transcended. They had passed beyond.

The fundamental laws of physics decree that once something reaches its ultimate summit, only one thing can happen.

CONTINUED AFTER NEXT PAGES...

Splash from FF *#63. At this point, all of Jack and Stan's greatest FF characters had been introduced, and their best FF stories had already been told. Despite that peak, the strip didn't show the slightest signs of deceleration.*

ON NEW DRAG STRIP— BEGINNING OF RACE BETWEEN
JOHNNY'S ROD AND GO-GO'S BUCKET CAR

GO-
GO
RAZZES
JOHNNY

FRIEND
WHIPS
DOWN
HAND-
KERCHIEF
TO
START
RACE

BOTH CARS ZOOM OFF

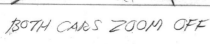

COPS ON DUTY TO SUPERVISE
CAREFUL RACING ON STRIP

Unused page from FF #68—fitting subject matter for the issue that would launch an "Age of Inertia" for the series.

THE TRANSITORY PERIOD

AT A GLANCE *FF* #39 (June 1965) Stone/Wood-cover inks *"A Blind Man Shall Lead Them"* 20p Giacoia-inks (Wood inks Daredevil figure only throughout; 1 collage page)

"A Blind Man Shall Lead Them" effortlessly surpassed everything the series had achieved up till now. It was the magazine's most dramatic and sophisticated tale to date. And readers got a glimpse of how majestic Kirby's art looked as embellished by master-inker Frank Giacoia.

Daredevil, Stan's blind costumed acrobat, had been slow out the gate. Kirby's pal Bill Everett was DD's initial artist, but he blew his first deadline. Joe Orlando took over after that, but Stan wasn't happy with Orlando's art and sales were disappointing.

Daredevil seemed like a lost cause until issue #5, when the brilliant Wally Wood came onboard. Woody quickly got moving on the character. He gave DD a complete facelift, changing his lurid yellow costume to a crimson bodysuit, 90% of which was imbued with patented Wally Wood spot blacks (which somehow remained opaque even in direct sunlight). Woody also improved DD's billy-club, converting it to an ingenious grapple and line device. And he would go on to produce a string of sleek, attention-grabbing *Daredevil* covers.

When Kirby drew this issue, DD's red costume hadn't yet been designed (or else Jack was unaware of it). Subsequently the King depicted Matt Murdock in his old costume in every panel. Wally Wood had to be called in for re-draws, and Frank Giacoia was asked to sit in Marvel's waiting room as Wood revamped and inked all of Kirby's Daredevil figures.

While Woody's work on *Daredevil* wasn't quite up to his old E.C. standards, it still had an undeniable clarity and grace. Wood was easily the third best artist that Stan had; maybe the second. Lee wanted some publicity for Wood's new improved Man Without Fear, hence Daredevil's appearance in *Fantastic Four*.

A change in the basic fabric of the stories began with *FF* #39. The Daredevil crossover ushered in *Fantastic Four's* most important crossroad so far: the five-issue Transitory Period that bridged the work of Chic Stone and Joe Sinnott. It was an era of new breadth and sophistication with a lurking sense of darkness that was heretofore absent from the series. During this phase lighthearted elements like Ben and Johnny's mock-brawls in the Baxter Building and the Thing's war against Yancy Street would disappear from the magazine entirely.

This Transitory Period that spanned *FF* #39-43 was characterized by stronger plots, broader character relationships, a deeper psychological depth and a greater sense of the epic. The stories would now take on an ominous intensity that under the microscope of hindsight seems like a change in writers.

From this point on, the storylines seem decidedly more Kirbyesque.

AT A GLANCE *FF* #40 (July 1965) Giacoia-cover inks *"The Battle of the Baxter Building"* 20p Colletta-inks

In *FF* #40, The Man Without Fear disappears from the storyline after page 13, and his absence from the book's final seven pages is unconvincingly explained by dialogue. The best guess is that Kirby forgot about Daredevil midway through the Baxter Building skirmish. Not that it mattered, because the concluding pages belong solely to the star of the series.

The intensity of aggression the Thing displayed in the final battle scene was beyond the reach of any other artist. Indeed, it had nothing to do with drawing skill. It came from deep within.

In order to defeat Dr. Doom, Reed was forced to turn the recently humanized Ben Grimm back into a monster without his consent and now it's payback time. The insidious Victor Von Doom throws everything he's got at the orange juggernaut; iron fists, flying boulders and nerve blasts. But Ben can't be stopped. His indomitable spirit pushes him on.

His vengeance will not be denied.

Driven past pain, past endurance, the unstoppable revenge-crazed Thing mows Doom down like a runaway train—battering him again and again until the once proud Lord of Latveria is a busted nothing.

This is not the wise-cracking nephew of Aunt Petunia who eventually morphed into the book's element of comic relief. This is the murderous, hate-filled Thing from the yellowing pages of the 1961 *Fantastic Four*. This is Jack Kirby's alter-ego at his most mythic, his most tragic, his most heroic.

Clinging in pain to his mangled, ironclad hand as it hangs in taters, what little there is left of Doctor Doom limps away in total defeat.

The Thing would never shine quite this glaringly bright again.

AT A GLANCE *FF* #41 (Aug. 1965) Giacoia/Colletta-cover inks *"The Brutal Betrayal Of Ben Grimm"* 20p Colletta-inks

A harbinger of what was to come suddenly appeared with "The Brutal Betrayal of Ben Grimm." *FF* #41 is a bona fide masterwork.

Due to the undeniable majesty of the stories that immediately followed it, the Frightful Four Trilogy is often overlooked and/or underrated. This seems somewhat inconceivable because throughout this eternally enduring epic, Lee and Kirby's storytelling instincts are sharp enough to draw blood.

"Cosmic" themes of space-age mythology and intergalactic demigods were still up ahead. During the Transitory Period, our heroes were still battling ordinary villains with typical comic book motives of world domination and revenge. Still, a host of fresh story elements are introduced in this superlative saga which will prove the series is soaring on an entirely new level.

Of all the startling innovations that would be launched during this Transitory Period, one of the most aesthetically satisfying was the further exploitation of multi-issue stories; a noticeable refinement of the direction that Lee and Kirby had explored briefly with the two-part Hulk/Thing battle seventeen months earlier.

FF #41-43 was the first three-part *Fantastic Four* adventure. The extra pages allowed Kirby to stretch his visual sense and narrate at his own pace. No longer confined to a 20-page format, the King was suddenly free from the tyranny of the small 9-panel grids that proliferated in all the early *Fantastic Four* tales. Kirby would now use these miniature panels with much less frequency. They'd be deployed to depict the quieter moments; scenes of subtle emotional nuance.

With more pages at his disposal the King increased his use of large 3-panel grids, 4-panel grids and elongated widescreen panels to facilitate his sweeping sense of the epic. Unquestionably, the big frames at the end of *FF* #40 made the Thing's battering of Dr. Doom a masterpiece.

From day one, *Fantastic Four's* most endearing quality was its juxtaposition of the mundane and the miraculous, and this story is chock-full of such contrasts. Reed, Sue and the Torch are eager to search for the Thing, who's quit the group in a fit of bitterness and frustration, but they can't. The landlord of the Baxter Building has castigated them for damages done to their headquarters during their battle with Dr. Doom, and they have to clean up the mess before they do anything.

Another fascinating cross between the ordinary and the incredible is the widescreen panel depicting a card game between Medusa and the Sandman. Medusa is using her dexterous red tresses to shuffle cards while using her hands to sip tea. And it would probably be safe to assume she's cheating.

The Lady of the Living Locks makes her debut in this story in a big showcase panel where she's seen reclining in an unquestionably provocative pose. Madam Medusa, the Frightful Four's ferocious *femme fatale*, will inject an erotic undercurrent into the storyline unlike anything the series has seen to date.

AT A GLANCE *FF* #42 (Sept. 1965) Colletta-cover inks
"To Save You, Why Must I Kill You?" 20p Colletta-inks

Apart from everything else, the Frightful Four Trilogy was an object lesson in impeccable panel choices. Note how many panoramic widescreen panels Kirby uses in this issue: 12 of them in 20 pages. They give the Kirby/Colletta artwork a distinctly cinematic flair.

Beyond that, Colletta's less-than-stellar delineation is proof of what Kirby always believed: No professional inker could ever ruin a well-drawn story. The series had suffered such doldrums before, during the Roussos Period.

By now it's become almost compulsory to castigate Vince Colletta for abridging Kirbys pencils and for not having the slick brushwork of Joe Sinnott or the boldly spotted blacks of Wally Wood. But above all else, the predominant problem with Vince was thematic incompatibility. While Colletta's scratchy, hair-thin lines worked beautifully in *Tales of Asgard*, *Fantastic Four* was unfolding on an increasingly technological front. The FF's intensely-detailed Kirbytech machinery needed a hard-edged metallic veneer that was simply beyond Colletta's grasp. Besides this, Vinnie was fundamentally useless at breathing life into Kirby's "explosion lines" which were now being deployed whenever Ben threw a clobberin' time right hook.

Fortunately, this thrilling three-part saga doesn't suffer from

Colletta's unsuitable inking as much as *FF Annual* #3 did. Reed and Sue's wedding day skirmish took place in New York, where Vince reduced Kirby's cityscapes to a series of unattractive checkerboards. *FF* #41-43 takes place in the secluded woodlands of New Jersey. The backdrops are knolls, lawns and trees; the type of organic elements that Colletta handled well. Vinnie's greatest strength, drawing attractive females, is also brought to the fore. Madam Medusa never looked better than she does in the Frightful Four Trilogy.

She of the Living Hair practically tops the bill in this second installment of the story. This is a woman so strong, so fierce, so domineering that at times she almost usurps the Wingless Wizard as the Frightful Four's licentious leader.

Madam Medusa is the *agent provocateur* of the evil FF—the matrix for most of the group's discord. She inaugurates sexual tension into the storyline; a disruptive element of jealousy that incites conflict between the Trapster, the Sandman and the Thing, all of whom are vying for her attention.

She's also responsible for some erotic undertones in the tale. As the unconscious Mr. Fantastic lies prone, helplessly glued to a table, Kirby depicts the titian-hared tigress eyeing him with delight as she declares "*he's almost too handsome to harm!*" Reed's state of bondage seems decidedly appealing to the Frightful Four's evil dominatrix.

Most significantly, in the next issue the Human Torch purposely hesitates and allows Medusa to escape justice. For reasons that even he can't fathom, Johnny can't bring himself to apprehend her. Whatever it was that the Torch found intriguing about Medusa, he'll find in spades when he meets her kid sister.

The about-to-conclude Frightful Four Trilogy wasn't merely a precur-

sor of the wonders to come. It was a story strong in its own right. Riveting and full of sap, it was a feast for the hungry mind.

Very few superhero sagas from the 1960s have stood the test of time as well as this one.

AT A GLANCE *FF* #43 (Oct. 1965) Colletta-cover inks
"Lo, There Shall Be An Ending" 20p Colletta-inks

The climax of the Frightful Four Triumvirate closed the curtain on *Fantastic Four's* astounding Transitory Period. It was an era of growing maturity in The World's Greatest Comic Magazine. Kirby's apparent domination of the plots, which seems to have begun with *FF* #39, brought an additional weight to the storylines. The series suddenly acquired a more somber, serious tone; a darker complexity and emotional depth that helped ease the magazine's transition between the optimistic *FF* stories of the early '60s and the apocalyptic *FF* stories of the late '60s.

The stage is now set for the cosmic concepts that will begin in the next issue.

Jack and Stan's *Fantastic Four* always focused on the Thing more than anyone. Being the first superhero who evoked pity more than admiration, Ben was easily the most complicated, neurotic and popular member of the group. In this dazzling finale the Thing comes to a new crossroad; another turning point in his characterization.

"Lo, There Shall Be An Ending" saw an ending to much of Ben's bitterness, resentment and pathos. He's finally learning to live with his monstrous deformity. Despite the occasional relapse into self-pity (see *FF* #51 and 55), from here on he'll play the FF's grumpy but endearing wise guy; a best friend to Reed, a protector to Sue and a big brother to the Torch.

Ben generally had the last word at the climax of every Lee/Kirby *FF* tale, and this story is no exception. In the final moments Kirby brilliantly employs three small panels (three 9-grid panels) to keep the emotion close and personal for one of the most heart-rending curtain closers in *FF* history.

As he gazes at the poignant symbolism of Reed and Sue's entwined hands, the weakened, bed-ridden Thing suddenly remembers the wedding. Sue hugs him, and then, just before losing consciousness, he wearily utters: "Mebbe someday you two'll come to *my* weddin! Mebbe I won't haveta remain a…a *Thing*…forever…! Mebbe…"

Thus, as the weary eyelids of tortured Ben Grimm slowly close, Sue and Reed clasp hands—With a prayer in their hearts, and new hope blazing in their souls! THE END.

It was for the best that Ben drifted off to sleep. As Reed's best man, he had a big day ahead of him.

AT A GLANCE *FF Annual* #3 (1965) Esposito-cover inks
"Bedlam At The Baxter Building" 23p Colletta-inks (1 collage page)/(r: *FF* #6) "Captives Of The Deadly Duo" 24p/(r: *FF* #11) "A Visit With The Fantastic Four" 11p/(r: *FF* #11) "The Impossible Man" 11p

What a bacchanalia of excess. *FF Annual* #3 remains one of the most enduring comic book classics of the 1960s and the first-ever example of guest-starring gone mad. There was almost no plot, but who needs one with action this big?

Reed Richards and Sue Storm weren't the first superheroes to tie the knot. DC's Hawkman and the Elongated Man were both married men. But no one ever capitalized on a comic book wedding like Jack and Stan.

Reed and Sue's long and winding road to matrimony was paved way back in *FF* #27, when Sue finally made her choice between Reed and the Sub-Mariner. After that, Reed's proposal, the big announcement to the press and the wedding rehearsal were all stretched out over the months leading up to *FF Annual* #3. The amount of mileage Lee and Kirby got from the whole thing was brilliant.

In Jack's original art and margin notes for this story, Dr. Doom was still recovering from his battle with the Thing in *FF* #40, and was still unable to use his shattered hand. To Kirby, this was the reason that Victor used a machine to disrupt the wedding; he was physically unable to tackle the FF personally. Stan ignored this directive and subsequently the three panels on page 2 (where Victor's hand is obviously hurting) were given incompatible dialogue.

Here's a list of all the characters featured on the cover who weren't seen in the story, in no particular order: Sub-Mariner, the Wasp, Medusa, the Leader, the Hulk, Loki, the Red Skull, Rick Jones, the Wingless Wizard, the Crimson Dynamo, Dragon Man, and most inexplicably the WWII era Sgt. Fury and the Rawhide Kid.

Just as *FF Annual* #1 was the perfect swan-song to the book's early period, *FF Annual* #3, which went on sale right before *FF* #44, seemed to perfectly cap-off the mid-period Lee/Kirby *Fantastic Four*, because with *FF* #44, the "Cosmic Era" began. It's a safe bet the writers didn't plan any of this, which makes it all the more astounding.

For detail-sticklers: On page 14, panel 4, Steve Ditko drew and inked the Spider-Man figure.

The Cosmic Era

AT A GLANCE *FF* #44 (Nov. 1965) Colletta-cover inks
"The Gentleman's Name Is Gorgon" 20p Sinnott-inks

"The Gentleman's Name is Gorgon" is one of the heftiest achievements in the entire checkered history of comic books. It is here that *Fantastic Four* begins to acquire real purpose.

Now that Joe Sinnott was inking the series, it's obvious the magazine was taking a quantum leap. But not just because of Sinnott's adroit brushwork. Now that Kirby had a little more time to spend on each page, his art would rise to match the wondrous new visions and vistas that were launched in this landmark issue.

Strangely enough, at first glance Gorgon seemed like a miscalculation. Coming on the heels of the series' greatest run of stories to date, a foe without much going for him besides a powerful kick seemed like a letdown. This might be the reason Dragon Man was thrown in. When you think about it, he really didn't belong in the Inhumans saga. He was a bit of a consolation prize.

As it turned out, Gorgon was just the tip of an iceberg. He held the key to a Pandora's Box of original

characters who would prove to be the most innovative group of comic stars since the FF themselves.

The prodigious originality of the Inhumans was stunningly obvious. The Royal Attilans owed very little to anything comics had ponyed-up in the past. Their roots could be traced back to ancient mythology more than anything.

With the advent of *FF* #44, the Cosmic Era is now underway. Thus begins the book's most fertile and influential period; an epoch that may never be surpassed.

Jack Kirby and Stan Lee would now take a bottom-rung art form— the comic book—and use it to create High Art; fantasy on par with the likes of Homer and Shakespeare. In doing so they would galvanize an entire generation of future writers and artists by proving that comics have limitless possibilities. Many of the characters from this period will prove to be as timeless and powerful as the Greek and Roman pantheon of mythological deities.

The comic book medium is about to transcend.

AT A GLANCE *FF* #45 (Dec. 1965) Sinnott-cover inks
"Among Us Hide The Inhumans" 20p Sinnott-inks

Fantastic Four's new era of cosmic complexity now shifts into high gear.

A potent plethora of new characters and first-time innovations are found in this magnificent milestone issue: Johnny falls for Crystal, the FF's jet-cycle is introduced, and the electrifying Black Bolt makes his startling entrance in the final panel.

Triton appears for the first time but he's literally under wraps, wearing a concealing water-bag cloak. Only his hideous scaly arm and webbed hand is revealed. Karnak the Shatterer also makes his debut, as does Lockjaw, the dimension-hopping bulldog.

On page 18 readers are mesmerized by the first-ever "suitable for hanging" Kirby/Sinnott full-page stunner: a street-level view of Reed, Sue and Ben on their new streamlined airjet cycle. How much more excitement could the writers cram into one issue?

The story kicks-off with one of the most riveting splash-pages that Kirby ever rendered. As Dragon Man flys off with the Invisible Girl, the entire building which houses Reed, Ben and the Torch suddenly collapses from the destructive tremors of Gorgon's concrete shattering kick.

This timeless masterwork ends with even more cement shattering as Black Bolt, one of the most powerful and godlike comic book characters ever seen, rips through a brick wall and comes crashing onto the scene in the last frame.

They really *don't* make comics like this anymore.

AT A GLANCE *FF* #46 (Jan. 1966) Giacoia/Sinnott-cover inks
"Those Who Would Destroy Us" 20p Sinnott-inks

1966 was the watershed year.

This era can easily be viewed as *Fantastic Four's* Second Coming. Everything seemed fresh, everything felt new and the exciting possibilities seemed boundless.

It's hard to imagine why the writers thought this storyline would require the presence of Dragon Man with all these astonishing new characters. The Inhumans and the Seeker surely would have been intriguing enough to stand on their own. But Dragon Man is still hanging around after three months running. Perhaps Lee and Kirby felt the presence of an older, more established character would help ease the readers into all these new innovations. Or maybe Jack just felt like drawing him. Who knows how Kirby's mind worked?

At any rate, some conspicuous storyline paradoxes were about to emerge between this issue and the next. In *FF* #45 and 46, Medusa and the Royal Family were fleeing in terror from the Seeker, whose mission was to return them to the Great Refuge. In this story, Triton emphatically tells the Seeker: *"You'll never send us back to the Great Refuge! We want to remain here! We want to live free!"* But as soon as the Inhumans return to the Great Refuge in *FF* #47, Medusa exclaims: *"We're safe at last! In the Great Refuge where we belong!"* The contradiction was confusing.

In the next issue Black Bolt usurps Maximus from the throne simply by removing his crown. If that's all it took, why did the Royal Family bother to flee the Great Refuge in the first place?

But those observations come with a backward glance of time and hindsight. In 1966, the overall effect of *FF* #46 was simply mesmerizing. The new Kirby/Sinnott artwork was virtually dripping with power and panache. It pulled the reader magnetically into this Shakespearian epic of secret civilizations, doomed young lovers and a super-powered race that shunned the outside world.

The cover alone was worth the price of admission.

AT A GLANCE *FF* #47 (Feb. 1966) Sinnott-cover inks
"Beware The Hidden Land" 20p Sinnott-inks

The Inhumans saga would prove to be long and labyrinthine.

At this point it had already spanned four issues with no end in sight, making it the most voluminous *Fantastic Four* story yet. With the Inhumans tale about to wrap up, and with the Galactus Trilogy just up ahead, the series' most fertile period is now coming to full fruition.

AT A GLANCE *FF* #48 deals primarily with Galactus, so for convenience's sake the end of the Inhuman's tale will be addressed here.

It's difficult to offer a gift-wrapped conclusion to a story that has so much intensity, so many innovations, so much strength and beauty. The central focus of this dark, grandiose 5-part opus was a stunningly original group of new characters who practically gave *Fantastic Four* another lease on life. The coming of the Inhumans was by far the most complex and compelling *FF* saga up to now.

The Royal Family's paranoiac distrust of mankind gave them a brooding sense of embitterment and an undercurrent of spiritual unease. This doesn't seem like something the sunny, positivistic Stan Lee would conjure up. This quasi-incestuous family of super-powered separatists was most likely engendered by the darker imagination of Jack Kirby, who seems to be doing the lion's share of the writing at this point.

The introduction of the reclusive Royal Family and the paring of Johnny and Crystal paved the way to a second and third *FF* storyline that would be initiated over the following months. The multi-pronged narrative which the series was about to acquire would launch an entirely new form of comic book storytelling. It would cause immeasurable changes in the way future writers and artists approached their craft.

On the debit side, *FF* #44-47's storyline paradoxes proved the danger of introducing too many new characters and ideas into the series over a short time. Most regrettably, Stan's talent for character-delineating dialogue was lost on the Inhumans. They had no individuality. The Royal Family's lack of differentia was a flaw that would become glaringly

apparent when their solo escapades were launched in *Thor* and *Amazing Adventures*.

The final conclusion: In the story's best moments, and there were many, the debut of the dark, distrustful Inhumans was the most sporadically brilliant tale the comics medium had seen to date. This ambitious, far-ranging storyline gave the magazine an entirely new veneer of significance; a heightened sense of prestige that was greatly facilitated by Joe Sinnott's masterful inking. Sinnott imbued Kirby's artwork with a dignified maturity that only one other inker—Wally Wood—had ever been able to evoke.

At this point the Lee/Kirby *FF* was giving the baby boomer generation some of the most powerful and memorable fiction of its time, and the incomparable spectacles of the Cosmic Era were just beginning. *Fantastic Four* now stands at the moment of its greatest potential.

AT A GLANCE *FF* #48 (Mar. 1966) Sinnott-cover inks
"The Coming Of Galactus" 20p Sinnott-inks (1 collage page)

This is the pinnacle.
This is *Fantastic Four* at the very height of its influence and ambition. There is so much of consequence in the forthcoming issues that we now enter a territory where critical commentary becomes almost purely subjective. The Galactus Trilogy, which was heralded as a masterpiece from the day of its release, can be seen as the peak of both Stan Lee and Jack Kirby's creative career. It's the kind of achievement which any writer or artist would be satisfied to regard as some kind of culmination to their life's work—no less than that.

No menace ever threatened Earth the way Galactus did. He was epic. He was nothing less than a world wrecker, the living embodiment of

Judgment Day. He was entirely above moral absolutes like evil or good. To Galactus, the annihilation of a planet was merely a change in its molecular structure.

Kirby's rendering of Galactus was so omnipotent that many True Believers were convinced the character had Biblical overtones. In the words of Jack Kirby: *"When I created the Silver Surfer and Galactus it came out of a Biblical feeling. I couldn't get gangsters to compete with all these superheroes, so I had to look for more omnipotent characters. I came up with what I thought was God in Galactus; a God-like character. Still thinking about it in the Biblical sense, I began to think of a fallen angel, and the fallen angel was the Silver Surfer. In the story, Galactus confines him to the Earth, just like the fallen angel. So you can get characters from Biblical feelings."*

With the coming of Galactus, the entire Marvel Comics line was bathing in *Fantastic Four's* iridescent glory.

AT A GLANCE *FF* #49 (Apr. 1966) Sinnott-cover inks
"If This Be Doomsday" 20p Sinnott-inks

By now their adventures had grown to mythic proportions. *FF* #49 was the showdown of the gods. Comicdom's collective consciousness was thunderstruck by Kirby's full-page *piece de resistance* on page 2. It demonstrated an unprecedented sense of scale and an opulence befitting religious art.

As they tower over the New York skyscrapers Galactus and the Watcher stand huge, ponderous and messianic, vying each other like rival gods on this Day of Reckoning. Meanwhile, the horrified denizens of Manhattan look on in disbelief, fear and awe. It was a cosmic spectacle of Biblical grandeur. It was a defining comic

book moment, a defining Kirby moment. It was probably the crowning achievement of the entire Silver Age. More than anything, it epitomized what this magazine was all about.

If one were forced to pick the exact point when the 1960s superhero comics peaked, page 2 of *Fantastic Four* #49 would undoubtedly be that moment.

Has there ever been a comic book page equal to this?

Stan first heard the phrase "the Galactus Trilogy" on one of his endless college-circuit appearances. He was astounded that intelligent young adults were analyzing the story as if it were High Art. Undoubtedly, for decades to come, the Trilogy's every panel will be dissected and analyzed by comic book creators, academics and fans as if it was oracular.

This story was Marvel Comics' grandest endeavor. Lee and Kirby were never more unified in their pursuit of magnificence and transcendence.

AT A GLANCE *FF* #50 (May 1966) Sinnott/Giacoia-cover inks
"The Startling Saga of the Silver Surfer" 20p Sinnott-inks

And with this final installment of the Galactus Trilogy, *Fantastic Four* was launched on its Gilded Age.

This was a period of great wealth, of aesthetic striving and achieving, of real grandeur and true elegance. A post-modern blend of classicism and bombast, it was comic's absolute epitome of confidence.

Kirby's self-assurance at this point was so immense that he threw conventional storytelling structure completely out the window. The final installment of the Galactus Triumvirate ended in the middle of *FF* #50, just as the beginning of the tale started in the middle of *FF* #48.

And what did it matter? In Kirby's mind everything was just one big story anyway; a story where everything connected to everything else, where everything intersected and entwined, then drifted apart. There was no beginning or end. It was an intricately interwoven cosmic jigsaw puzzle of interlocking relationships and ironic coincidences; the sum of whose parts formed a labyrinthic but cohesive Universe.

The Human Torch began his college days in this issue, which seemed yet another colossal Marvel innovation—a two-pronged narrative which would soon evolve into a triangulated storyline. And why not? At this point it seemed that nothing was impossible.

To comic fandom down through the years, the Galactus Trilogy and its long term repercussions would become the center of rapt attention, to be studied and analyzed and written about. And underneath the central equation was the startling Silver Surfer whose intrinsic worth, over time, would significantly eclipse his master's. He would soon become Marvel's most tragic and philosophical figure.

In the words of Stan Lee: "*The Silver Surfer looked so pure, so guileless, so noble that I felt I couldn't let him speak like any other comic book character. His personality had to be as special as his demeanor. And so, I decided to let the Silver Surfer become the voice of Marvel's conscience. He mouthed all the philosophical thoughts and observations that I myself always harbored and dwelled upon. Within a short time he, more than any other of our creations, came to symbolize all that was good and true about life and the human condition.*"

In the end, inevitably, the Galactus Trilogy took the comic book medium to a level that no one had dared to dream was possible. A level that had been unknown before

and that has remained unequalled since.

And still Kirby's ambitions were infinite.

And still Kirby's drives were phenomenal.

And still Kirby's energies were volcanic.

After fifty issues, *Fantastic Four* shows no signs of abating.

AT A GLANCE *FF* #51 (June 1966) Sinnott-cover inks
"*This Man, This Monster*" 20p Sinnott-inks (1 collage page)

This is a timeless tale of heroism, courage, self-sacrifice and redemption. And those qualities belong not to the heroes, but to the *villain* of the story.

Talk about a twist.

"This Man, This Monster" is probably the greatest single-issue story in the entire Lee/Kirby *FF* cannon. Intrinsically it lacks nothing. It has a Zen-like perfection; it is whole, like a perfect circle which cannot be added to or subtracted from without upsetting its flawless balance.

Since the principal storyline of *FF* #51 is discussed in the main text, this segment will focus on the book's subplot, Johnny Storm's recent arrival at Metro College. At this point it would seem that the writers, or maybe Kirby alone, decided to give *Fantastic Four* a twin-storyline like the Earth/Asgard duality that was occurring in the pages of *Journey Into Mystery*.

FF #50 devoted an entire page and then some to a character called Sam Thorne. Coach Thorne, his wife Belle and Whitey Mullins, the football team's star quarterback, were all inseminated into the storyline. Thorne's career is fading and he desperately needs a great athlete to replace the arrogant and egotistical Mullins.

Obviously, Wyatt Wingfoot, who was also introduced in *FF* #50, was

going to be the answer to Thorn's dilemma. Three pages in *FF* #51 are devoted to the Wingfoot/Mullins subplot. But the story-threads woven in this tale were left forever hanging, and the entire Metro University scenario was dropped after this issue.

It's been speculated that after *FF* #51 the notoriously absent-minded writers simply forgot that Johnny had gone off to college. But it's more likely that Jack and Stan quickly decided the Metro College subplot was too dull a premise. Let's face it, after Galactus, "Whitey Mullins" didn't quite cut it.

And after *FF* #52, Johnny would never be seen at college again. Wyatt however, would be seen at Metro one final time in *FF* #61, when Lockjaw leads Crystal there.

Despite the forever unresolved Metro subplot, *Fantastic Four* #51 stands as a high-water mark of the Silver Age. It can easily be seen as some kind of peak. If nothing else, it's certainly the series' most unforgettable 20-page story.

Of course this appreciation is largely retrospective. At the time it was just the latest issue of *Fantastic Four*.

Fantastic Footnote: Stan recalls that he spent several hours agonizing over the title of this story. "I didn't know whether to call it *This Man, This Monster* or *This Monster, This Man*," said Lee. "*This Man, This Monster* just seemed to have a better ring to it."

AT A GLANCE *FF* #52 (July 1966) Sinnott-cover inks
"*The Black Panther*" 20p Sinnott-inks

At this period in our nation's history the civil rights movement was growing bigger and more confrontational, building a wall between blacks and whites as well as the white North and the white South.

In a time when social forces

seemed to be polarizing people, not uniting them, Lee and Kirby were ready to unmask the shame of societal inequity without any apparent concern for sales in the South. It was in this political climate that comic's first Black superhero was created. It was another fantastic first in a comic series that spawned so many other first-time innovations.

It could be speculated that Wally Wood's recently revised Daredevil costume, with its great abundance of ink-absorbing spot blacks, influenced Kirby's final Black Panther design. The two costumes look suspiciously alike.

And regarding the Black Panther's attire, the unused cover of *FF* #52 proves that Kirby's first take on T'Challa's uniform was significantly revamped. Or maybe Jack did the cover first, then forgot the original costume when he drew the interior pages.

Whichever the case, this "cover under reconstruction" resulted in the house ads for *FF* #52 being blocked-out and replaced by a blurb which hyped the Panther's coming with Stan's usual flair for the dramatic.

In this story the FF find themselves in the tribal village Wakanda, a technological wonderland in the heart of the African jungle. They're being hunted like big-game by a mysterious costumed chieftain who possesses the fighting ability of Captain America and the scientific prowess of Reed Richards.

Under the close scrutiny of hindsight, this two-part Black Panther debut was a four-color *tour de force*—one of Lee and Kirby's best realized *FF* tales of all time.

AT A GLANCE *FF* #53 (Aug. 1966) Sinnott-cover inks
"*The Way It Began*" 20p Sinnott-inks

Intrigue in the heart of the jungle

continues as the FF learn "The Way it Began."

In this issue we discover that T'Challa was born into an isolated African tribe in the land of Wakanda, which had no contact with modern civilization. T'Challa's father was murdered by a Westerner named Klaw, who had come to Wakanda to plunder the rare metal "vibranium."

Young T'Challa vowed vengeance, then went abroad to study science. On his return from the West, he survived a ritual that earned him the right to wear the mask of the Black Panther, Wakanda's symbol of strength and nobility.

In the above paragraphs, if you change the name "T'Challa" to "Doom," and "Wakanda" to "Latveria," you almost have the origin of Doctor Doom as seen in *FF Annual #2*—not that anyone seemed to notice at the time.

The flaws and recycled themes found in *FF #44-53* are only evident under the intense glare of retrospection. At the time, the magazine's amazing new characters were so mind-boggling that any blemishes in the storylines went largely unnoticed.

It was at this point that the introduction of unforgettable new characters ended. *Fantastic Four's* Cosmic Era was far from over, but there would be no more immortal Lee/Kirby icons like the Inhumans, the Silver Surfer, Galactus or the Black Panther.

It was understandable. No one could keep up that level of creativity indefinitely.

AT A GLANCE *FF #54* (Sept. 1966) Sinnott-cover inks
"Whosoever Finds The Evil Eye" 20p Sinnott-inks

Inevitably there came a point when *Fantastic Four's* storyline had grown too complex, too immense, and much too various to be contin-

ued in a single direction. And at this point, in *FF #54*, the magazine broke apart into different factions and directions.

Having tested the waters of a two-sided plot structure with Johnny's short stint at college, the writers now had wider ambitions. Now that comic fandom had applauded thunderously for *Fantastic Four's* multi-issue story arcs, Lee and Kirby knew they could seize the moment and complexify the *FF's* storyline into a totally new format; a format unlike anything comics had ever seen.

Various characters and coincidences would now overlap and intertwine for unspecified periods as the Inhumans' adventures became a regular subplot in the book. Likewise, the Torch would now randomly drift in and out of his teammate's lives and then spin off on his own with Wyatt Wingfoot.

Obviously, *Fantastic Four's* new triple-storyline was a stunning development in terms of complex thematic variation. But it also presented problems which were instantly apparent. Occasional plot threads were left unresolved, as seen on page 6 of this story. Gorgon is trying to trick Mad Maximus into creating a device which will shatter the Great Barrier. Right before the scene segues back to the FF, Medusa's dramatic thought-balloon reads: *Will he do it? Or is he too mad? Everything depends on what happens next!*

In fact, *nothing* happened next. The next time we see Maximus he's happily tinkering with Triton's saline apparatus. These disjointed developments weren't all Kirby's fault. As Jack's editor, Stan Lee—one half of comicdom's most absent-minded duo—should have caught these incongruities.

Comic theologians claim the Prester John character was based on a 12th century Christian Priest King with the title of "Presbyter

John," who appears in Medieval Jewish legend. Obviously, at this stage Kirby was going back further than old comics and pulps for his inspirations.

AT A GLANCE *FF #55* (Oct. 1966) Sinnott-cover inks
"When Strikes The Silver Surfer" 20p Sinnott-inks (1 collage panel)

No document on Earth gives stronger proof of *Fantastic Four's* storyline being a joint-effort than *FF #55*.

We know what Stan contributed to this tale because it was reported by Nat Freeland in the 1/9/66 *New York Herald-Tribune*. The main storyline, where Ben finds the Silver Surfer with Alicia and attacks him in a jealous rage, was Lee's idea. Ergo, we know what Kirby contributed to the plot—all the elements not mentioned in Freeland's article. And this entails some very significant story points.

The first *FF* tale to incorporate a three-pronged storyline was the previous month's issue (*FF #54*) which devoted a whopping 14 out of 20 pages to the adventures of the Inhumans in the Great Barrier and to Johnny and Wyatt's search for Crystal. During the *FF* story conference that Freeland was privy to, Lee apparently forgot about these subplots.

Kirby didn't. In "When Strikes the Silver Surfer," Jack shifted the storyline from Ben and Alicia on the Atlantic Coast to the snow-covered Himalayas, where Wyatt and the Torch encounter Lockjaw, Crystal's dimension-bouncing bulldog. At this point, Johnny and Wyatt abandon T'Challa's gyro-cruiser and allow Lockjaw to lead them wherever he sees fit. It's clear this development was entirely Kirby's idea.

This was the second of three consecutive self-contained *FF* stories. All three were topnotch examples of *Fantastic Four* in the heyday of its

Gilded Age, and this totally absorbing tale was probably the best of the lot.

Fantastic Four #55 still stands as a classic of its kind.

AT A GLANCE *FF #56* (Nov. 1966) Sinnott-cover inks
"Klaw, The Murderous Master Of Sound" 20p Sinnott-inks

It's odd that the new Klaw only appeared in one issue of the Lee/Kirby *FF*.

As difficult as it was for Jack and Stan to come up with competent villains for the series, one would think this much-improved "master of sound" would be a better return prospect than someone like the Mole Man.

At the end of *FF #53*, Klaw climbed into his sound-transformer which altered the structure of all living things but had never been tested on a human. After that, he wasn't seen again until now.

When he emerged from the transformer he was invariably magnificent; all scarlet and satanic, with a mechanical sonic-force transmitter in place of his useless hand. He looked quite imposing.

Klaw's no-return in the series might be attributed to the fact that he was too easy to defeat. All it took to bring him down was an uppercut from Mr. Fantastic with a set of vibranium knuckles, compliments of the Black Panther.

The two sub-storylines continue as Johnny and Wyatt find themselves transported by Lockjaw to a shadowy and frightening realm which they suspect is not on Earth. Now that the Torch and Wingfoot have united with Crystal's canine, their quest takes on an ominous undercurrent. They are no longer in control of their own destiny.

Meanwhile, deep in the Himalayas, Medusa goes ballistic on Maximus when he tells her he can penetrate the Great Barrier at will, but chooses not to. At this point Stan is calling the Great Barrier the "Negative Zone." At some future date, he would decide the Negative Zone was the region that was referred to as "Sub-Space" in *FF #51*. (The original concept of Sub-Space was first introduced in *FF #37*.)

Despite this breach of continuity, *Fantastic Four #56* is a classic example of Lee, Kirby and Sinnott at the peak of their prodigious powers; and between them the creative sparks fly.

The series may not have been gathering steam at this point but it

was certainly still steaming.

AT A GLANCE *FF SPECIAL* #4 (Nov. 1966) Sinnott/Giacoia-cover inks
"The Torch That Was" 19p Sinnott-inks/(r: *FF* #25) "The Hulk Vs. The Thing" 22p/
(r: *FF* #26) "The Avengers Take Over" 23p

Fantastic Four seemed the ideal place to reintroduce characters from the dull yellowing pages of the Golden Age Timely comics. This practice undoubtedly thrilled older fans who longed for the return of their childhood heroes.

Johnny's prototype, the original android Torch, makes his first appearance since 1954 in this impressive tale which is fundamentally a Human Torch solo story. Obviously, there hadn't been any reason to reinstate the old Torch with Johnny on the scene, so here's the question: Why bring back the Golden Age Torch just to kill him off at the story's end?

In 1966, Carl Burgos initiated a lawsuit against Marvel over rights to the original Human Torch. That might have been the impetus for this story in *FF Annual* #4.

Burgos had drawn the Torch for Goodman in the 1940s, '50s and '60s. His last shot at drawing the character was seen in the early 1960s *Strange Tales* series. The Torch/Thing *Strange Tales* adventures were among the weakest stories Marvel ever produced.

Stan Goldberg claims that Burgos never got along with Stan Lee, which made working at Marvel an unpleasant experience for him. Maybe this had a bearing on Burgos' lawsuit which, by all accounts, amounted to almost nothing. The suit was settled out of court, and Carl's daughter recalls that on the day it was settled, Burgos' was so upset he threw away all his Golden Age comics. Burgos' career as a comic book

artist was completely finished by 1967.

For collectors of useless information, this was the last ever Lee/Kirby *FF* story with a "symbolic" splash page. The last regular issue of *Fantastic Four* with a symbolic-splash was *FF* #56.

AT A GLANCE *FF* #57 (Dec. 1966) Sinnott-cover inks
"Enter, Doctor Doom" 20p Sinnott-inks

The element of incongruity is introduced right off the bat as the story begins not with Doctor Doom, but with a 3-page skirmish between the FF and the Sandman at the prison where Sandman and the Wizard are serving time. Sandman escapes and then disappears, not to be seen again for months. With this done, the writers have set the stage for *FF* #61. It's odd how Lee and Kirby, both with incredibly bad memories, were occasionally capable of these far-ranging storyline strategies.

According to Kirby-historian Mike Gartland, "It was Jack's original intention for the Silver Surfer to enter mankind as a blank slate, absorbing new lessons about the human condition with every subsequent adventure." Gartland's remark was totally on-target. In *FF* #49 the Surfer learned the value of human life. In *FF* #55 he learned about human emotion through Ben's jealousy. Here, in *FF* #57, he discovers human treachery.

And in this tale Dr. Doom is Treachery Personified. On page 15, as the Lord of Latveria gloats over the fallen alien, Kirby imbues Doom with a sense of evil that almost runs off the page. If any readers doubted that *Fantastic Four* was "The World's Greatest Comic Magazine," *FF* #57 laid those doubts to rest. At this point the series had acquired an opulence that surprised even the most

optimistic Marvel fans.

Fantastic Fact: Joe Sinnott said that *FF* #57 featured his all-time favorite Kirby cover.

AT A GLANCE *FF* #58 (Jan. 1967) Sinnott-cover inks
"The Dismal Dregs Of Defeat" 20p Sinnott-inks

Even the most hard-nosed critic would be sorely pressed to find any shortcomings in *FF* #58. This adventure is a powerhouse presentation from its terrifying splash page to its final panel where Dr. Doom soars serenely above the waves on his stolen surfboard.

Page one is spellbinding. Doom's ghastly negative image flashes with every burst of lightning during a midday New York rainstorm. It's a brilliant and terrifying opening moment. Even the courageous Thing becomes a nervous wreck as Dr. Doom sadistically toys with his old enemies.

The story offers page after page of riveting action juxtaposed with eerie moments of quietude; the very same sophisticated contrasts that made the Galactus saga so compelling. This four-part Dr. Doom opus has other similarities to the Galactus tale as well. Here's the connection: Our heroes are faced with a menace too powerful to defeat by might. The only way he can be toppled will be to outsmart him.

Victor's cataclysmic battles with the Thing and the Torch individually are both conclusive victories for the Lord of Latveria. And in the story's closing moments, Mr. Fantastic admits defeat as his teammates recoil in shock and disbelief.

This is Victor Von Doom in all his ignoble glory. Never again will he seem so dark, so powerful, so foreboding.

AT A GLANCE *FF* #59 (Feb. 1967) Sinnott-cover inks

"Doomsday" 20p Sinnott-inks

Black Bolt's end-of-civilization roar was a transcendent moment in comic book history. All the thrills, all the glory, all the splendor that four-color fantasy had promised since the dawn of the Silver Age suddenly came to full fruition and crystallized on a comic book page that was dark, ominous, and catastrophic. The shattering of the Great Barrier was a cataclysm of Biblical magnitude; a spectacle of Old Testament grandeur.

It was the mind-bending answer to why he never spoke.

Black Bolt's universe-shattering scream, which scattered the Great Dome to the four corners of the Earth, was a vision that rivaled the Galactus/Watcher full-page masterpiece in *FF* #49. The panels contained huge, frantic outpourings of wrath and supernatural apocalypse; magnificent and chaotic, bombastic and bloated into Wagnerian proportions. This is Jacob Kurtzberg's ghetto-bred anger manifested on a comic book page. This is Jack Kirby's rage, terror, and power. After numerous months of confinement, the Incomparable Inhumans are suddenly free.

The Doom/Surfer story cycle hadn't yet reached its full, ferocious climax, but it peaked here.

AT A GLANCE *FF* #60 (Mar. 1967) Sinnott-cover inks
"The Peril And The Power" 20p Sinnott-inks

As the sun began to set on *Fantastic Four*'s Gilded Age, Stan Lee and Jack Kirby had left the entire comic book industry ridiculously in back of them. They were in their own world now.

Given any kind of close examination, the exoticism of the magazine's Cosmic Era—which hadn't entirely ended—seems to have exerted no lasting influence on the final years

of Kirby's *Fantastic Four*. In fact, it was almost as if it never happened.

The mystery, force and sense of wonder that the Cosmic Era possessed would not dissipate immediately; it would simply channel and flow in other directions. As the publisher and writers began to suspect that the long sweeping sagas were only satisfying a limited subculture, other approaches would be tested. Simpler storylines and more big action would soon be the New Order; and after that, no more continued stories.

Certain aspects of issues #44 through #60 have undergone some reassessment.

Under a microscope, these Cosmic Era stories suffered some noticeable weaknesses which weren't perceptible at the time because the pacing was fast and the characters were mesmeric. The problems were myriad: A writer with no editor to catch his mistakes, an artist whose pencil could barely keep up with his exploding imagination, and the most absent-minded creative duo the comics industry had ever known. None of these things helped stabilize the storylines. One solution might have been to put Roy Thomas in charge of continuity. He would have been perfect for the job.

FF #60 concluded one of the most impressive multi-issue sagas in the annals of comic book history. With this issue the series has reached a breaking point. It was far from decline, but it would never peak this high again.

Fantastic Four has seen its ultimate summit.

AT A GLANCE *FF* #61 (Apr. 1967)
Sinnott-cover inks
"Where Stalks The Sandman?"
20p Sinnott-inks

The rush of adrenaline that had sustained the magazine from *FF* #44-60 was about to exhaust itself,

but its immediate aftermath would show no signs of artistic fatigue.

In this tale the new improved Sandman becomes an honorary Jack Kirby villain; and why not? Since the coming of the Frightful Four way back in *FF* #36, Jack had been getting more mileage out of the character than his creator, Steve Ditko.

Sturdy Steve's Sandman, who first appeared in *The Amazing Spider-Man* #4, was the type of colorful urban hoodlum that Ditko specialized in. However, by the late 1960s his trademark striped shirt was a bit of an anachronism; especially in the technologically advanced *Fantastic Four*, with its complex Kirby-contraptions and costumes.

Sandman's ally, the Trapster, had received a Kirby facelift ages ago. The Trapster's new look and new name converted him from one of the most ludicrous comic book characters ever created ("Paste-Pot Pete") into a formidable foe. In *FF* #78, the Wizard would receive a patented Kirby makeover as well. This time it was the Sandman's turn.

Johnny's faithful Indian companion Wyatt Wingfoot has a quick cameo with Crystal at Metro College. This will be the final mention of the campus from which the Torch has apparently dropped out.

This is an exciting, beautifully drawn tale. From its power-surge opening to its runaway train ending, it's a non-stop roller coaster ride of action and thrills.

Superhero comics don't come too much better than this.

AT A GLANCE *FF* #62 (May 1967)
Giacoia-cover inks
"And One Shall Save Him" 20p Sinnott-inks (2 collage pages)

Bearing more than a passing resemblance to *FF* #51, "And One Shall Save Him" finds Reed once

again hopelessly adrift in the terrifying anti-matter universe called the Negative Zone.

Despite the recycled plot, this harrowing companion piece to "This Man, This Monster" is an electrifying story where a lot of important events emerge. After Crystal obtained Black Bolt's permission to search for Johnny in the previous issue, Lockjaw finally brings her to the Baxter Building where she finds the Torch, Sue and Ben in utter turmoil over Reed's hopeless predicament. After all the months of Johnny and Wyatt searching for Crystal, it was she who found him.

The couple's reunion triggers major changes in *Fantastic Four*. Obviously, from this point on there would be no more "Johnny searching for Crystal" subplots. Likewise, the Inhumans' sub-storyline in the series ended after this issue as well.

The writers could have continued to keep tabs on the Royal Family in the pages of *Fantastic Four*, but they chose not to because Goodman was telling Stan the Inhumans would soon have their own magazine. As it happened, he was wrong.

The fate of Triton subsequent to this issue is interesting. After saving Reed from the murderous miasma of the Negative Zone (and thereby paying Richards back for saving his life in *FF* #47), Triton begins an extended stay in New York, residing at the Baxter Building. The aquatic Inhuman appears to be acting as Crystal's chaperone; a duty which he will perform for the next two issues.

Despite the fact that *FF* #44-60 had been the magazine's highest peak, the adventures which immediately followed were tremendously exciting in both stories and art. The changes, progression and growth that made *Fantastic Four* the leader in the field were still quite prevalent at this illustrious juncture.

AT A GLANCE *FF* #63 (June 1967)
Sinnott-cover inks
"Blastaar, The Living Bomb-Burst" 20p Sinnott-inks

The splash page of *FF* #63 hits you like a Kirby punch.

Could there be a more exciting way to begin a story than having the roof cave in? This is action on an epic scale.

Although it wouldn't be apparent for years to come, at this point all of Jack and Stan's greatest *FF* characters had been introduced, and all of the best Lee/Kirby *FF* stories had been told. In that sense, *Fantastic Four* had already peaked. But at this phase there wasn't the slightest sign of deceleration. If anything, the magazine's pace had intensified.

Blastaar, who was introduced in the previous issue, was a real contender. He was a ruthless monarch whose subjects overthrew him and sent him adrift in the Negative Zone. He possessed superhuman strength and could generate blasts of concussive force from his fingertips. He was certainly one of Stan and Jack's most impressive antagonists.

On page 8, we have a mesmerizing full-page illustration of Blastaar gone mad, clinching his fists, raving and enraged as if he's completely unhinged. Even his ally the Sandman seems fearful of him.

Triton's presence in the story is a welcome change of pace, as two masterfully drawn pages are devoted to his encounter with Blastaar on the roof of the Baxter Building. Triton's quirky air gun (first seen in the previous issue) was the type of ingenious device which Kirby could have found countless uses for. Unfortunately, Jack forgot about it after this story.

Fantastic Four #63 has everything a superhero story needs in order to be great: action, drama, suspense, humor, romance, a ferocious battle and the inevitable happy ending. Not a single element is missing.

AT A GLANCE *FF* #64 (July 1967)
Sinnott-cover inks
"The Sentry Sinister" 20p Sinnott-inks

Although the magazine's peak period was over, *Fantastic Four* was still basking in the warm affluent afterglow of the most incendiary hot streak comics had ever seen. At this point Kirby was still keen to offer up ever new innovations and characters. There was no way anyone could have predicted the

lethargy to come.

A new element of the Marvel Universe is introduced as we get the first preamble of the Kree race, the only extraterrestrial civilization that Lee and Kirby would introduce into the series besides the Skrulls; a concept that future generations of writers would get acres of mileage from.

In this entertaining tale, two archeologists follow the trail of an ancient civilization and discover a giant alien robot still living in the ruins. The robot, Inter-Galactic Sentry 459, was left behind by the space-traveling Kree race to protect his outpost. As fate would have it, the outpost just happens to be located on an island in the South Pacific that Reed, Sue and Ben have chosen as a vacation spot.

One sideline of this story is the final glimpse of Triton in New York, where he's seen soaring above the city on Johnny's jet cycle. The Attilan aquanaut had been ensconced in the Baxter building since FF #62. His extended stay in the Big Apple may have been a brief and aborted attempt to give Triton a sub-storyline in the series like the quickly discarded "Metro College" subplot that lasted two issues (see FF #50 and 51).

Either way, the writers goofed. In the next issue Sue would say that Triton and Lockjaw went back to "the camp" that the Royal Family has established. But four months later in FF Annual #5, Jack depicted the fish-man materializing on Panther Island with Ben and the Torch from the Baxter Building as if he'd been there all along.

AT A GLANCE FF #65 (Aug. 1967) Sinnott-cover inks
"From Beyond This Planet Earth" 20p Sinnott-inks

"From Beyond This Planet Earth" is Jack Kirby's second infatuation with a new extraterrestrial race

called the Kree, which began in the previous issue.

Had Kirby not left Marvel in 1970, it's a safe bet he would have done more with this new alien culture. The Inhumans' back-up features in Thor would establish that the Attilan race was the by-product of a Kree experiment, and a new series called Captain Marvel would also have a Kree underpinning. But Fantastic Four wouldn't rekindle a Kree theme until issue #98, right before Jack left the book.

In this fine story Ronan the Accuser comes to Earth to indict the FF for destroying the Kree Sentry in the last issue. The "Him" storyline from FF #66-67 begins here with Alicia being whisked through a solid wall by a mystery man with a strange wristband.

All's well that ends well. Our heroes kick Ronan's accusing ass all the way back to the Kree Galaxy, and that's the last we see of him in Jack Kirby's Fantastic Four.

At the beginning of this story we see that Ben and Johnny are sharing the same bedroom in the FF's headquarters; even sleeping in the same double bed. Contrarily, a special-feature page from FF #8 revealed that Johnny had his own fireproof bedroom in the Baxter Building.

One wonders if the writers were making a point to assure the readers (and perhaps the Comics Code) that there was nothing inappropriate about Johnny and Crystal's cohabitation of the Baxter Building.

AT A GLANCE FF #66 (Sept. 1967) Sinnott-cover inks
'What Lurks Behind The Beehive?" 20p Sinnott-inks

Much ink has been absorbed writing about this two-part story and its effects. The reasons for this are numerous. First, it's known that Stan bastardized Kirby's original intent story-wise. Second, this two-part

tale would pretty much be the last FF adventure to which Kirby would wholeheartedly apply his creative genius. After this, the King mostly did the book on autopilot.

Just as Lee and John Buscema's "Norrin Radd" totally inverted Kirby's Silver Surfer character, Lee turned the tables on Jack's "cocoon" storyline as well. Kirby wanted the golden, godlike "Him" to turn on the well-intentioned scientists who created him simply because they didn't meet his standards. Conversely, Stan made the scientists evil geniuses bent on world domination.

At the risk of being tarred and feathered by the Kirby community, it should be noted that changing storylines to reflect their own personal vision is simply what comic book editors did. It was an everyday occurrence in the industry. Stan Lee was the King's editor as well as his co-author. People tend to forget that in their passion to prop Kirby up as the wronged artiest.

Does anyone really think that Stan would frivolously subvert Jack's ideas just to piss him off, or just because it was his prerogative? Lee was the only person in the Marvel management who appreciated Kirby. Martin Goodman certainly didn't, and the company's imminent new owners would value Kirby even less than Goodman.

It's possible that Stan felt the King's version of FF #66 and 67 had no clear cut division of good and evil, and to make the tale more accessible, more commercial, he made it simpler.

On the other hand, a directive from Martin Goodman might have been the impetus for Stan to simplify the "Him" storyline. Around this time Goodman began to worry that Marvel's stories were mainly targeting college kids, and the younger readers were finding them too hard to follow.

AT A GLANCE FF #67 (Oct. 1967) Sinnott-cover inks
"When Opens The Cocoon" 20p Sinnott-inks

Kirby biographer Mark Evanier told Mike Gartland that this "cocoon" story was influenced by Kirby's take on the philosophy of Objectivism, as spouted by its chief architect Ayn Rand. Steve Ditko was said to have been greatly influenced by Rand as well. But there's little trace of Ayn Rand's philosophy in FF #66 and 67, so maybe this connection is similar to Jack claiming his late 1963 stories were greatly influenced by JFK's death. One has to dig very, very deep to uncover that correlation. It may exist only in the most abstract terms; or maybe only in Kirby's mind.

Some comic book theologians believe that certain Outer Limits episodes such as The Boarderland, The Architects of Fear and The Bellero Shield influenced this story. Other historians list various sci-fi movies as the matrix for this tale.

Whatever the case, it's unarguable that Fantastic Four would change quite drastically after this story, and not for the better. Beginning with FF #68, Kirby would never again contribute complicated plots which touched on things that intrigued him like science, mythology, politics, religion or philosophy. He would never again contribute any stupendously original characters like the Silver Surfer that Marvel could compromise or turn into long-term bread-winners (which is exactly what happened to "Him," who became "Adam Warlock" in 1972). From here on, the King would habitually reinstate previously established characters to the series or concoct mindless androids and robots; most of whom were speechless and entirely generic.

And so Fantastic Four's Gilded Age, the "Cosmic Era" draws to a close; not with a celebrated send-

off, but with a story full of compromises and conflicting ideas.

But what a glorious epoch it had been. It was a time of reaching and achieving, of breaking boundaries and testing limits, of ultimately learning there are no limits. It was a shinning, stunning apotheosis; a period that by its very nature proved ephemeral, fleeting, not meant to last.

Such intensity couldn't possibly sustain.

AT A GLANCE *FF SPECIAL* #5 (Nov. 1967) Giacoia-cover inks "*Divide And Conquer*" 30p Giacoia-inks (accredited to Sinnott)/"*This Is A Plot?*" 3p Giacoia-inks/*Black Bolt/Gorgon/ Medusa/Karnak/Triton/Crystal/ Maximus/Supporting Characters* 8p Giacoia-inks/*Fantastic Four* 2p Sinnott-inks/"*The Peerless Power Of The Silver Surfer*" 12p Giacoia-inks

The explanation for the numerous flaws in *Fantastic Four Annual* #5 only became apparent decades later, after copies of the original pencil art surfaced (see below).

In the published version, Crystal stayed with Reed and Sue at the Baxter Building while the others went off to battle Psycho-Man. Contrarily, the book's cover depicted Crys battling Psycho-Man alongside Ben, Johnny, the Black Panther and the Inhumans.

Here's the reason: In the original art, Kirby had Crystal travel to Panther Island along with Ben, Johnny, Triton and Lockjaw to

defeat Psycho-Man, but the King forgot to draw her in the story after page 20. Subsequently, Stan had to have all the Crystal figures after page 14 erased, which left unsightly gaps in every panel she was deleted from. The composition of panel 5, page 20 (below), is significantly unbalanced by Crystal's erasure.

Besides this, the Panther's skirmish with "Cat-Beast" seems to be another thread that Jack left hanging. The King apparently forgot about it midway through the story, and its outcome was unconvincingly explained by dialogue.

Despite these incongruities (which no one noticed in 1967), this was the most opulent *FF Annual* since *Annual* #2. The Inhumans pin-ups are among the most splendid that Kirby drew in the Silver Age; they're simply magnificent. The inks on the main story were obviously done by Frank Giacoia, but were accredited to Joe Sinnott.

About the back-up story: The way Mark Evanier tells it, this Silver Surfer tale was drawn because

Martin Goodman wanted to give The Hulk his own magazine and fill the Hulk's *Tales to Astonish* slot with *Tales of the Silver Surfer*. That never happened, hence the appearance of the Silver Surfer back-up story in *FF Annual* #5. The coincidence was incredibly appropriate because this Silver Surfer adventure picks up exactly where *FF Annual* #4 left off the previous year, with the "Quasimodo" storyline.

In lucid hindsight, it's an incredible coincidence that every other *FF Annual* wrapped up one phase of *Fantastic Four* and ushered in the next. *Annual* #1 signaled the end of the Dick Ayers era and Sue's conflict over Namor. *Annual* #3 rang in the Cosmic period because *FF* #44 was the issue which immediately followed it. *Annual* #5 would be immediately followed by *FF* #68; the exact point where inertia set in.

In that sense, *Fantastic Four Annual* #5 is the final story from the series' Gilded Age; the unforgettable "Cosmic Era."

GALACTUS

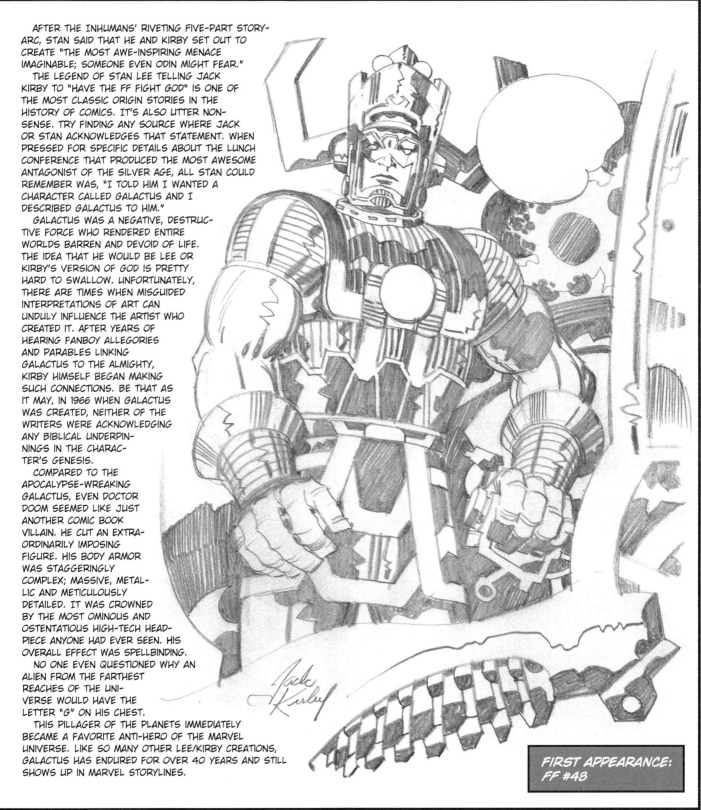

AFTER THE INHUMANS' RIVETING FIVE-PART STORY-ARC, STAN SAID THAT HE AND KIRBY SET OUT TO CREATE "THE MOST AWE-INSPIRING MENACE IMAGINABLE; SOMEONE EVEN ODIN MIGHT FEAR."

THE LEGEND OF STAN LEE TELLING JACK KIRBY TO "HAVE THE FF FIGHT GOD" IS ONE OF THE MOST CLASSIC ORIGIN STORIES IN THE HISTORY OF COMICS. IT'S ALSO UTTER NON-SENSE. TRY FINDING ANY SOURCE WHERE JACK OR STAN ACKNOWLEDGES THAT STATEMENT. WHEN PRESSED FOR SPECIFIC DETAILS ABOUT THE LUNCH CONFERENCE THAT PRODUCED THE MOST AWESOME ANTAGONIST OF THE SILVER AGE, ALL STAN COULD REMEMBER WAS, "I TOLD HIM I WANTED A CHARACTER CALLED GALACTUS AND I DESCRIBED GALACTUS TO HIM."

GALACTUS WAS A NEGATIVE, DESTRUCTIVE FORCE WHO RENDERED ENTIRE WORLDS BARREN AND DEVOID OF LIFE. THE IDEA THAT HE WOULD BE LEE OR KIRBY'S VERSION OF GOD IS PRETTY HARD TO SWALLOW. UNFORTUNATELY, THERE ARE TIMES WHEN MISGUIDED INTERPRETATIONS OF ART CAN UNDULY INFLUENCE THE ARTIST WHO CREATED IT. AFTER YEARS OF HEARING FANBOY ALLEGORIES AND PARABLES LINKING GALACTUS TO THE ALMIGHTY, KIRBY HIMSELF BEGAN MAKING SUCH CONNECTIONS. BE THAT AS IT MAY, IN 1966 WHEN GALACTUS WAS CREATED, NEITHER OF THE WRITERS WERE ACKNOWLEDGING ANY BIBLICAL UNDERPIN-NINGS IN THE CHARAC-TER'S GENESIS.

COMPARED TO THE APOCALYPSE-WREAKING GALACTUS, EVEN DOCTOR DOOM SEEMED LIKE JUST ANOTHER COMIC BOOK VILLAIN. HE CUT AN EXTRA-ORDINARILY IMPOSING FIGURE. HIS BODY ARMOR WAS STAGGERINGLY COMPLEX; MASSIVE, METAL-LIC AND METICULOUSLY DETAILED. IT WAS CROWNED BY THE MOST OMINOUS AND OSTENTATIOUS HIGH-TECH HEAD-PIECE ANYONE HAD EVER SEEN. HIS OVERALL EFFECT WAS SPELLBINDING.

NO ONE EVEN QUESTIONED WHY AN ALIEN FROM THE FARTHEST REACHES OF THE UNI-VERSE WOULD HAVE THE LETTER "G" ON HIS CHEST.

THIS PILLAGER OF THE PLANETS IMMEDIATELY BECAME A FAVORITE ANTI-HERO OF THE MARVEL UNIVERSE. LIKE SO MANY OTHER LEE/KIRBY CREATIONS, GALACTUS HAS ENDURED FOR OVER 40 YEARS AND STILL SHOWS UP IN MARVEL STORYLINES.

FIRST APPEARANCE:
FF #48

THE SILVER SURFER

LEE AND KIRBY IMBUED THE SPACE-FARING SILVER SURFER WITH AN UNPRECEDENTED SENSE OF NOBILITY. HE SEEMED THE VERY ESSENCE OF MORAL VIRTUE. HE HAD A SPIRITUAL QUALITY AND NEAR-RELIGIOUS FERVOR IN HIS ATTITUDE AND DEMEANOR. THE SADNESS HE ENDURED FOR THE MISERY HE FOUND ON THIS PLANET WAS AKIN TO THE AGONIES SUFFERED BY THE EARLY RELIGIOUS MARTYRS.

STAN MATCHED THE PURITY THAT KIRBY DEPICTED IN THE CHARACTER BY GIVING HIM EXCEEDINGLY VIRTUOUS SPEECH PATTERNS. HIS DIALECT WAS NAIVE, TRUSTING, OTHER-WORLDLY AND TINGED WITH REGRET. REGRET FOR THE UNFULFILLED PROMISE THAT HE RECOGNIZED IN THE INHABITANTS OF EARTH.

THE STORY OF KIRBY CREATING THE SILVER SURFER ON HIS OWN WITH NO INPUT FROM STAN IS WELL-KNOWN. LEE FREELY ADMITS HE HAD NOTHING TO DO WITH THE SURFER'S CONCEPTION OTHER THAN GIVING HIM HIS DISTINCTIVE DIALOGUE. SOME KIRBY PUNDITS CLAIM THE ONLY REASON STAN HAS ADMITTED TO THIS IS BECAUSE ROY THOMAS WAS STANDING BY HIS SIDE WHEN THE PAGES TO *FF #48* ARRIVED.

BUT THIS SHOULD BE NOTED: SOL BRODSKY TOLD THOMAS THAT THE CREATION OF THE SILVER SURFER BY KIRBY, WITHOUT LEE'S INPUT, WAS THE EXCEPTION TO THE RULE. NOT THE NORM.

FIRST APPEARANCE: *FF #48*

BLACK PANTHER

ACCORDING TO THE PEOPLE WHO WERE THERE, IT HAPPENED LIKE THIS:

THE YEAR WAS 1965, AND THE ENTIRE COMIC BOOK INDUSTRY WAS SCRAMBLING LIKE MAD TO PRODUCE NEW SUPERHERO COMICS TO CASH-IN ON THE UPCOMING *BATMAN* TV SERIES. MARTIN GOODMAN BECAME WORRIED WHEN HE HEARD ABOUT THE NEW LINE OF ACTION HERO BOOKS THAT JOE SIMON HAD CONTRACTED TO LAUNCH FOR HARVEY COMICS. GOODMAN'S RESPONSE WAS TO INTRODUCE SEVERAL NEW CHARACTERS INTO EXISTING MARVEL TITLES AND THEN SPIN THEM OFF ON THEIR OWN. MARTIN WOULD THEN ASK INDEPENDENT NEWS TO ALLOW HIM TO PUBLISH MORE SUPERHERO COMIC BOOKS.

LEE PASSED GOODMAN'S WISHES ON TO KIRBY, AND OVER THE COURSE OF A WEEKEND THE KING CAME UP WITH TWO NEW CONCEPTS. ONE WAS A FAMILY OF STARTLING NEW CHARACTERS CALLED THE INHUMANS. THE OTHER WAS A BLACK SUPERHERO CALLED THE COAL TIGER.

THE WRITERS QUICKLY CHANGED THE COAL TIGER'S NAME TO THE BLACK PANTHER. THE INHUMANS AND THE BLACK PANTHER WERE TO BE THE FIRST NEW MARVEL SUPERHEROES TO GET THEIR OWN TITLES. BUT MARTIN'S PLAN NEVER CAME TO FRUITION. IN THE END, IND. TURNED A DEAF EAR TO GOODMAN'S EXPANSION DEMANDS.

AS FAR AS KIRBY'S BLACK SUPERHERO WAS CONCERNED, IT MIGHT HAVE BEEN BETTER TO KEEP THE ORIGINAL "COAL TIGER" MONIKER. THE BLACK PANTHER'S NAME WAS IDENTI-CAL TO THE NAME OF THE MILITANT BLACK POLITICAL PARTY. STAN SAID THIS UNLUCKY COINCIDENCE CAP-SIZED T'CHALLA'S CHANCES OF GETTING HIS OWN BOOK IN THE 1960S. IT EVEN CAUSED MARVEL TO LIMIT HIS APPEAR-ANCES. CONSEQUENTLY, THE WAKANDA WARRIOR WAS ONLY FEATURED PROMINENTLY THREE TIMES IN THE LEE/KIRBY *FF* (SEE *FF* #52, 53 AND *FF ANNUAL* #5). "I DIDN'T WANT IT TO SEEM THAT WE WERE ESPOUSING ANY PARTICULAR CAUSE," SAID STAN.

THE SAD PART IS, MARVEL HAD THE NAME FIRST. BOBBY SEALE AND HUEY P. NEWTON, THE BLACK PANTHERS' FOUNDING MEMBERS, KEPT STRICT RECORDS OF THEIR ORGANIZATION'S BEGINNINGS FOR POSTERITY. THE PANTHERS WERE FOUNDED IN OAKLAND, CALIFORNIA ON OCTOBER 15, 1966, ABOUT SIX MONTHS AFTER *FF* #52 WENT ON SALE.

WHETHER OR NOT T'CHALLA HAD AN INFLUENCE ON THE NAME OF SEALE AND NEWTON'S GROUP IS A TOUGH GUESS. IT'S CERTAINLY POSSIBLE. THEN AGAIN, THE NAME "BLACK PANTHERS" WOULD BE A LOGICAL CHOICE FOR A BLACK POLITICAL PARTY, REGARDLESS OF THE COMIC CHARACTER.

THE BLACK PANTHER POS-SESSED EXTRAORDINARY NIGHT VISION AND DEVELOPED A FIGHTING STYLE THAT INCORPORATED STEALTH, ACROBATICS AND ADVANCED HAND-TO-HAND COMBAT TECH-NIQUES. KIRBY ALWAYS MADE A POINT TO RENDER T'CHALLA IN CAT-LIKE STANCES AND WITH FELINE GRACE.

FIRST APPEARANCE: FF #52

WYATT WINGFOOT

FIRST APPEARANCE: FF #50

IN A PECULIAR BREACH FROM THE NORM, THE GALACTUS TRILOGY DIDN'T END WITH THE FF SAVING THE EARTH FROM THE GREAT GALACTUS. IT CONCLUDED WITH THE TORCH WALKING DOWN THE CORRIDORS OF METRO UNIVERSITY WITH HIS NEW ROOMMATE, WYATT WINGFOOT.

ACCORDING TO STAN, MARVEL'S FIRST NATIVE AMERICAN HERO WAS BASED ON THE STAR ATHLETE JIM THORPE, AN AMERICAN INDIAN FROM OKLAHOMA. THE VERSATILE THORPE EXCELLED IN FOOTBALL, TRACK, BASEBALL AND BASKET-BALL. THE ASSOCIATED PRESS NAMED HIM THE GREATEST ATHLETE OF THE FIRST HALF OF THE 20TH CENTURY.

THE WYATT WINGFOOT/ JIM THORPE NEXUS APPARENTLY CAUSED LEE SOME CONFUSION. WINGFOOT'S FOOTBALL COACH APPEARED IN THE SERIES ONLY THREE TIMES, AND STAN LABELED HIM WITH A DIFFER-ENT NAME EACH TIME. IN FF #51 HE WAS "SAM THORNE." IN FF #52 HE WAS "JIM THORPE," AND IN FF #61 HE WAS CALLED "SAM THORPE."

WINGFOOT PLAYED A SIGNIFICANT ROLE IN THE LATTER-DAY LEE/KIRBY FANTASTIC FOUR. IN FF #54 JOHNNY AND WYATT BORROWED THE BLACK PANTHER'S GYRO-CRUISER IN AN EFFORT TO FIND THE GREAT BARRIER. INSTEAD, THEY FOUND PRESTER JOHN AND A WEAPON CALLED THE EVIL EYE. IN FF #55, THEY ENCOUNTERED LOCKJAW, CRYSTAL'S TELEPORTING PET POOCH, AND THEY CAST THEIR LOT WITH HIM, HOPING HE WOULD EVENTUALLY LEAD THEM TO THE INHUMANS. SOMETIME LATER, ALONGSIDE THE KEEWAZI TRIBE, WYATT AND THE FF BATTLED THE TOMAZOOMA ROBOT.

DESPITE HIS LACK OF SUPER-POWERS, WINGFOOT IS AN EXCELLENT ATHLETE, MARKSMAN, TRACKER AND HAND-TO-HAND FIGHTER. HE'S ALSO ONE OF THE FEW MODERN NATIVE AMERICAN CHARACTERS IN COMICS.

FF #64 pencils. Stan Lee's tinkering with the "Him" plotline is thought to be the last straw for Kirby, after which he put less effort into creating sophisticated, complex storylines for the FF, and ceased creating major new characters.

DECLINE

In the months following the Inhumans' return to society, there was virtually no perceptible deterioration in *Fantastic Four*. At this stage the book showed hardly any signs of dying down or even slowing up. The Kree in *FF* #65 (Aug. 1967), and "Him," whose flesh gleamed like gold in *FF* #67 (Oct. 1967), both appeared to have exciting long-term possibilities.

FF Annual #5 (Nov. 1967) seemed to atone for everything the previous year's Annual lacked. It featured great pin-ups, guest-stars galore and a staggering surprise. After two years of marriage (i.e., long enough to avoid any nasty gossip), Sue announced she was pregnant. It was totally unexpected. It was another first for the superhero genre, another explosion of Marvel Age innovation.

But something had changed. It wasn't as if cracks were showing; it was more a vague sense of tapering off. Beginning with *FF* #68, the storylines became less ambitious, the innovations fewer. Straight-ahead battle sequences began to fill the pages of *Fantastic Four*, and themes of cosmic significance began to disappear.

The faceless android on the cover of *FF* #70 (Jan. 1968) didn't seem as mesmerizing as Klaw, or Blastaar the Living Bomb-Burst. And almost inevitably, the second Galactus tale in *FF* #74 (May 1968) wasn't nearly as awe-inspiring as the first. The magazine's once-unstoppable rate of progression was now degenerating into a state of inertia. Despite this, *Fantastic Four's* early erosion barely showed. When imbued with the combined force of Kirby and Sinnott's incomparable artwork, even the most uninspired story became a thing of rare beauty.

Fantastic Four's main problem at this point seems to be a reluctance on Kirby's part to contribute anything but lukewarm concepts and recycled ideas. Many historians feel that after Stan changed Jack's plot to the "Him" tale in issue #66 (see **AT A GLANCE** *FF* #66), Kirby pretty much shut down. He considered it a waste of time to create innovative, thought-provoking storylines, only to see them cannibalized and turned into clichéd comic book plots—which is basically what happened to the King's "cocoon" story.

There's also evidence that in the late 1960s Goodman directed Stan to target younger readers by focusing on simpler stories with more action and battle sequences. When the Lee/Buscema *Silver Surfer* began to decline in sales, Goodman ordered Stan to give the magazine a more action-oriented framework with more fighting and less philosophical leanings. Martin may have told Lee to use this approach across the board as well. According to Goodman, "I think when Stan developed the Marvel super-heroes, he did a very good job and he got a lot of

college kids reading us. They make up a segment of our readership, but when you play it to them you lose the very young kids who just can't follow the whole damn thing. We try to keep a balance. Because I read some stories sometimes and I can't even understand them. I really can't!"

Another factor that contributed to the downslide was Stan spreading himself too thin. At this point Marvel was in a state of expansion, the type of which hadn't been seen since Goodman's wild binge and splurge days.

Due to the success of the Marvel line, Independent News was finally allowing Martin to publish more titles. By January 1966, Goodman had convinced Jack Liebowitz to increase the number of comics he could publish to thirteen, including *Fantastic Four*,

Here in FF #95 (Feb. 1970), *Kirby seems to be paying tribute to Steve Ditko's classic scene of Spider-Man overcoming a tremendous weight in* Amazing Spider-Man #33.

Amazing Spider-Man, Journey Into Mystery, Tales of Suspense, Tales to Astonish, Strange Tales, Avengers, X-Men, Daredevil, Sgt. Fury, Kid Colt Outlaw, Two-Gun Kid and Millie the Model. But four of these titles were non-superhero books, and Martin knew that superheroes were Marvel's cash cows. One report said that at the time of FF #1, Goodman was selling 18 million comics per year, and by 1968 that figure had increased to 50 million comics annually.

Martin wanted more superhero product and he wanted it right away, but Jack Liebowitz was playing hard to get. Independent News gradually and cautiously allowed Goodman to expand under strict parameters. In 1966, Martin was allowed four new titles providing they were sold in the less-profitable 25-cent format. First there was Fantasy Masterpieces (Feb. 1966), featuring Captain America's Golden Age adventures by Jack Kirby. Next was Marvel Collector's Item Classics (Apr. 1966), with a line-up of Fantastic Four, Hulk, Iron Man and Dr. Strange reprints. Three months later Marvel Tales (July 1966) became a staple of Goodman's line

On FF #82 (Jan. 1969), Lee had John Romita rework Kirby's Reed figure, which he deemed too effeminate.

featuring Spider-Man, Thor, Human Torch and Ant-Man reruns. To help support a new minimally-animated television show called *Marvel Super-Heroes* produced by Gantray-Lawrence, Goodman told Stan to create yet another reprint anthology called *Marvel Super-Heroes* (Oct. 1966). It collected the early adventures of the Avengers, the X-Men and Daredevil.

After that, Goodman was offered another compromise. He could expand further, providing that none of his new titles were superhero books. The results were *Ghost Rider* (Feb. 1967) and *Not Brand Echh* (Aug. 1967). Both of these comics were geared to superhero fans even though they were technically in the western and humor genres. A forgettable *Sgt. Fury* spin-off called *Captain Savage and His Leatherneck Raiders* (Jan. 1968) soon followed.

Jack Liebowitz had been holding the reins tightly on Goodman. He undoubtedly feared that any new Marvel comics would thrive at the expense of current DC titles. But by 1968, he finally agreed to let Martin publish twenty-four comics a month, including more superhero books. Soon, Marvel's three "split books," *Tales to Astonish, Tales of Suspense* and *Strange Tales* morphed into six monthly titles. First came *The Incredible Hulk* and *Captain America* (Apr. 1968), followed by *Iron Man* and *Sub-Mariner* (May 1968), then finally *Nick Fury, Agent of S.H.I.E.L.D.* and *Dr. Strange* (June 1968). In May 1968, a new series called *Captain Marvel* was rushed into publication to capitalize on Marvel's newly-acquired rights to the character's name.

The Spectacular Spider-Man (July 1968) was a 35-cent magazine-sized black-and-white publication released in hopes that it would crash the adult market. Its second (and last) issue was printed in color. *The Spectacular Spider-Man's* unspectacular sales proved that the world wasn't ready for such an ambitious project. Another drain on Stan's time and energy would be *The Silver Surfer* (Aug. 1968). After a mere 18 issues, Lee and Buscema's "Norrin Radd" surfed into oblivion.

Goodman had been shopping around to sell his entire company since 1966, and he knew that increased grosses, even in the short term, could lead to a better sales price. All this expanding and frantic restructuring of titles meant that Stan had to juggle all his artists and inkers, plus hire new ones. It didn't help that Kirby stopped doing layouts around this time because the page rates weren't worth his time and effort. Lee had

This powerful FF #95 *page (Feb. 1970) is a good example of Kirby simplifying his style—solid draftsmanship, but relying more and more on heavy blacks by Sinnott.*

Kirby recreated the cover to FF #96, when Marvel needed a new cover for Marvel's Greatest Comics #77 in 1978. He basically re-pencilled a flopped version of his original Sinnott-inked cover, then handed it off to Mike Royer to ink.

always relied on Kirby's layouts to break-in new pencilers.

All these pressures on Stan may have impacted his work on *Fantastic Four*, because readers were beginning to see more and more recycled storylines. In *FF* #62 (May 1967), Triton plunged headlong into the nightmarish vortex of the Negative Zone to save Reed from an out-of-control spiral toward oblivion. It was a slightly altered rewrite of *FF* #51. In *FF* #68-71 (Nov. 1967 through Feb. 1968), an evil genius turns Ben into a revenge-crazed killer who's bent on destroying his teammates. It was *FF* #41-43 *redux*.

FF #71 (Feb. 1968) opened with Kirby's all-time biggest head-shot to date. It depicted Sue screaming in anguish because she thought Ben had killed Reed and Johnny. There may be a reason for Kirby opening the story with this extreme close-up. This issue was penciled shortly after Marvel switched from large art-boards that had a 12" x 18" image area, to smaller ones that were 10" x 15".

The smaller boards had a tendency to make Kirby draw everything bigger, particularly heads and figures. He now began to use 4-grid pages more than ever before, almost *ad nauseam*. Kirby was never entirely comfortable with the change to smaller art. But like it or not, he adjusted to the new boards admirably, making the action bigger and bolder even as his creative intensity was dwindling.

Ironically, while Jack's enthusiasm was shrinking, Marvel was growing in every way. By now Marvel was successful enough to vacate Magazine Management's offices and relocate into a space of its own. It was a necessary move. By this time Marvel's fan base had grown so large and clamorous that the True Believers were becoming a disturbance at the office.

The company's new headquarters was at 635 Madison Avenue, just one block from the 625 offices which were still occupied by Goodman's Magazine Management Corporation. After the move, Marvel's indicia and letter-pages still listed 625 Madison Avenue as the address of Marvel Comics. This was a ploy to keep the fans away from Marvel's new location.

A strange paradox: "Let There Be... Life!" *FF Annual* #6 (Nov. 1968). At forty-eight pages this was by far the longest, most exhaustive single-issue *FF* story to date. By now the pattern of saving the book's most important events for the *FF Annuals* had been well established. It was a cinch this would be the issue where Reed and Sue become parents.

FF Annual #6 had all the hallmarks of a bravura Lee/Kirby *FF* epic: five "suitable for framing" full-page drawings and an impressive double-page photo-collage. The story ended with one of the most dramatic events of the entire Silver Age; the birth of Franklin Richards. And yet, despite the verve and volume of the tale, it somehow seemed contrived—almost as if the writers were doggedly trying to sustain an era of greatness that was slowly but undeniably slipping away from them.

Paradoxically, *FF Annual* #6 exhibited everything that was glorious about the 1960s *Fantastic Four* while at the same time giving evidence that the book's glory days were dwindling. There was a persistent sense that something was coming to an end. The birth of Sue's baby should have been a brilliant new dawn for the Lee/Kirby *FF*. Instead, it proved to be a melancholy sunset.

An interesting turn of events: In *FF* #81 (Dec. 1968), Sue went on maternity leave from the group and Crystal took her place. It was a fine idea; it was logical and entirely fitting. Somehow it never amounted to much.

And Sue Storm wasn't the only girl at Marvel who needed a break. By 1968 even the unflappable Flo Steinberg was losing ground. Since that fateful Spring of 1963 when she first signed on, she'd been Stan Lee's sweet and sassy "Gal Friday," the company's cheerleader, confidant and tough gatekeeper; deflecting office tensions with a joke or calming logic. Steinberg had dutifully answered every single letter to Marvel personally, endearing thousands of True Believers to the Marvel Comics brand and producing the most rabidly loyal fan base since the days of E.C. Comics' "fan–addicts."

But it had taken its toll on Steinberg. In later years she would remember it like this: "I was just tired. The last years were so long because the fan mail was overwhelming. Bags of it would come in, and all the letters had to be acknowledged. I became so overwhelmed with the fan mail and the Merry Marvel Marching Society fan club

As the series wore on and art-size shrank, Kirby resorted to more full-page panels in his FF *work, like this one from #72 (March 1968). They're beautifully constructed, but do little to advance the story.*

whatever was on *The Prisoner* that night (*FF* #84-87), or *Star Trek* (*FF* #91-93), or a late-late broadcast of *The Creature from the Black Lagoon* (*FF* #97). It was a far cry from the spellbinding cosmic odysseys of the past.

Simply, the ideas were gone. It was as if the very heart of the book had been wrenched out because Kirby's heart was no longer in it. He was still capable of imbuing every line he drew with a latent sense of power, but now it felt almost perfunctory. Even True Believers without the slightest inkling of the King's discontent could tell something essential was missing.

For the first time, Kirby seemed to be taking shortcuts. Previously, he would never have rendered a full-page drawing just to advertise his virtuosity. His use of the full-page panel always gave the reader a sense of wonder and enchantment. They either propelled

that Stan started. There was just so much work! I needed extra help and had gotten this wonderful letter from a college girl in Virginia by the name of Linda Fite. She came up and was hired to help me out, though she eventually went on to do writing and production work."

Flo's position, even after five years, was not particularly well-paid and she quit after Goodman wouldn't give her a five-dollar raise. Marie Severin, recalling the day of Steinberg's going-away party, made this observation: "I was thinking, what the hell is the problem with these people? She's a personality. She knows what she's doing. She handles the fans right. She's loyal to the company. I think the stupidest thing Marvel ever did was not give her a raise when she asked for it."

Flo wasn't the only one having trouble at Marvel. Around this time Kirby's problems with the company were becoming irreconcilable. As far back as 1965, Kirby noticed that Lee was getting a disproportionate share of publicity for Marvel's success. This upset him greatly. Besides this, Kirby was making story contributions that he felt were under-credited and under-compensated. Martin Goodman had promised him payment for Marvel merchandising and for siding with Marvel during Joe Simon's 1969 lawsuit over the rights to Captain America. Goodman reneged on both.

It was around this time, according to John Buscema, that Martin Goodman decided Kirby was earning too much money. Apparently, Martin tried to cut Kirby's page rate, and only when Jack threatened to quit did Goodman back off from the idea.

But above all, Kirby's contract had expired. By this time the company had new owners, Perfect Film and Chemical Corporation, and they were giving Jack the bum's rush every time he asked about renegotiating. The contract they finally offered him was so Draconian that no sane man would have considered it. This was the final affront. Now the rift between Kirby and Marvel was unbridgeable. He didn't want to leave the company but he felt he had no choice. The situation had become so unbearable that he was practically forced out. At this point he began hoarding his new characters and concepts. They would now be his bargaining chips for a new contract with a new publisher.

Kirby's unwillingness to contribute exciting new characters or high-quality storylines produced an extremely odd hybrid. Readers were now seeing beautifully drawn Kirby/Sinnott pages depicting the weakest *Fantastic Four* stories since the Impossible Man. It was a dichotomy that made no sense.

One can easily imagine Kirby drawing the latter-day *FF* with the television on. The storyline for the next issue would inevitably be

(top) Some of the panels in FF *#96 (March 1970) don't even look like 1960s Kirby art. The thrill was gone. (above) Unused page from* FF *#100, inked by a fan.*

moving backwards.

Meanwhile, the entire Marvel line-up seemed to be spinning out of control at this frustratingly unstable juncture. Since Marvel had been purchased by Perfect Film and Chemical, it had grown even larger. The new owners had deep enough pockets to break off completely with Jack Liebowitz and Independent News and cut a deal with Curtis Circulation.

Now that Marvel finally had a wide-open distribution deal with none of Liebowitz's conflicts of interest, Goodman was unleashed again. Soon even more new titles flooded the market, including two new split-books: *Astonishing Tales* (Aug. 1970) showcased a Lee/Kirby Ka-Zar story, and *Amazing Adventures* (Aug. 1970) featured an

the storyline relentlessly or slowed it down for great effect. Either way, he'd always used them sparingly. But by 1969, as the decade stumbled to a close, nearly every issue of *Fantastic Four* would contain at least two full-page drawings, if not three. *FF* #89 (Aug. 1969) had four of them. Undoubtedly, Marvel's change to smaller art was the biggest contributing factor in this, and many of Kirby's single-panel drawings were mesmerizing. On the other hand, a lot of them felt almost gratuitous; like the King was trying to finish up faster. Unquestionably, at this point the Lee/Kirby *Fantastic Four* was limping toward a dismal conclusion.

FF Annual #7 (Nov. 1969) was a staggering letdown. It had no new stories and no new pin-ups—nothing but leftovers. Even Jack's cover-art was markedly substandard. If the readers had any doubts that Kirby's run on *Fantastic Four* was in its death-throes, this miserable rotting corpse of an Annual dispelled those doubts decisively.

As the final curtain closed on the decade, Kirby's artwork wasn't the only eroding element in *Fantastic Four*. After going line for line with the King for almost five years, Joe Sinnott was completely wiped out. In an exclusive correspondence, the Prince of Pen and Ink elaborated on his dilemma: "I had worked for Timely/Atlas and Marvel Comics since 1950 and had never had a vacation, other than taking a day or two off here and there, but never missing any work. I called Stan and said that I needed a break to take a few weeks off, and get away with the family for a nice vacation. Had I known that Kirby would soon be leaving Marvel, I certainly would have stayed on the book until after Jack left, and taken my vacation then."

Joe's request was understandable. Keeping up with Jack Kirby was an exhausting task, so Stan had Frank Giacoia pinch-hit on inks for *FF* #93, 96 and 97 (Dec. 1969 and March-April 1970). Giacoia's bold, confident brushstrokes had often served Kirby well, but he wasn't Joe Sinnott. Sinnott was in a class by himself.

Another factor that made the series lose much of its depth and direction was a mid-1969 mandate from Goodman: No more continued stories. Pulling back from elaborate, multi-issue narratives seemed to hamstring Kirby's loose, sprawling storytelling instincts. Action and drama had to be drastically hemmed-in to fit the confines of twenty pages. At this point *Fantastic Four* began to lose its growing sense of inertia. In fact, it now seemed to be

(top left) Unused pencils from FF #94's debut of Agatha Harkness, who some think originally looked a lot like Kirby's wife Roz. (above and right) More full-pagers, from #89 and #93.

Inhumans series written and drawn by Kirby.

Inevitably, as Goodman's comic book line spread, its style became diverse, diluted and directionless. It lost much of its cohesiveness and identity. Gone was the sense of unity and connectedness that had marked the Chic Stone era. The newly expanded Marvel was beginning to seem bloated, self-indulgent and out of touch with its readers.

As the 1960s ran down, Martin Goodman's comic book line seemed increasingly barren. With the new decade just up ahead, new artists had come up to replace Steve Ditko, Wally Wood and Jim Steranko, but they weren't in the same class. Although highly competent, none of the new Marvel artists had the wonderfully idiosyncratic styles of the old guard.

Unquestionably, the final Lee/Kirby *Fantastic Four* tales were the saddest. There was an unmistakable jadedness and exhaustion in both the stories and art. On far too many panels the King didn't even bother to draw backgrounds. Looking at the last page of *FF* #99 (June 1970), one can't help but feel the art had regressed considerably when viewed with an eye to its former greatness.

To commiserate the magazine's centennial, *FF* #100 (July 1970) should have been the mother of all battles. *FF Annual* #3, a similar free-for-all, had been a riot of inspired excess with heroes and villains plunged deep into epic madness. Disappointingly, in the anniversary issue, the FF and their adversaries battled without passion or any real sense

I SHALL FINISH YOU *QUICKLY*-- WITH AS LITTLE *PAIN* AS POSSIBLE!

(top right) FF #99's (June 1970) sloppy full-page Inhumans splash shows a stiff, almost androgenous Medusa—a far cry from Kirby's early take on the femme fatale. And where's Karnak's mask?

of combat. The book's once-inexhaustible vitality now seemed atrophied, used up.

Looking back on the last twelve Kirby-drawn *FF* stories, one can't help but notice how often Reed, Sue, Ben and Johnny were portrayed in their street clothes. Whether or not the King did this deliberately is unknowable. But here's the final irony: between the lack of costumes and the retrogressive art, the Fantastic Four, in the end, looked much like they did in the beginning, in 1961.

In a strange sense it was a completing of the circle.

When Jack Kirby left Marvel for the beckoning vistas of DC Comics in 1970, the True Believers were filled with a sense of unredeemable loss. Not everyone saw the Fourth World as a satisfying alternative to the Lee/Kirby masterpieces of the Silver Age. Not everyone saw the Lee/Buscema *Fantastic Four* as a logical encore to Jack and Stan's version. Beyond the ruins of the Silver Age *FF*, the future looked undeniably bleak. Many fans had to lower their expectations or simply walk away from comics altogether.

Somehow the unfathomable had happened. The day Jack Kirby went to DC, the Silver Age Marvel Renaissance, which had once seemed eternal, suddenly ended. The era was torn asunder. The odyssey was over.

Somehow after that, the summers never seemed quite as glorious or golden. Somehow they seemed shorter with each passing year. Somehow the trees seemed quicker to exfoliate, and the ground seemed quicker to turn desolate and barren. The snow came harder that year, and it brought on the dusk.

The Wonder Years had quietly perished.

CONCLUDED AFTER NEXT PAGES...

The Age of Inertia

AT A GLANCE *FF* #68 (Nov. 1967)
Sinnott-cover inks
"His Mission: Destroy The Fantastic Four" 20p Sinnott-inks

This will be a lean aesthetic period in view of what preceded it.

If one studies the Lee/Kirby *Fantastic Four* canon, it's obvious that a major change in the basic framework of the magazine occurred at this point. The issues after *FF* #67 represented a definite tapering off of complexity and innovation. In fact, the tale of "the cocoon" would be the book's last storyline aimed at a more sophisticated faction of the comic buying public.

A variety of authors have claimed that the deterioration of *Fantastic Four* after issue #67 was a direct response from Kirby to what Lee did to his "cocoon" tale.

It's been said that from here on, Kirby made the storylines so uncomplicated that no amount of conflicting dialogue could compromise their intent. By playing it safe and creating simple stories that Stan could script without demanding redraws, Kirby's life became much less frustrating.

The theme of this four-part story bears a strong resemblance to the plot of *FF* #41-43. "Dr. Santini" turns the Thing against his teammates just as the Wizard did in the Frightful Four Trilogy. And yet, despite the storyline's lack of originality, there's no sense of atrophy whatsoever in the art itself. The Kirby/Sinnott synergy shows no sign of erosion, and that's the odd paradox.

Over the next two years the artwork in the Lee/Kirby *FF* would become even more magnificent than the art seen in the previous worthier period. This exasperating dichotomy of increasingly brilliant art and decreasingly brilliant stories

would usher in the next phase of *Fantastic Four*.

Welcome to the Age of Inertia.

AT A GLANCE *FF* #69 (Nov. 1967)
Sinnott-cover inks
"By Ben Betrayed" 20p Sinnott-inks

"By Ben Betrayed" is a less-than-impressive rewrite of "The Brutal Betrayal of Ben Grimm." For the most part, it's a fairly discouraging effort despite the undeniably superlative artwork.

In the heat of the battle with the Thing, Reed orders the Torch to jet-cycle Sue and Crystal to the safety of the police station. Sue's absence from the FF's adventures right before and after the birth of her son will become a mainstay of the series in the forthcoming issues.

Meanwhile, the evil Dr. Santini reveals his true identity as the Mad Thinker, a revelation which registered a solid zero on the reader's personal Excitograph.

Coming on the heels of its Cosmic Era antecedents, this second installment of The Big Green Android story offers a grim glimpse into the unpromising future of *Fantastic Four*—a comic book whose readers had almost become jaded from seeing so many mesmerizing characters and dazzling innovations over the years.

The True Believers were now in for a rude awakening.

AT A GLANCE *FF* #70 (Jan. 1968)
Sinnott-cover inks
"When Fall The Mighty" 20p Sinnott-inks

Now comes the onslaught of the Mindless Minions.

Over the next ten months readers would see page after page of sinister, super-powered androids, panel after panel of straight-ahead battle scenes, and issue after issue of miserably monotonous storylines.

One can't help but speculate that

Kirby's reluctance to contribute potent ideas at this point was the death knell for the Lee/Kirby FF.

In particular, Stan's contributions seemed immeasurably harmed by this change of direction. Big-action slugfests with mute robots left little room for characterization. What sort of inspired dialogue could Lee come up with when the antagonist was speechless and most of the panels showed the characters exchanging blows? Even creating a decent name for these generic creatures was nearly impossible. Thus, "killer androids," "indestructible androids" and "android men" would forge a droning presence in *Fantastic Four* for almost a year to come.

The Kirby/Sinnott artwork was as magnificent as ever; in fact, better than ever. But this tale didn't measure up to the Cosmic Era stories that preceded it—not by a long shot.

AT A GLANCE *FF* #71 (Feb. 1968)
Sinnott-cover inks
"And So It Ends" 20p Sinnott-inks

The cover of *FF* #71 made it glaringly obvious that the main salient point of this brainless, battle oriented tale was the "sizzling big action" slugfest between the FF and the Mad Thinker's faceless android. For the first time in ages, Lee resorted to his early 1960s practice of front-cover hyperbole: *"SIZZLING BIG ACTION ISSUE!"* was indeed the best way to describe *FF* #71. No plot, no character development and definitely no memorable dialogue from the android—just lots of sizzling big action.

On can't help but speculate on Kirby's motives during this period. By this time the King was sick of creating comics via the Marvel Method; a method that made the artist do most of the plotting with no credit and no extra pay. Is it possible that Jack was now using Stan's self-serving Marvel Method to trip Lee up?

By allowing the pages to be drawn first, Stan could only be subservient to Kirby's ideas. In this way, Lee had painted himself into a corner. What kind of emotional developments or character nuance could Stan possibly contribute to a story like this?

Fantastic Four now begins to fall into despair with ever-increasing frequency. The art was still unquestionably majestic, but the stories were losing their power. Little by little they turned into mere formalities; dry and deprived of sensation, they left the discriminating readers unimpressed and unsatisfied.

In fact, this story's only saving grace is the shock ending where Reed announces that he and Sue are quitting the group. Aside from that, *FF* #71 is a dead-end on almost every level.

AT A GLANCE *FF* #72 (Mar. 1968)
Sinnott-cover inks
"Where Soars The Silver Surfer" 20p Sinnott-inks

The sword of Damocles had been hanging over the head of the Watcher for some time now.

Endless thematic repetition had short-circuited his effectiveness. Since he had sworn never to interfere (a vow he'd broken on occasion), his main function was to warn the FF of impending danger; usually from the Great Beyond. How many more times could he do that before the premise wore itself out?

FF #72 marked the Watcher's ninth appearance in the series. Readers were beginning to sense a prevailing exhaustion about the character, and the writers knew it. This would be his last stand in Jack Kirby's *Fantastic Four*.

The startling Silver Surfer returns in this magnificently drawn tale and he's never looked better. Witness the godlike grace and power that Kirby evokes in the full-page Surfer illustration on page 6. This is the

Silver Surfer's defining portrait in *Fantastic Four*. It's one of those rare "sense of wonder" comic book moments that sent chills down the reader's spine.

Stan often used his comic book heroes to express his own thoughts and philosophy. In the very last panel that the Watcher would be seen in Kirby's *FF*, Stan once again proved himself to be the greatest dialogue man of the Silver Age. When a worried Sue Storm asks the Watcher what chance Reed has against the all-powerful Silver Surfer, the cosmic sage replies: *All-powerful? There is only one who deserves that name! And his only weapon is love!*

AT A GLANCE *FF* #73 (Apr. 1968) Sinnott-cover inks
"The Flames of Battle" 20p Sinnott-inks (Romita assist on Spider-Man)

Readers who thought that *Fantastic Four's* flowering of space age mythology and technological complexity had ushered out the uncomplicated fun of a Jack Kirby free-for-all would be pleasantly surprised by this story. "The Flames of Battle" undoubtedly made many True Believers wistful for the action-packed Marvel crossover battles of yesteryear.

Aside from being a pleasant, nostalgic stroll down 1964 Chicstone Lane, this charmingly insubstantial guest-star gala amply demonstrates why Jack Kirby would have been the wrong artist for Spider-Man, and why Joe Sinnott would have been the wrong inker for Thor.

That aside, Daredevil never looked better.

AT A GLANCE *FF* #74 (May 1968) Sinnott-cover inks
"When Calls Galactus" 20p Sinnott-inks

The strong element of disciplined

understatement that characterized the original Galactus story is noticeably lacking in this Galactus sequel.

All the subtleties, complexities and sophistications found in *FF* #48-50 are swept away in favor of large-panel action scenes, clobberin' time punches and patented Stan Lee/Artie Simek sound effects. This second Galactus story cycle (which would absorb four issues) is mostly Reed, Ben and the Torch engaged in hand-to-hand combat with the Punisher, the "soulless replicas," Psycho-Man, and the Indestructible Android.

The differences between the first and second Galactus tales are microcosmic of the changes that distinguish the 1966 *Fantastic Four* from the 1968 model. Quiet scenes in the Galactus Trilogy such as Sue admonishing Reed to shave and come to dinner (while the Earth hangs by a thread) are what made the original story ageless. Sadly, there's no similar dramatic contrast in this second Galactus/Surfer adventure. This might be why comic book historians haven't written a lot of erudite essays on "the Galactus Quadrilogy."

There was however a consolation prize. In 1968 Kirby began to offer at least one full-page illustration in every issue. These full-pagers were among the most astonishing drawings the King ever produced. There are two mesmerizing full-page Galactus portraits in this story cycle that can be matched only by the full-page Galactus illustrations found in *Thor* #134 and *Thor* #160. That's about the best that can be said for this Galactus sequel when one considers the splendor of the original story.

Infinitely less impressive than its predecessor, "Galactus redux" is a triumph of style over substance; a sad reminder of what the series once had achieved.

AT A GLANCE *FF* #75 (June 1968) Sinnott-cover inks

"Worlds Within Worlds" 20p Sinnott-inks

One of the many promotional innovations that Stan Lee pioneered in the 1960s was the concept of the "lead-in" story. In many cases when a Marvel superhero was about to get his own series, Stan would feature him as a guest-star in another Marvel title right before the new series debuted. For example, Captain America's battle with Iron Man in *Tales Of Suspense* #58 was the lead-in to Cap's new series that began in *Tales of Suspense* #59.

FF #74-77 was the multi-issue lead-in that paved the way for the Lee/Buscema *Silver Surfer* series. And it's a safe bet that it wasn't *Kirby's* idea to concoct a grand four-issue lead-in for a series that Jack was passed over on—a series that bastardized his Surfer to the point where Kirby could barely recognize him. One wonders if the King even realized he was doing a lead-in at the time.

A few generalizations: Reed, Ben and Johnny's battle with the "soulless replicas" is trite. And the idea that the heroes switch opponents and battle a replica other than their own isn't exceeding brilliant.

What *is* exceedingly brilliant is the full-page illustration of Galactus seen from a "worm's eye view" on page 4.

And again, it's emblematic of almost all the 1968-1969 issues where the artwork is much more impressive than the story it depicts.

AT A GLANCE *FF* #76 (July 1968) Sinnott-cover inks
"Stranded In Sub-Atomica" 20p Sinnott-inks

In 1968 the Psychedelic Experience was alive and well. *Fantastic Four's* phantasmagoric purview formed by Jack Kirby's boundless imagination (one coincidentally well-matched with the

consciousness expanding youth culture of the 1960s) can be seen on almost every page of "Stranded in Sub-Atomica." The full-page Silver Surfer illustration on page six is *maxigasmic*, and Psycho-Man's micro-world is a surrealistic wonderland of hallucinatory weirdness; a fantastic journey through an endless string of enormous molecules.

This is mind-expansion from a rational mind.

High points: The return of Psycho-Man, last seen in *FF Annual* #5, and the unmitigated joy the Silver Surfer displays on discovering an environment which he can soar through like outer space.

Low point: the now-compulsory appearance of yet another generic super-powerful android. This one is called "the Indestructible." Oddly enough, Kirby's margin notes for *FF* #76 reveal that he originally intended the Indestructible to speak. Lee unaccountably ignored this directive and rendered the character mute. This is somewhat curious when one considers how verbose Stan normally was.

AT A GLANCE *FF* #77 (Aug. 1968) Sinnott-cover inks
"Shall Earth Endure?" 20p Sinnott-inks

The entire point of this four-part Silver Surfer story cycle, which apparently was Lee's brainchild more than Kirby's, was to introduce the new Lee/Buscema *Silver Surfer* series, which went on sale to overlap with this issue.

Kirby felt he had lost the Surfer at this point. He would never again draw him in the pages of *Fantastic Four*. Nevertheless, he did draw the skyrider of the spaceways one last time in the 1960s, in *Silver Surfer* #18 (Sept. 1970). Jack handled that job with at least a soupcon of resentment, and it showed in the art.

Stan totally altered Jack's concept of the character for the

1968 *Silver Surfer* series. Where Kirby had envisioned the Surfer as an alien who gradually becomes more human, Stan inverted that idea and turned the Silver Surfer into a human who becomes an alien.

The new Lee/Buscema Silver Surfer was all solemnity and portentousness. With his arms gesturing in exaggerated emotion, he'd launch into melodramatic monologues spouting Stan's maxims to the masses.

One's reaction to this new Silver Surfer was entirely a matter of perspective. Some felt Norrin Radd's projected emotion and self-righteous speeches sounded very real and carried great wisdom. Some felt it was Lee's finest hour. Others felt the sanctity was stultifying, and that it became increasingly grating with each subsequent issue.

Unsurprisingly, Stan called *The Silver Surfer* "the finest series I know." But the True Believers were suitably unimpressed. Readers got bored and the book was unceremoniously canceled after 18 issues.

"Shall Earth Endure" contains some very impressive full-page and large-panel illustrations of Psycho-Man's sub-atomic world: Exotic dreamscapes and apocalyptic wastelands compliments of your tour guide Jack Kirby. Incredibly, there's not a single mindless robot or mute android anywhere to be found.

That alone rates two thumbs up.

AT A GLANCE *FF* #78 (Sept. 1968) Sinnott-cover inks
"The Thing No More" 20p Sinnott-inks

In this issue the Wizard returns and the story's premise takes a giant step toward the implausible. This *Strange Tales* leftover couldn't defeat the FF in the context of the Frightful Four, but he's now going to tackle them solo?

The stunningly powerful Kirby/Sinnott art just about makes up for

the weak storyline. The four-panel grid depicting Ben's return to human form was one of those phantasmagoric "sense of wonder" moments that would be seen less and less.

The Age of Inertia was now well underway. The plots were becoming unadorned and uncomplicated. The innovations were fewer, and the straight-ahead battle segments were beginning to dominate every issue.

Throughout this period *Fantastic Four* was in a stalemate. Kirby's reluctance to contribute any worthwhile concepts wouldn't allow the series to move forward, yet too much advancement had occurred in the Cosmic Era for the magazine to go back. Wedged in from all sides by paradox, the series now stood still and would continue to do so for roughly 16 more months—at which point it would begin a slow, agonizing decline.

AT A GLANCE *FF* #79 (Oct. 1968) Sinnott-cover inks
"A Monster Forever?" 20p Sinnott-inks

By now the androids were wearing thin.

The relentless succession of brainless, non-human powerhouses that plagued the series since *FF* #70 had produced the weakest string of *Fantastic Four* stories since the days of Kurrgo and the Impossible Man. It was an invasion of impotency that began with the Mad Thinker's killer androids in *FF* #70-71, and continued with the half-robot Punisher, the pit bull of Galactus, in issue #74.

In *FF* #76 there was Psycho-Man's Indestructible Android (who wasn't), and Ben now faces the mundane menace of the Android Man, another mediocre machine-man brought to you by the Mad Thinker.

Lee and Kirby's biggest failure in *Fantastic Four* was always their inability to produce worthwhile villains. Granted, they hit the jackpot

with Dr. Doom and Galactus, but they were notable exceptions. In the early days, whenever the writers were stumped for a foe they would whip-up one of their tried and true Atlas-style monsters or aliens. Now it was androids.

The manifold mindlessness of the FF's android adversaries nullified the motivations and character nuance that made the team's greatest rival's palatable. Most of these humanoids couldn't even speak, and the ones who could, like Android Man, filled the pages with dialogue like this: *"What? The little human gnat dares to attack me again?"* It was moronic.

The book's one shining moment is the poignant full-page portrait of Reed and Sue in the maternity ward. Kirby's full-page illustrations from this period were sometimes even better than his *FF Annual* pin-ups.

Fantastic Four's elaborately woven 1966 plot structures have now given over to the looser, simpler, battle-oriented storylines of 1968. Because they featured page after page of brutally energetic Kirby fight sequences, these android altercations undoubtedly thrilled younger readers on a purely action-packed level. But they soon became agonizingly repetitive.

A pox on it.

AT A GLANCE *FF* #80 (Nov. 1968) Sinnott-cover inks
"Where Treads The Living Totem" 20p Sinnott-inks

By *FF* #80, Jack and Stan had played out the android angle to the point of nausea. But still having no solid ideas for a new *FF* villain, Kirby resorted to the old habitual tactic of cranking out another carnage-wreaking colossus.

Welcome back to the Atlas Age of monsters.

Tomazooma's American Indian overtones can't disguise the fact that he's merely the latest in a long

line of classic Atlas-type monstrosities with a double "o" in his name like Groot, Tim-Boo-Ba, Vandoom, Goom, Oog, Googam, Fin-Fang-Foom and Taboo.

Taboo? The only thing taboo in *FF* #80 was an antagonist with real potency.

The backstory to this issue is noteworthy. It's been said that Lee and Kirby had originally decided on an entirely different storyline for *FF* #80, and that Kirby either forgot it or rejected it. Instead, he turned in the tale of the Tomazooma robot without Stan's input or prior knowledge.

One can't help but wonder if the duo's original idea might have been better.

AT A GLANCE *FF SPECIAL* #6 (Nov. 1968) Sinnott-cover inks
"Let There Be Life" 48p Sinnott-inks (2 collage pages)

According to Stan Lee, "*FF Annual* #6 is the first comic book story I know in which a heroine is pregnant. Lots of people told us we were crazy to introduce the theme of a heroine's pregnancy in a fantasy/action strip, but, as usual, lots of people underestimated the intelligence of our readers—readers who have always enjoyed the fact that we managed to combine far-out fantasy with believable, empathetic realism."

Upon closer analysis, this final Lee/Kirby *FF Annual*, though highly commendable, doesn't sustain the same type of natural momentum as the story in *FF Annual* #5 that led up to it. One would think the Big Event which unfolds at the end of this lengthy saga would epitomize the true ethos of all great *Fantastic Four* stories. And yet somehow it falls short.

By now it was obvious to the regular readers that a great deal of attrition had occurred in *Fantastic Four* since the previous year's

Annual. The art was still opulent, but the stories were becoming increasingly mundane, and very few impressive new characters were anywhere to be found.

Annihilus, the gigantic insectoid terror of the Negative Zone, was the last worthwhile FF nemesis that Lee and Kirby would ever produce. And yet, despite the harrowing magnificence of Annihilus, some vital element seems missing.

Perhaps Sue was that element. Her maternity-related absence from the group's adventures underscored how essential she was to the FF's chemistry; to their balance, their completeness.

The verdict: This story, which by all rights should have been one of the most unforgettable *Fantastic Four* adventures of all time, is a causality of the Age of Inertia doldrums. The marathon 48-page duration only reiterates that mass and masterpiece don't always go hand in hand.

AT A GLANCE *FF* #81 (Dec. 1968)
Sinnott-cover inks
"Enter, The Exquisite Elemental"
20p Sinnott-inks

After the odious onslaught of the mindless androids and the dismal disappointment of Tomazooma, the search for a decent new antagonist had become a tangle of exhausted possibilities.

So beginning with issue #81, *Fantastic Four* would showcase no new evildoers for 14 months running. The Wizard, Maximus, Dr. Doom, the Mole Man, the Skrulls and the Frightful Four would all be dusted off and reinstated to prolong the inevitable anticlimax of a new Lee/Kirby opponent.

When the series finally did cough up some new adversaries, beginning with "the Monocle" in issue #95, Jack and Stan's final string of super-villains would be the weakest since the era of the Molecule Man

and the Infant Terrible.

In this story the Wingless Wizard is back and he tackles the FF solo. He's got some new improved "wonder gloves" that look great, but not half as great as Crystal looks on the splash-page in her new FF uniform. Crys has sewn herself a blue costume, hoping to join the team while the Invisible Girl is on maternity leave.

This is a fine little comic book. The Exquisite Elemental shows the guys what she can do against the Wizard and officially becomes Sue's temporary replacement. The whole story is neatly wrapped up in 20 pages and it concludes with a classic *FF* happy ending. In the last panel the smiling heroes walk away arm-in-arm, with Ben having the last word as usual: *"From now on the super-hero biz is gonna be a blast!"*

Crystal seems to have given the team a new dynamic, yet at the same time an old familiar feeling; as if she and the Torch were a younger version of Sue and Reed.

AT A GLANCE *FF* #82 (Jan. 1969)
Sinnott-cover inks
"The Mark Of The Madman" 20p
Sinnott-inks

In this exquisitely drawn tale, Crystal returns to the Great Refuge to obtain the Royal Family's permission to join the FF in Sue's absence. This issue contains two of the now-obligatory full-page drawings that characterized the Kirby/Sinnott artwork of this period. These striking full-page portraits of Maximus on his throne and the Inhumans in captivity prove that Jack's art was still full of power and enthusiasm at this stage.

Under the magnifying glass of retrospection, it dawns on the reader how slick and highly-polished the 1968-1969 *Fantastic Four* had become. At this point it had the most sleek and stylized artwork of any American comic book. And now

that Marvel was expanding, Lee wanted Jack's dynamic drawing style to be featured in his entire superhero comics line; a line that would soon topple DC from the number one sales slot. Lee was telling all his artists to "draw like Kirby." Thus, the Kirby-style became the Marvel house-style of artwork.

Of course, far away in the background, one occasionally recalled that *Fantastic Four* had begun as a guerilla. Once upon a time it had seemed dangerous, subversive, a threat to all things drab and dismal in the industry—like the concept of a "house style" that stifled an artist's individual vision.

How things change.

Note to original art enthusiasts: On page 2 panel 2, Reed's figure was reworked by John Romita. Kirby originally had Richards standing in a rather odd pose, which Lee may have deemed effeminate. Stan was always telling Gil Kane his heroes looked "too homosexual."

AT A GLANCE *FF* #83 (Feb. 1969)
Sinnott-cover inks
"Shall Man Survive?" 20p
Sinnott-inks

In an obscure fanzine called *Excelsior* published in 1966, a fan interviewed Lee and Kirby separately. Kirby was asked point blank, "Who created the Inhumans, you or Stan?" And Kirby answered: "I did." Since Jack was still working for Marvel at this point, it's inconceivable that he would make this claim if it weren't true.

According to Kirby, the Inhumans and the Black Panther were both created the same weekend with no input from Lee. Unsurprisingly, Stan denied this. It's odious to add fuel to the "who did what" debates, but all things considered, the *Excelsior* interview is a strong argument for Kirby's sole authorship of the Royal Attilans.

"Shall Man Survive" is the finale

of the two-part Inhumans tale which began in the previous issue. Note how muscular both Reed and Johnny look on the splash-page compared to how Kirby first drew them. The slim scientist and the skinny teenager from 1962 are gone. Their arms have hypertrophied and they now have biceps worthy of Captain America.

This Inhumans adventure was pretty much characteristic of the entire Age of Inertia: majestically drawn pages inked with perfect precision, an overabundance of four-panel grids and full-page portraits (about half of which seem like mere pin-ups, extraneous to the story-line), and the painfully repetitious battles with yet another set of Mindless Minions; the Alpha Primitives and a "multi-powered android" named "Zorr." Unsurprisingly, Zorr was another throwback from the days of the Atlas monsters, right down to the double-consonant in his name.

The main noteworthy point of *FF* #83 occurs during the first three panels of page 11. Back at the Baxter Building, we see Sue covering her sleeping baby in his crib. Sue wishes Reed could be there to help her choose a name for the infant.

It was another heartwarming ordinary human moment juxtaposed with the fanciful world of Marvel superheroes. Hundreds of such scenes could be found in past issues. This contrast of the everyday and the extraordinary had always been the key to the magazine's greatness.

AT A GLANCE *FF* #84 (Mar. 1969)
Sinnott-cover inks
"The Name Is Doom" 20p
Sinnott-inks

"The Name is Doom" begins a four-part story where Kirby incorporates elements of Patrick McGoohan's TV thriller *The Prisoner.*

 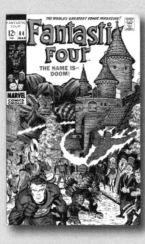  

The Prisoner was a 1967-1968 British television series which combined elements of science-fiction, allegory and psychological drama. It followed the adventures of an unnamed British agent who abruptly resigns his job, then finds himself in an isolated seaside "village" which is secured by numerous monitoring systems and security forces, including a mysterious device called "Rover" that captures those who try to escape. The city's population seems to be tranquilly living out their lives, when in reality they are living a nightmare of captivity.

This story begins with a cameo by S.H.I.E.L.D. agents Fury and Dugan, just in case anyone thought the Marvel Age of crossovers was over.

At this stage *Fantastic Four* would begin a series of "last ever" events in regard to the Lee/Kirby *FF*. This four-part story will be the last FF vs. Doctor Doom adventure drawn by Jack Kirby. And it's off to a fine start.

Fantastic factoid: *FF* #84 featured inker Mike Royer's all-time favorite Kirby cover.

AT A GLANCE *FF* #85 (Apr. 1969) Sinnott-cover inks
"Within This Tortured Land" 20p Sinnott-inks

"Within This Tortured Land" is a majestic title that befits the story's atmospheric artwork. In fact, the entire *FF* #84-87 story cycle is chockfull of realistically rendered castles, cottages, outdoor cafés and Balkan street scenes, masterfully drawn by Jack Kirby and inked with meticulous organic detail by Joe Sinnott.

The only sign of cancer in this gradually unfolding drama is the appearance of Doom's "omnipurpose robot"—another speechless, faceless, green-hued mechanical man.

Regrettably, the dire and droning

Mindless Minions were about to descend once more.

AT A GLANCE *FF* #86 (May 1969) Sinnott-cover inks
"The Victims" 20p Sinnott-inks

The tale opens with the FF about to tackle the forces of Doctor Doom without their powers, which is basically what happened in *FF* #39 and 40. Obviously, the most banal characters in this multi-issue story are Doom's robot army; the latest in a long line of mute, mindless humanoids of incalculable strength.

Despite these annoying androids, the Latverian landscapes are drawn with stunning beauty. The battle segment with the town ablaze generates real excitement, and Sue's unexpected return at the end is a complete shock; a brilliant way to save the day and another shining moment for the ever-unpredictable Invisible Girl.

Even the last panel is compelling. Ben, Crystal and the Torch stand ready for combat as the Thing announces it's time to kick some Balkan butt.

Next issue: The Wrap-up.

AT A GLANCE *FF* #87 (June 1969) Sinnott-cover inks
"The Power And The Pride" 20p Sinnott-inks

Marvel's takeoff of *The Prisoner* concludes as we see the last appearance of Victor Von Doom in Jack Kirby's *Fantastic Four*. The book's cover promises *"THE MOST OFF-BEAT ENDING OF THE YEAR"* and the hype is entirely justified.

The ending isn't the only off-beat element in the story. Doom isolates Sue and Crystal from their partners, and when the girls open a beautifully ornate double-door they find the most bizarre spectacle imaginable: the horrifying Dr. Doom acting as the perfect congenial host, graciously welcoming them to a luxurious

banquet.

All throughout *FF* #84-87 there are numerous full-page portraits of Victor, and almost every one of them seems like eye-candy; splendid to look at, but irrelevant to the storyline. Not this one. This astonishing illustration of Doom and his servants is spellbinding, and it advances the storyline exquisitely.

Because of the deep insights into Dr. Doom's persona that we've acquired since *FF Annual* #2, we can believe the story's unique ending. In the closing scenes, Victor's aristocratic appreciation for the arts causes him to sacrifice his victory over the FF to save his art gallery; a collection of priceless masterpieces that he's plundered from all over the globe.

This is a thoroughly satisfying wrap-up to Jack and Stan's final Dr. Doom story in an era when *Fantastic Four* was becoming less and less satisfying.

AT A GLANCE *FF* #88 (July 1969) Sinnott-cover inks
"A House There Was" 20p Sinnott-inks

"We feel that the old villains have never really been explored. We may like to explore another aspect of their lives. For instance, I did this Mole Man story in Fantastic Four where he had built a house. I stressed the fact that Mole Man might be a crybaby when a lot of less-talented people are going through life with a lot more courage with their afflictions, and Mole Man becomes human that way. It humanizes him. And then he retreats into his own insanity and goes underground. He's ready for another episode." —Jack Kirby from a 1969 interview for *The Nostalgia Journal*.

Obviously, much of *Fantastic Four's* preeminence started to wane after Kirby's discontent with Marvel made him reluctant to contribute

any worthwhile new characters. And by now the King's creative no-show was beginning to wreak havoc on the series.

At this point Kirby was only willing to provide the magazine with evildoers of a throwaway variety or revive the FF's past adversaries. For this issue he chose the latter. Subsequently, the subterranean Mole Man surfaces once again.

The Kirby/Sinnott synergy is as powerful as ever, but both of the full-page drawings on pages 6 and 7 are totally superfluous. They could be pulled out of the book without affecting the story one iota. Do we really need a full-page portrait that depicts the group (with their backs to us) walking into a house? The large-panel drawing of the maniacal Mole Man on page 18 is much better.

AT A GLANCE *FF* #89 (Aug. 1969) Sinnott/M. Severin-cover inks
"The Madness Of The Mole Man" 20p Sinnott-inks (1 collage page)

At the time you couldn't put your finger on it, but a pervading sense of apathy was creeping in.

Under the deep analysis of hindsight it can be seen that some of the FF's classic villains—like the Mole Man—should have stayed in the early 1960s where they belonged. In this mostly-forgettable tale we find the undefeatable Fantastic Five (counting Crystal), battling a foe who's legally blind and not much taller than Franklin Richards. And for twenty pages, he manages to keep our heroes at bay *with a stick*.

Just as he did in *FF* #48, Kirby introduces a completely new storyline midway through *FF* #89—the Skrulls are back.

Regarding this issue's record number of full-page illustrations (four total), they're all knockouts, and only the full-page drawing of the Torch on page 16 seems

Talk about superfluous! Kirby used not one, but two consecutive single-page splashes in FF #88, just to propel the characters through a doorway.

unnecessary to the plot. It's the type of "pin-up panel" that the fans had come to expect at this stage. The overall impression is that the artist is using these big drawings to finish the job faster.

And "job" is the only applicable description. At this point, what had once been a labor of love for Jack Kirby was now just a labor.

Worse was yet to come.

AT A GLANCE *FF* #90 (Sept. 1969) Sinnott-cover inks
"The Skrull Takes A Slave" 20p Sinnott-inks

Just when you thought our heroes had put the kibosh on the sinister subterranean Mole Man, he shocks the FF and the readers by unexpectedly leaping up and making his great escape. He then wraps up

the "House That Was" storyline by vanishing into the dread reaches of the Earth from whence he came.

Obviously, Kirby hadn't lost the knack for surprise.

At a rather late point in the tale (page 9), the new Skrull storyline which began in the previous issue is revisited. It felt like a return to 1966, where important story points were randomly injected without

regard for traditional comic book beginnings or endings.

While the stage is being set for the new Skrull saga, there's very little action in the storyline and a lot of plot points to establish. To cover all the details, Kirby employs more 9-panel grids than he's used in ages; 15 in a row on pages 10 and 11. These small, dense frames effectively set the mood in welcome contrast

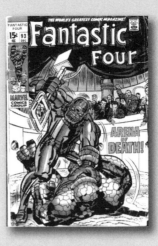

to issues like *FF* #82, which featured nothing but sweeping layouts facilitated by big-panel page grids.

The new Skrull adventure is showing considerable potential at this point.

AT A GLANCE *FF* #91 (Oct. 1969) Sinnott-cover inks
"The Thing Enslaved" 20p Sinnott-inks

Kirby had always been fascinated with gangsters. He'd grown up with them in New York, he owned several books about mobsters, and the gangster movie was a genre that Kirby had loved since his boyhood. The themes in Hollywood gangster epics from the 1920s and 1930s were subject matter that the King exploited throughout his entire career.

FF #91-93 finds its roots in classic gangster films and two episodes from the second season of *Star Trek*. One show called *A Piece of the Action* featured the crew of the Enterprise dressed as mobsters, while another, *The Gamesters of Triskelion*, was a take-off on the 1960 film *Spartacus*. It featured Kirk in a restraining collar like the one that Ben was forced to wear in this story.

One of the characters introduced in this issue, "Napoleon G. Robinson," is a dead-ringer for Edward G. Robinson, who along with Kirby look-alike Jimmy Cagney was one of the King's favorite big-screen bad guys.

AT A GLANCE *FF* #92 (Nov. 1969) Sinnott-cover inks
"Ben Grimm, Killer" 20p Sinnott-inks

Upon closer examination, one sees that at this stage the writers were seeking fresh aesthetic pastures. For the first time in years, the series began making various forays into new ground.

At this point, with ever-increasing

frequency, the storyline of *Fantastic Four* was moving away from the Baxter Building. In this issue for example, the action takes place in the Skrull Galaxy. It wasn't unusual for the group to have adventures in space, but now even the earth-bound stories were becoming progressively independent of New York City.

The Mole Man adventure which preceded this story-cycle occurred in a wooded area outside of the city; and the Agatha Harkness tale that follows it takes place in a secluded site in upstate New York.

The recent Inhumans and Dr. Doom adventures took place in the Himalayas and the Balkan Peninsula. *FF* #97 would depict the quartet vacationing in "The Lost Lagoon," while the moon-landing story in *FF* #98 finds the group on an island in the Pacific.

Coinciding with these changes of venue was a growing tendency for the FF to be seen out of uniform. Most of the final Kirby episodes show the foursome in their civilian clothes for the first half of the story. In other issues, like *FF* #94, 96 and 97, they don't bother to suit-up at all. Could it be that Jack was sick of costumed superheroes at this point? Kirby historian Mike Gartland opined that since the birth of Franklin, the FF had become a more "normal" family. As such, the King was portraying them in normal attire.

Whatever the case, this installment of the multi-issue Skrull story features some interesting new characters. Having met the mechanical slave gladiator Torgo in the previous issue, Ben meets the Cat-Man, the quirky Rhinogon and the oddly fascinating Magno Man who has a huge horseshoe-shaped magnet extending from the sides of his head.

AT A GLANCE *FF* #93 (Dec. 1969) Giacoia-cover inks

"At The Mercy Of Torgo" 20p Giacoia-inks

With this "straight out of *Spartacus*" wrap-up, Kirby's final multi-part *Fantastic Four* adventure draws to a close.

The storyline in this tale is fairly entertaining, but despite the novelty of the FF dressing like Prohibition era gangsters, it was clear the rot was setting in. The art in this issue looks hurried and haphazard; and Kirby wasn't the only FF artist who was winding down. Joe Sinnott told Stan he hadn't had a vacation in almost 20 years, and needed some serious time off. Subsequently, Coach Lee called in his favorite pinch-hitter, Frank Giacoia.

It proved to be a bad call. Giacoia's normally superlative inks are totally ineffective in *FF* #93. In almost every panel, and particularly on page five's full-page drawing, the Thing's rocky exterior looks like a one-dimensional jigsaw puzzle due to the absence of spot blacks. It harks back to the George Roussos Period.

By now the series seems dispirited. It was losing momentum. Kirby's input seems constrained, half-involved. At this point the rift between Kirby and Marvel was rapidly widening. An essential balance had been shattered and it wouldn't be long before this intractable situation manifested itself in the full-blown deterioration of Marvel's flagship magazine.

AT A GLANCE *FF* #94 (Jan. 1970) Trimpe-cover inks

"The Return Of The Frightful Four" 20p Sinnott-inks (assist by Trimpe)

In a time when *Fantastic Four's* splendor was being increasingly despoiled by dross and dissipation, this story was a shining oasis in the desert. It was the heroic exception to the mediocrity that preceded it

and the morbidity that followed it.

The tale begins with a poignant scene where Ben learns that Sue and Reed have named their baby "Franklin Benjamin Richards" in his honor, and after Johnny and Sue's father. Next, for a brief tantalizing moment the reader is led to believe that the greatest bad girl of the Silver Age, the magnificent Madam Medusa, has returned to her evil ways. Unfortunately it was just a tease. It soon becomes apparent that the Lady of the Living Locks has rejoined the Frightful Four only to subvert their plans from the inside.

The creepiest babysitter who ever lived, Agatha Harkness, is introduced in this issue. Harkness was one of the few reoccurring characters who emerged from Lee and Kirby's latter-day *FF*, and the genesis of this gothic sorceress is yet another subject of debate. Some speculate that Stan created her because at this point Kirby had stopped giving Marvel any new characters. Others say the unpublished *FF* #94 page where Harkness looks like Roz proves the character was Jack's.

Despite the fact that Kirby's art has noticeably devolved from its peak period, "The Return of the Frightful Four" is fantasy of a thoroughly nourishing variety.

Regrettably, in the months ahead it would prove to be the exception, not the norm.

The New Order, said the Publisher, was no more continued stories, and within this constricting framework the action was severely limited. To his credit, Kirby rose to the challenge and produced this exceptional 20-page thriller. But the new restriction would ultimately hamstring the final Kirby *FF* tales.

The Age of Inertia, where the series stood stock-still, is now over. At this point *Fantastic Four* began a backwards lurch to a new Dark Age.

THE AGE OF DECLINE

AT A GLANCE *FF* #95 (Feb. 1970)
Sinnott-cover inks
   "Tomorrow, World War Three"
20p Sinnott-inks (assist by Romita)

While unsatisfying on many levels, *FF* #95 isn't entirely dismissible. Unlike the previous issue, this tale suffers somewhat from the tyranny of the 20-page format.

While the Faustian "Monocle" is merely another Lee/Kirby throwaway villain, the book's redeeming qualities can be found on two magnificent full-page drawings that evoke the old *FF* magic. On page 8 we see the impossibly heroic Thing holding up an entire building which was about to fall on a crowd, thereby saving countless lives. Joe Sinnott said this was his all-time favorite Jack Kirby page.

Johnny's close-up on page 13 shows the King doing his "when in doubt, black it out" Wally Wood impression, imbuing the Torch's face with moody and highly idiosyncratic spot black shadows. Over the years the True Believers had developed ravenous appetites for these dramatic full-page portraits. But as striking as they were, they couldn't reverse *Fantastic Four's* inevitable descent into despoilment.

With the initiation of Goodman's brutally restrictive "no more continued stories" mandate, the series has fallen even further. It seemed to be suffering from a drastic loss of direction, and this issue's new "Fantastic Four" cover logo didn't help one bit.

There's a definite pattern to all artistic movements. They begin with raw innocent vigor, pass into healthy adulthood and ultimately atrophy into an overwrought, feeble old age. Something of this process can be observed in the overall omnibus of Lee and Kirby's

Fantastic Four. Without question, at this point the series was in serious trouble.

The Age of Decline has now set in and the end is near.

AT A GLANCE *FF* #96 (Mar. 1970)
Sinnott/M. Severin-cover inks
   "The Mad Thinker And His Androids Of Death" 20p Giacoia-inks

Unsurprisingly, *FF* #96 is plagued by the usual bound-for-oblivion blues found in all the final Lee/Kirby *Fantastic Four* stories: sloppy art, bare backgrounds and a sense of indifference that nearly drips off every page. Frank Giacoia's fill-in inking doesn't help in the least. Some of the panels (on page 7 in particular) don't even look like Jack Kirby artwork. Everything now felt used up, despoiled, second-hand.

And did the series really need more of the Mad Thinker's Androids? At least this latest set of humanoids could actually speak. In fact, they were exact replicas of the Fantastic Four.

The only thing that made the story even marginally interesting was its unusual line-up: Reed and Ben fly solo because the Storm siblings were under sedation and thus removed from the action.

One almost envies them.

Fantastic Four is now swimming against the tide with ever-diminishing energy.

AT A GLANCE *FF* #97 (Apr. 1970)
Verpoorten-cover inks
   "The Monster From The Lost Lagoon" 20p Giacoia-inks (assist by Romita)

This story and the one after it gave readers a brief respite from the truly unexceptional issues which surrounded them on both sides.

There are two nods to Marvel's past which stir the embers of nostalgia (at least in this reader). First,

the "lagoon monster" seems like a good old-fashioned Goodman rip-off. You can almost hear the old knockoff champion telling Lee: "Maybe we should do a *Creature from the Black Lagoon* story!"

The other trip down memory lane occurs on page five, when the Torch explains the reason his clothes don't burn is because they're made of unstable molecules. This probably hadn't been mentioned since *FF Annual* #1. It's amazing that the writers remembered.

At any rate, Frank Giacoia's inks look somewhat better here than they did in *FF* #96.

AT A GLANCE *FF* #98 (May 1970)
Sinnott-cover inks
   "Mystery On The Moon" 20p Sinnott-inks

It would be naive to think that Kirby would produce anything other than lukewarm storylines after he stopped creating worthwhile characters for *Fantastic Four*. This story however has its moments; especially when juxtaposed with what came after it.

Good news: Joe Sinnott is back and obviously revitalized. His return was sorely needed to cover up Kirby's increasingly desultory artwork. But even Sinnott's highly polished finishing of Jack's art couldn't pull the series out of the deepening malaise that had taken root by this time.

This tale, which takes place in July 1969, is about the Kree's attempt to sabotage the U.S. flight to the moon. The story is noticeably stronger than the four which will follow it, but it's nonetheless trifling compared to the book's glory days.

For the first time in ages, the cover featured twin elements of hard-sell. There was a boxed-in blurb promising *"THRILLS AND DRAMA AS ONLY MIGHTY MARVEL CAN PRESENT THEM!"* There

were also three excitement-enhancing dialogue balloons, the likes of which hadn't graced a *Fantastic Four* cover since issue #22. Both gave further proof that the magazine was in a state of regression.

As if any were needed.

AT A GLANCE *FF* #99 (June 1970) Verpoorten-cover inks
   "The Torch Goes Wild" 20p Sinnott-inks

Here again is another lamentably dismal offering.

We're now well into the Age of Decline, where decay and morbidity lurk everywhere in the pages of *Fantastic Four.* But even in the magazine's darkest days, the taste of death was almost always sugarcoated by an occasional flash of brilliance from Lee and Kirby or from Kirby and Sinnott.

That is to say *almost* always.

The sympathetic reader can painstakingly comb every page of *FF* #99 searching for the slightest glimmer of greatness, or even for a pennyweight nail to hang a kind word on. It's simply not to be found.

The superfluous full-page drawing of the Inhumans could have been the book's one saving grace, but Medusa looks stiff; almost androgynous. And there's no mask on Karnak. During the story's closing moments the backgrounds are nonexistent, and Kirby uses a very unconvincing shadow pattern at the top of page 20 to fill the overabundance of empty space. The loyal readers who'd been around since the beginning couldn't deny how dour it was all becoming.

Stan really drops the ball on the final page when his dialogue reveals that Black Bolt is Crystal's *brother.* Which would make him Medusa's....

This would be a good point to move on.

By FF #99, Kirby was pretty much phoning the book in. Note the unconvincing shadow-pattern in the top panel, and the lack of background in panels 3-6. Lee was slipping too—in the top panel, he decided Black Bolt was Crystal's brother, which would make him Medusa's brother!

108

AT A GLANCE *FF* #100 (July 1970) Sinnott-cover inks
"The Long Journey Home" 19p Sinnott-inks

By now the once-magnificent series had even lost the ability to entertain its readers in a purely simplistic action-oriented context.

Mark Evanier told us that *FF* #100 was originally meant to be an expanded-length Centennial Special, but for some reason the idea got shelved. Consequently, Kirby had to redraw much of the book to fit everything into 20 pages. Hence the story's choppy pacing and over-abundance of 9-panel grids.

This explains the page of unused art from *FF* #100 that depicts the Puppet Master examining the Hulk-android on an operating table. The page is composed of six panels and seems to be more leisurely paced than the finished story. It was probably cut after the book's page-count was reduced because it didn't advance the storyline fast enough.

The *FF* Anniversary Special wasn't special by any standards. It was Marvel's biggest disappointment of 1970. It stands as an impotent, slapdash throwaway featuring the quartet and Crystal engaged in battle with another set of androids created by the Mad Thinker. Despite the fact that these robots resemble some of the greatest adversaries of the past, the centennial battle lacks fervor and seems oddly devoid of any real passion.

At this point *Fantastic Four* couldn't even rally for Clobberin' Time.

AT A GLANCE *FF* #101 (Aug. 1970) Sinnott-cover inks
"Bedlam In The Baxter Building" 19p Sinnott-inks (assist by Romita)

The Lee/Kirby *FF* now teeters precariously on the edge of oblivion.

One really does regret continually pouring disparagement on Jack and Stan's latter-day *Fantastic Four*, but

really, what else can the objective reader do? This story encapsulates everything that had gone wrong: the stiff, hurried art, the copious 9-panel grids that Jack now had to employ because of the "no continued stories" mandate, and worst of all, the total lack of Kirby inspiration.

There's one humorous note in this sad state of affairs. In the previous issue's final panel, Stan wrote "Next: Bedlam at the Baxter Building!" Someone must have reminded him that *FF* Annual #3 had that exact same title. By the time *FF* #101 appeared, Lee had changed the preposition: Now the story is called "Bedlam *in* the Baxter Building!"

It was bedlam alright, because at this stage Jack was merely cranking out the book by rote.

In this story the FF battle gun-totting hoods from "the Maggia," which was the Marvel Universe counterpart to the Mafia. In 1969, the Mafia had become a household name due to the success of *The Godfather* by Mario Puzo. Mario was Stan's old crony from Magazine Management Company. In the early 1960s Puzo wrote for Goodman's men's magazines like *Swank* and *Male* under the pseudonym "Mario Cleri."

In *FF* #101 we see the same super-team that once stood up to Galactus being threatened by a cheap thug with a machine gun. It was in this dismal morning-after spirit that the series limped, at last, to a sad conclusion.

In gloomy retrospect, perhaps it was fortunate that the curtain was closing on the Lee/Kirby *FF*. If the writers had continued to churn out trite, directionless stories like this, it would have been a travesty of everything the magazine once stood for.

Either way, it would all be over in a month.

AT A GLANCE *FF* #102 (Sept. 1970)
"The Strength Of The Sub-

Mariner" 19p Sinnott-inks

And finally the circle was closed. With this less-than-illustrious finale, the most important and influential comic book partnership of the 20th Century goes out not with a bang, but a whimper. Except for an unfinished story that was butchered for *FF* #108 (March 1971), and the halfhearted 1978 *Silver Surfer Graphic Novel*, Stan Lee and Jack Kirby would never collaborate in comics again.

The story's splash-page seems to indicate a return to the book's former greatness. In a beautifully drawn opening sequence worthy of the 1966 *FF*, we see Crystal patiently spoon-feeding an obviously flu-stricken Thing; gently holding his nose as she carefully administers his medicine. This is the last poignant scene that the Lee/Kirby *Fantastic Four* will ever offer—the final ordinary human moment in a magazine whose greatness was spawned from a marriage of the commonplace and the cosmic.

The book's always prevalent sense of humor is introduced on page 2, as Ben begins to sniffle, then lets loose a hurricane-velocity sneeze that demolishes the entire area. Of course, at this point Reed enters the room, disconcertedly wondering what all the commotion is about.

Classic.

After that it's all downhill. The plot sounds like something Stan would reel off to Kirby over the phone in three seconds: "*Have them battle Namor and Magneto.*" We then find two of Marvel's most impressive antagonists uniting to wage war against the surface world. The odd thing is, they don't seem to remember that they already tried this a few years back in *X-Men* #7 (Sept. 1963).

Despite the impressive full-page drawing of Namor on his throne in repose, by page 16 Kirby's enthusi-

asm has begun to wane. In many panels the figures look stiff, the backgrounds are negative space and a feeling of tiredness creeps in; the same sense of lethargy that plagued all the 1970 *FF* stories.

The final page ends with Reed acknowledging Sub-Mariner's declaration of war. Readers are given no indication that another war—a war between Jack Kirby and Marvel—would result in this continued story being the final episode in the massive Lee/Kirby *FF* cannon.

The greatest comic book run of the 20th Century should have gone out with a glorious, golden sunset; a magnificent final toast. But it wasn't meant to be.

Fantastic Four #102 stands as an unworthy epitaph, a cardboard tombstone, a sad and tatty end to the partnership of two brilliant comic book rebels whose fusion wiped clean and drew again the face of superhero comics.

PENCIL ART GALLERY: INERTIA & DECLINE

On the next few pages are copies of Kirby's pencil art from the latter era of *Fantastic Four*:

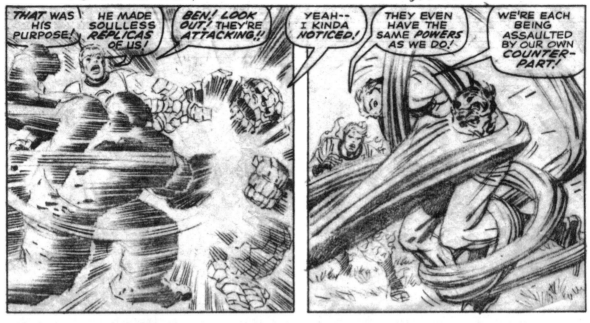

TORCH FLAMES ON — THE GET MY OPONENT FIRST

BUT EVIL TORCH DOESN'T SHOOT FLAME HE SHOOTS COSMIC FORCE IT PICKS UP UN-BALANCES TORCH

IN REED'S LAB--SURFER ... AND VANISHES INTO CHEMICAL ON SLIDE--

110

SKRULL SAYS - I'VE MEMORIZED THIS PLASTI-MOLD OF DEAD RICHARDS - I DON'T NEED IT NOW

PLASTI-FACE DISINTEGRATES-- ON STRIKING GROUND--

I NO LONGER NEED THIS PLASTI-MOLD...

FOR I HAVE THOROUGHLY MEMORIZED THE FACE OF REED RICHARDS!

AND SO, I SHALL ALLOW IT TO DIS-INTEGRATE!

NOW TO CHECK MINITIURIZED EQUIPMENT IN GLOVE

THE TIME IS COME TO CHECK THE MINITIURIZED EQUIPMENT HIDDEN IN MY GLOVE...

A SINGLE TOUCH CAN ACTIVATE IT...

...BRINGING IT TO FULL SIZE IN THE SPACE OF A HEARTBEAT!

IT IS THIS VERY NERVE RAY WHICH SHALL FELL... THE THING!

BUT, FOR NOW... IT MUST AGAIN BE CONCEALED!

NEXT, I MUST TEST MY HIGHLY-POTENT SHAPE-CHANGER!

THOUGH WE SKRULLS CAN CHANGE OUR OWN APPEARANCE IN AN INSTANT...

...IT IS NECESSARY FOR US TO USE MECHANICAL DEVICES TO CAUSE SUCH CHANGES ON OUR EQUIPMENT!

10

WEAPON GROWS SMALL AGAIN --

NOW HE TAKES OUT MINIATURE-SHAPE-CHANGER

SKRULLS CAN CHANGE THEIR OWN SHAPE - BUT THEY MUST USE MECHANICAL MEANS ON THEIR EQUIPMEN

114

AFTER MASTERING THE ART OF *SPACE TRAVEL*....

TO *ME*, THIS VEHICLE IS LIKE A *TOY!*

THE SIGNAL GROWS *STRONGER!*

MY *QUARRY* MUST BE DIRECTLY *AHEAD!*

THERE CAN BE *NO MISTAKING* THE BROAD, MASSIVE *BACK* THE WIDE, MIGHTY *SHOULDERS*...

TRULY, HE SHALL BE THE GREATEST *PRIZE* THAT I HAVE EVER *ENSLAVED!*

HE IS SURROUNDED BY *FEMALES* OF THE SPECIES!

EVEN ON *EARTH*, WHAT A MIGHTY *MAGNET* IS *FAME!*

JUST WRITE "LOVE TO BARBARA ANN"...AND SIGN IT *THE THING!*

HOW'S ABOUT I SPELL IT *DUSTIN HOFFMAN?*

I'LL *STILL* BETCHA A SAWBUCK HE'S WEARIN' A *MASK!*

WAIT! YOU DIDN'T SIGN *MINE!*

JUST *ONE* MORE... BEFORE YOU GO!

SORRY, LADIES ---THAT'S *ALL* FER NOW!

'YA WANT I SHOULD GIT *WRITERS' CRAMP?*

AHH, GOOD... *GOOD!* HE IS *ALONE* AT LAST!

NOW TO PUT MY STUDY OF *REED RICHARDS'* FACE TO *USE!*

16.

THE MENACE OF
THE MEGA-MEN!

ONE FACE OF STATUE IS CALM — WHOLESOME
OTHER FACE IS EVIL — SAVAGE

WHY SHOULD STATUE HAVE
BEEN UNEARTHED AT THIS
PARTICULAR TIME? STRANGE

Epilogue

In the end so much remains, and in a way, so little.

There is, in the annals of legendary magazine moguls, a publisher who is best characterized by an absurd paradox. After 30 years of blatantly plagiarizing other people's ideas, Martin Goodman's relentless pursuit of unoriginality somehow netted him an entire universe of the most original comic book characters ever created.

After stepping down from Marvel Comics in 1972, Goodman made one last, brief foray into comic book publishing in June 1974 with Seaboard Periodicals. His new comic book line revived the old Atlas name and knocked-off almost every 1960s superhero Marvel had. The entire venture was a dismal flop, and by December 1975 Goodman had thrown in the towel.

In June 1992, the Depression-bred publisher of pulps, men's magazines and funnybooks died peacefully in a geriatric home in Palm Beach Florida. He was 84 years old.

Martin's last sleazy, spectacular stunt for the House of Ideas was an ingenious price-increase scam. In the summer of 1971, Goodman raised the price of his comics from 32 pages for 15 cents to 48 pages for 25 cents. Around this same time, DC raised their prices and page-counts to 64 pages for 25 cents. Just one month after Marvel's price-increase, Goodman lowered his cover price to 32 pages for 20 cents. This gave the readers five Marvel comics to their dollar as opposed to four DC titles.

In effect, Goodman had created the illusion of a bargain when in fact he'd raised his price by one-third. The increased profits enabled Martin to give his wholesalers a 50 percent discount off the cover price. Since DC could only offer a 40 percent discount, Marvel comics were more widely distributed than ever before.

The sting worked brilliantly. DC stubbornly stuck to their guns and kept their prices up for a year. During that year, they took a bath. When the smoke cleared, the unthinkable had happened. The once-untouchable publishers of *Superman* suddenly found themselves in second place.

The blood-splattering newsstand circulation wars of the 1930s had taught Goodman how to fight dirty. After Jack Liebowitz stepped down in 1971, the post-war greenhorns who headed up DC's sales division didn't stand a chance against the old knockoff champion from the hobo jungles.

Despite the occasional anomaly like "The Death of Superman," Marvel comics have out-sold DC titles ever since. Thirteen years after the fall of Atlas, Martin Goodman took what was once the losing-est comic book company in the industry and made it the unchallenged leader of the field—a position it holds to this day.

Not bad for a man with a fourth-grade education.

There is, at Pierce Brothers Memorial Park in Westlake Village California, a gravesite marked by a memorial plaque no bigger than any of the hundreds of others that dot the lawn of the cemetery. The modest headstone is dedicated to the beloved husband, father and grandfather who sleeps below with no more pages to draw, no more deadlines to meet. On the memorial's bottom left corner is the Star of David. One can't help but think the monument is far too small for a man who—in the eyes of his fans—stood as tall as Galactus. One also wonders how many thousands of mesmerizing new characters and wondrous concepts rest in that grave with Jack "King" Kirby.

(left) Kirby harks back to his days in romance comics in this touching page from FF #79 (Oct. 1968).
(above) The sense of "family" never faded during the Lee/Kirby series, as this 1970 page from #102 attests.

There is, on a hilltop in Los Angeles, a very old man who is a millionaire many times over. He has reaped all the financial rewards that his ex-partner Jack Kirby equally deserved but never attained. Despite his advanced age, there's still something youthful and vibrant about his persona that makes him easy to like. It's easy to forgive him for failing to understand either the nature or the depth of Jack Kirby's discontent.

Although he's no longer officially connected to the company he cultivated, Stan Lee dedicated the majority of his life to Timely, Atlas and Marvel Comics; rolling with the company's changes, working his way to the top and staying there for nearly half a century. Like the shape-shifting Skrulls from *FF* #2, he changed his role many times: Writer, Editor, Art Director, Publisher, Company President,

Chairman Emeritus—you name it, he's worn the hat.

His detractors, and there are many, believe that Lee lucked into his fame and fortune through nepotism and through Marvel's desire to be represented by a media-savvy Founding Father figure; someone from the family who is paid well enough to never sue for copyrights to the characters that he created or co-created. His critics also say the great majority of ideas in the early Marvel comics came from Kirby and Ditko. To prove this, they point out that Lee never created any comics of merit after Marvel's two hottest flames departed.

On the other side you have the three people who were closest to him when it all happened: Flo Steinberg, Roy Thomas and the late Sol Brodsky. All three have gone on record to say that Stan spearheaded the whole Marvel phenomena and was a veritable fountain of ideas. In the end, Lee's final artistic legacy will undoubtedly remain a topic of heated debate.

At the time of this writing, that career he wanted as a "serious" writer still eludes him.

Stan Lee and Jack Kirby were two of the 20th Century's greatest fantasists. We owe some of our fondest childhood memories to these two daring, visionary comic book rebels who took what was once a junk medium and elevated it to unprecedented heights. They transformed the comic book into an art form of limitless possibilities, and in the process they liberated it from its subculture status and made it a vital force in mainstream entertainment.

The Fantastic Four's revolutionary adventures had energy, power and style; and in their refracted light you could feel your own life intensify. *Fantastic Four* was the first comic book to aspire to be taken seriously, and the first to achieve that lofty goal. Its effect was extraordinarily powerful on those it captivated. This is why most of us who grew up reading the Lee/Kirby *FF* are lifelong True Believers.

There is, in The Big Apple, a pretty and exuberant lady named Flo who has fond memories of her first job in New York back in 1963. After leaving Marvel Comics she went to work for the American Petroleum Industry. She eventually moved to Oregon and later to San Francisco before returning to New York City to head the Captain Company, the merchandising division of Warren Publishing.

In 1975 she published *Big Apple Comix*; a historically important link between underground comix and modern-day independent comics. From the late 1970s to the late 1980s Steinberg was the Managing Editor of the prestigious *Arts Magazine*, a glossy periodical that focused on traditional art in America. Flo eventually ended up back at Marvel where she worked part-time as a proofreader from the early to mid-1990s.

Steinberg's devotion to the 1960s Marvel mailbag and her determination to acknowledge every single kid who wrote to Marvel Comics produced the most loyal fan base any comics

Kirby seemed to have the same empathy for Bill Everett's aquatic anti-hero Prince Namor as he did for his own characters. Up to the end, Jack immortalized Sub-Mariner in majestic full-page panels like this from #102.

company ever had. All these years later, Flo Steinberg still occasionally responds to letters from True Believers with warm, personal replies; her youthful exuberance is evident in every line she writes. She's as fabulous as ever.

There is, in New York, a multi-billion-dollar octopus-like corporate entertainment complex that changes its name so often the mass media isn't sure what to call it anymore. Lately it's been known as Marvel Worldwide Inc. or Marvel Enterprises. Before that, it was the Marvel Entertainment Group. Before that, it was just Marvel Comics. But Marvel's main concern isn't comics anymore. Not by a long shot. Many believe the comic book is a dying medium, just as it was in the

The FF's first cover logo change was on #95 (Feb. 1970), as Sol Brodsky's original font was thickened up a bit.

Stan, Sol, Flo, and (a very rocky) Jack Kirby, from What If? *#11 (Oct. 1978). Pencil art by Kirby.*

days before the Fantastic Four. These days Marvel's primary focus is on movies, cartoon shows, toys, video games, and licensing their iconic characters for everything under the sun.

Over the past two decades Marvel has published several expensive and lavishly illustrated "history" books that focus on the company's continuing evolution. In these books, the minimal text that's wedged between the innumerable color pictures will explain that once, long ago, the Fantastic Four dominated the Marvel Universe. Nowadays however, they've been eclipsed in popularity by Spider-Man, Iron Man, Wolverine, the Avengers, the X-Men, the Hulk and others. At the dawn of the Marvel Age that idea would've been laughable. In those days the Fantastic Four ruled unchallenged. They were the ones who soared. The rest just existed.

In the last analysis, if current predictions come true and comic books cease to exist, and even if superhero movies fall by the wayside, Marvel will somehow bounce back, just as it bounced back from bankruptcy after 1996. No matter how many times the company might fall to ruin, Marvel will always find a way to make yet another fortune from its Silver Age superheroes. And just like Dr. Doom, The House of Ideas will rise again and again.

That's how sturdy Jack and Stan built that house.

There is, at your nearest comic book shop, still a magazine called *Fantastic Four*. The cover usually has a modern computer-generated "Fantastic Four" logo, but once in awhile the original Sol Brodsky masthead is dredged up, dusted off and reinstated, complete with *"THE WORLD'S GREATEST COMIC MAGAZINE!"* blurb from *FF* #4. When this happens, the book is somehow transformed. It seems to revert back to something older, something more atmospheric. Something more fulfilling.

In the years after 1970, many generations of *Fantastic Four* writers and artists would spend decades reviving and elaborating on the characters and concepts of Stan Lee and Jack Kirby. All those mesmerizing Lee/Kirby supporting-characters are still there, every bit as prevalent as they were in 1966; the Watcher, the Silver Surfer, the Black Panther and the Inhumans, along with Doctor Doom and the great Galactus. They still shine on.

Lee and Kirby dug a yet-undrained well of richness, innovation and myth that the magazine still draws from month after month, year after year, decade after decade. When one picks up the latest issue of *Fantastic Four*, they're overcome with an uncanny sense of changelessness; a reassuring sameness. Each new issue is a celebration of the magazine's astonishing characters: their triumphs, tragedies, myths, props and backdrops; their ironies, sentimentalities and their ever-changing, never-changing rituals.

Amazingly, the four stars of the book still look exactly as they did in 1962. That's comforting to know. It also goes to show that no one, as of yet, has been able to improve on them. ★

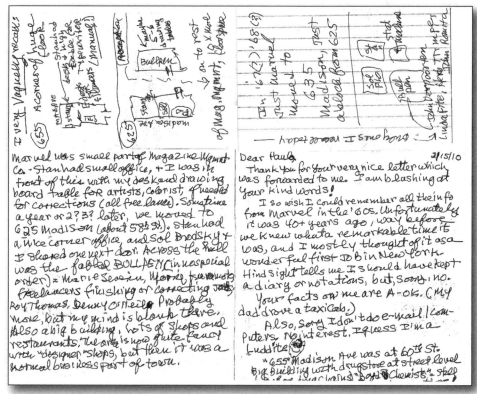

"Fabulous" Flo Steinberg took time to document her recollections of '60s Marvel for this book. Thanks, Flo!

A New Take On An Old Classic

Presented here, in its entirety, are Jack Kirby's storyboards for the Depatie-Freleng *Fantastic Four* cartoon "The Mole Man" from 1978. Kirby and Lee worked together on the series, marking their final creative project together. This episode introduced the Mole Man to Saturday morning cartoon audiences, as the FF meet the villain in sort of an expanded version of the *Fantastic Four* #1 and #22 stories. For a fascinating comparison, view Jack's storyboards while watching the finished episode online at *http://youtu.be/qiEY6y0sS8o.* ★

FANTASTIC FOUR

JACK KIRBY

"THE MOLE MAN.."

STAN LEE

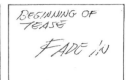

BEGINNING OF TEASE

FADE IN

POWER PLANT SOMEWHERE IN EUROPE

WORKERS AT NORMAL ROUTINE

SUDDENLY ALARM SOUND.

TREMORS CAUSE PANIC!

WORKERS FLEE PLANT

TREMORS INCREASE

PLANT BEGINS TO SINK

ITS DRAWN BELOW GROUND

--AND VANISHES!

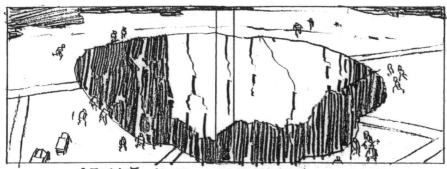

PEOPLE ARE MYSTIFIED!

AUTHORITIES BAFFLED.

DISCUSSION OF INCIDENT IS HELD AT HIGH LEVEL CONFERENCE

LET'S NOTIFY THE U.N.

GET ME OUR AMBASSADOR AT U.N.

AMBASSADOR PUTS PROBLEM TO COLLEAGUES!

ONE DELEGATE POINTS TO BAXTER BLDG.

LET'S CALL IN THE F.F.

DISSOLVE TO REED RICHARD ADDRESSING U.N.

REED ACKNOWLEDGES THE EMERGENCY.

IT'S HAPPENING EVERY- WHERE!

THIS FILM CLIP SHOWS SITE OF PLANT VANISHING'' IN SOUTH AMERICAN

THIS INDICATES SIMILAR HAPPENINGS IN OTHER PARTS OF GLOBE.

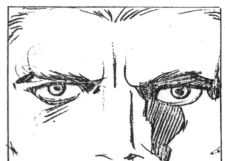

THERE HASN'T BEEN A CLUE.

-- ONLY A WHISPERED NAME''

-- THE MOLE MAN!--

SOMETHING HAS TO BE DONE!!!

OR THE WORLD WILL SOON BE WITHOUT POWER''

AT THE MERCY OF THE MOLE MAN.. -- END OF TEASE..

DISSOLVE TO F.F. HEADQUARTERS..
REED AND OTHERS DISCUSS MYSTERY..

F.F. DISCUSS MYSTERY

REED DESCRIBES A MOLE.

MAYBE IT'S A GIANT MOLE!

IT'S WORSE!

THERE'S A HUMAN BEHIND THIS..

I DON'T BUY IT

SOUNDS LIKE A FAIRY TALE.

YOU'D KNOW ALL ABOUT THAT..

IT'S YOUR FAVORITE READING MATTER

BEN ENGAGES HERBIE IN BANTER..

HOLD IT, YOU TWO..

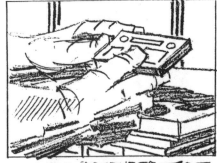

REED PRODUCES TAPE OF SEISMOGRAPHIC ACTIVITY..

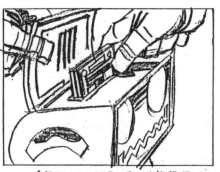

FEEDS IT TO HERBIE FOR ANALYSIS.

COMPUTE IT AND PREDICT LOCATION OF NEXT ATTACK

HERBIE COMPUTES DATA.

THEN MAKES CALCU- LATION"

TAPE IS THEN REJECTED!

REED STUDIES PREDICTION!

THE NEXT ATTACK WILL BE --

-- IN RUSSIA!

DISSOLVE TO HANGAR IN WHICH POGO PLANE IS KEPT"

F.F. WILL FOLLOW UP LEAD" THEY FUEL POGO PLANE!

THEY'LL FLY TO RUSSIA"

ROOF HANGAR OPENS"

ALL OF FF BOARD THE PLANE!

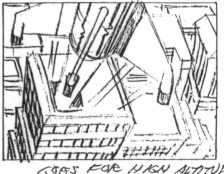

POGO PLANE LEAVES FROM BAXTER BLDG.

IT RISES ON ROCKETS LIKE MISSILE"

GOES FOR HIGH ALTITUDE

CITY SHRINKS BELOW

PLANE HEADS FOR OPEN SEA!

RUSSIA LIES AHEAD..

PLANE SOON REACHES RUGGED SIBERIAN COUNTRY..

APPROACHES POWER PLANT

LANDS NEAR INSTALLATION!

DISSOLVE TO
GUARD TOWER
AT PLANT
ENTRANCE

GUARD TOWER SPOTS DE-SCENDING PLANE..

GUARDS ON ALERT AS F.F. APPROACH!

LET US IN..

NOT ALLOWED!

127

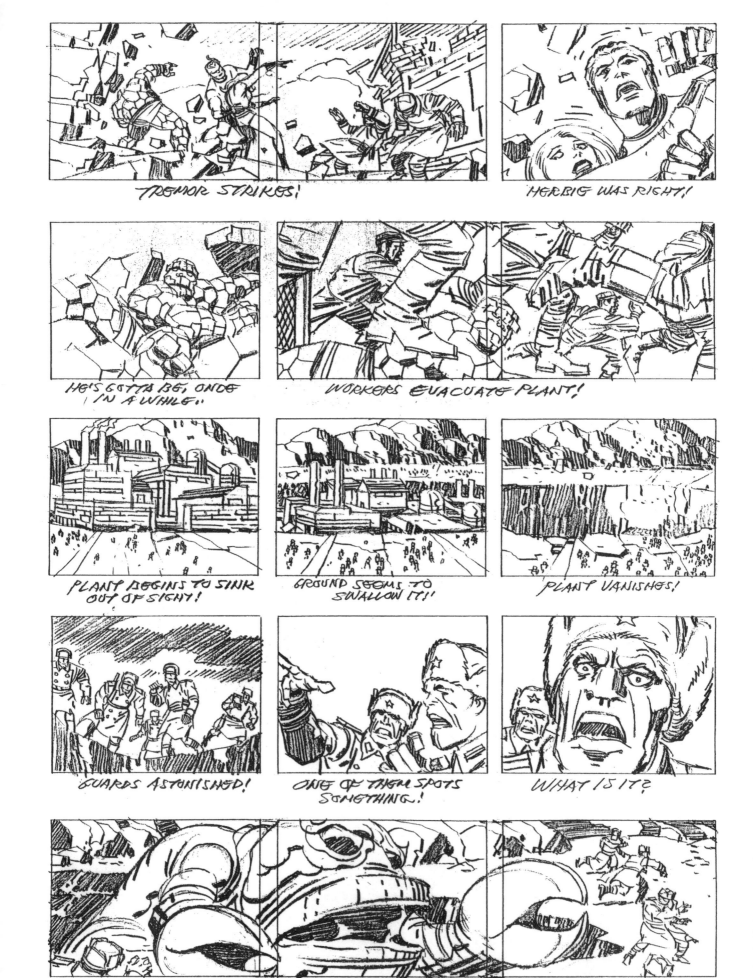

TREMOR STRIKES!

HERBIG WAS RIGHT!

HE'S GOTTA BE, ONCE IN A WHILE!!

WORKERS EVACUATE PLANT!

PLANT BEGINS TO SINK OUT OF SIGHT!

GROUND SEEMS TO SWALLOW IT!!

PLANT VANISHES!

GUARDS ASTONISHED!

ONE OF THEM SPOTS SOMETHING!

WHAT IS IT?

HUGE CREATURE APPEARS AT VANISHING SITE!

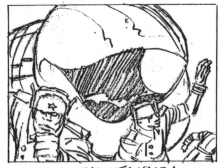
GET THE TANKS!

TANKS ROLL TOWARD CREATURE!

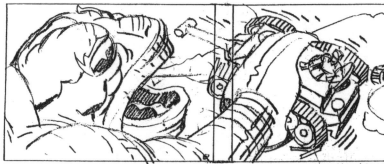
CREATURE SEIZES LEAD TANK AS OTHERS TURN AND FLEE!

CREW ABANDONS TANK

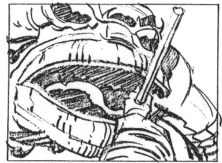
THEN TANK IS CRUSHED!

-- AND TOSSED AWAY LIKE JUNK!

SUDDENLY, CREATURE IS STOPPED

STRANGE HUMAN APPEARS..

HE ORDERS CREATURE TO DIG HOLE.

HE VANISHES WITH IT BENEATH GROUND.

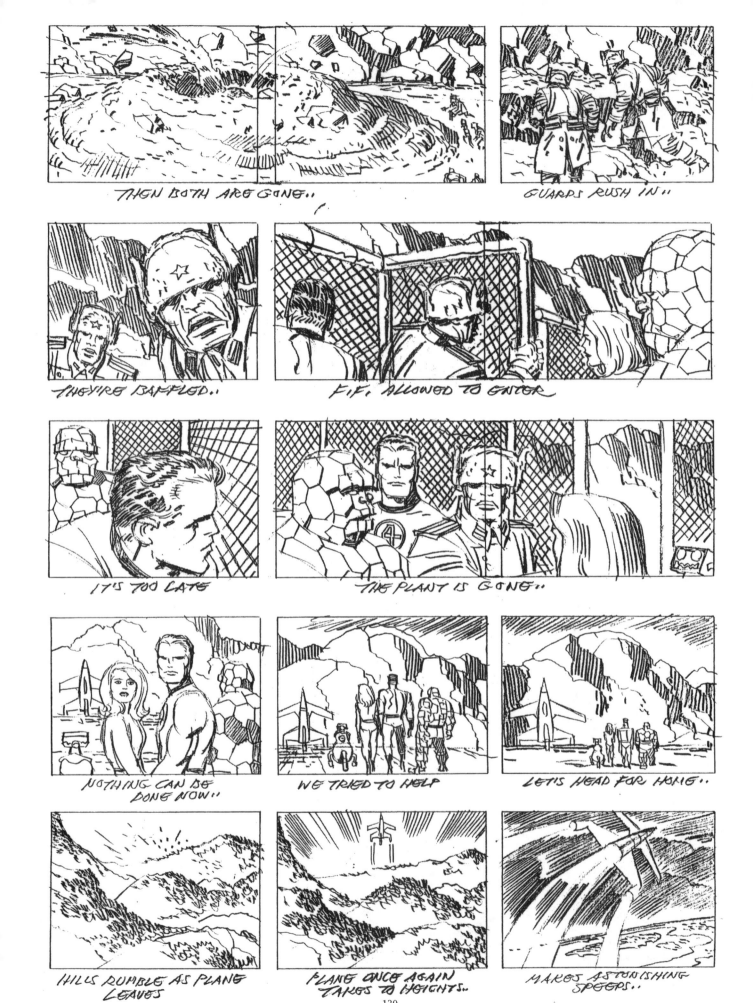

THEN BOTH ARE GONE..

GUARDS RUSH IN..

THEY'RE BAFFLED..

F.F. ALLOWED TO ENTER

IT'S TOO LATE

THE PLANT IS GONE..

NOTHING CAN BE
DONE NOW..

WE TRIED TO HELP

LET'S HEAD FOR HOME..

HILLS RUMBLE AS PLANE
LEAVES

PLANE ONCE AGAIN
TAKES TO HEIGHTS..

MAKES ASTONISHING
SPEEDS..

SHOOTS ACROSS OCEAN

AND FADES INTO HORIZON!

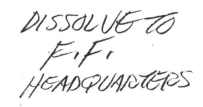

DISSOLVE TO
F.F.
HEADQUARTERS

BACK AT HQ, EXPERIENCE IS
DISCUSSED.

THIS IS GROWING
SERIOUS!

WE SAW IT HAPPEN!

I SUPPOSE HERBIE CAN
PREDICT AGAIN!!

I THINK HE CAN

LET'S SEE YOU DO IT!

ARM SHOOTS FROM HERBIE
WITH PLUG!

HERBIE LINKS UP WITH
MAP MECHANISM.

MAKES CALCULATION.!
SPOT ON MAP REACTS!

BEN RIBS HERBIE!!! "THERE'S NO SUCH
PLACE!!!"

131

NOW THAT'S A FAIRY TALE!

NO, IT'S A LEGEND..

YOU CAN'T TAKE HERBIE SERIOUSLY..

NO BELIEVES IN "MONSTER ISLE!"

I BELIEVE IN HERBIE!

THANKS REED..

I'LL GO WHERE YOU GO!

EVERYONE'S NUTTY!

I'LL GO ANYWHERE!

DISSOLVE TO VIEW OF BAXTER BLDG...

PLANE TAKES OFF AGAIN!

HEADS OUT FOR SEA..

STORM DEVELOPS.

PLANE TRIES TO RISE.

—BUT IS CAUGHT IN TUR- —BULENCE!

132

SITUATION GET HAIRY.

PLANE IS TOSSED ABOUT!

REED LOOKS FOR ESCAPE FROM STORM

HE ZOOMS THRU OPENING IN CLOUDS..

--AND CLEARS STORM..

"MONSTER ISLE" IS SIGHTED!

PLANE APPROACHES VOLCANO..

CAUGHT IN GAS CLOUD.

SPUT!
SPUT
SPUT

ENGINE CUTS OUT..

REED USES ALL HIS SKILL TO CONTROL PLANE.

VOLCANO CRATER LOOMS UP

REED AND SUE ABANDON PLANE TO LIGHTON IT...

REED BECOMES PARA- -CHUTE...

'LANDS SAFELY...

BEN TRIES TO GLIDE PLANE TO SAFETY!

BUT PLUMMETS INTO CRATER...

VANISHES BELOW...

WHAT WILL HAPPEN TO THEM

WE'VE GOT TO FIND A WAY TO HELP THEM!

THEY FACE UNKNOWN DANGERS,

THERE ARE STRANGE STORIES ABOUT THIS PLACE!

THEY SAY ISLAND IS GUARDED BY FLYING TREE

134

THERE IT IS!

SUE BECOMES INVISIBLE AS TREE ATTACKS!

REED LASSOES TREE.

FLINGS IT OUTWARD!

IT VANISHES ACROSS SEA!

REED NOW REACHES FOR SUE. SHE'S VISIBLE.

LET'S LEAVE THIS SPOT! --

-- AND FOLLOW BEN AND HERBIE!

REED, ONCE MORE, IS PARACHUTE.

DRIFTS INTO CRATER WITH SUE!

DISSOLVE TO
BEN & HERBIE
IN UNDER-
GROUND CELL..

THIS IS A FINE SPOT TO BE IN

WE'RE IN A CELL
NO LESS!

BUT I'M NOT STAYING!

BEN APPLIES PRESSURE
TO WALL

IT CRACKS!

BEN IS OUT--

HE SEES GLOWING
OBJECT!

IT'S A BIZARRE SERPENT

BEN REACHES FOR
IT.

SHOCK JOLTS DUO!

BEN AND HERBIE FALL
BACK..

MOLE MAN APPEARS,

IT'S USELESS TO DEFY ME!

THIS IS MY STORY!

DISSOLVE TO TALE TOLD BY MOLE MAN

MOLE MAN WAS REKNOWNED SCIENTIST..

I BELIEVE IN MONSTER ISLE!"

YOU CAN'T BE SERIOUS!

BELIEVE IT!!

MOLE MAN IS RIDICULED BY COLLEAGUES..

HE LEAVES MEETING..

DENIED WORK ..

BUT DETERMINED TO FIND ISLAND..

--"AND WREAK REVENGE ON SCOFFERS!

137

SOON FINDS MONSTER ISLE.

CLIMBS VOLCANO.

STORM JOLTS HIM INTO CRATER

PLUMMETS INTO DEPTHS

BUT LANDS UNHARMED.

HE FINDS CREATURES OF ISLAND.

LEARNS TO CONTROL THEM..

BECOMES THEIR MASTER.

AND VOWS TO MASTER SURFACE WORLD!

NARRATIVE ENDS. DISSOLVE TO MOLE MAN ONCE MORE FACING THING AND HERBIE

I CAN OUTMANEUVER YOU TWO!

I'VE DEVELOPED A RADAR SENSE!

TRY TO HIT ME!

I'M WILLING!

BEN SHOOTS FORWARD.

MOLE MAN AVOIDS HIM

I'LL TRY IT AGAIN!

MOLE MAN VAULTS OVER HIM WITH STAFF!

MOLE MAN TAUNTS THEM

HE'LL DEMONSTRATE HIS POWER

EACH CIRCLE IS POWER PLANT!

ONCE I'VE STOLEN THESE I'LL CONTROL ENERGY SUPPLY

MY CREATURES WILL ATTACK SURFACE!

THEY'LL DEFEAT NATIONS

—AND CONTROL CIVILIZATION..

YOU CAN SAVE YOURSELVES--

-- IF YOU JOIN ME!!

REED AND SUE BREAK IN!

MOLE MAN PANICS!

GROUND SLAB OPENS..

MOLE MAN ESCAPES BY CHUTE!

BEN IS TOO LATE TO STOP HIM

SOMETHINGS HAPPENING!

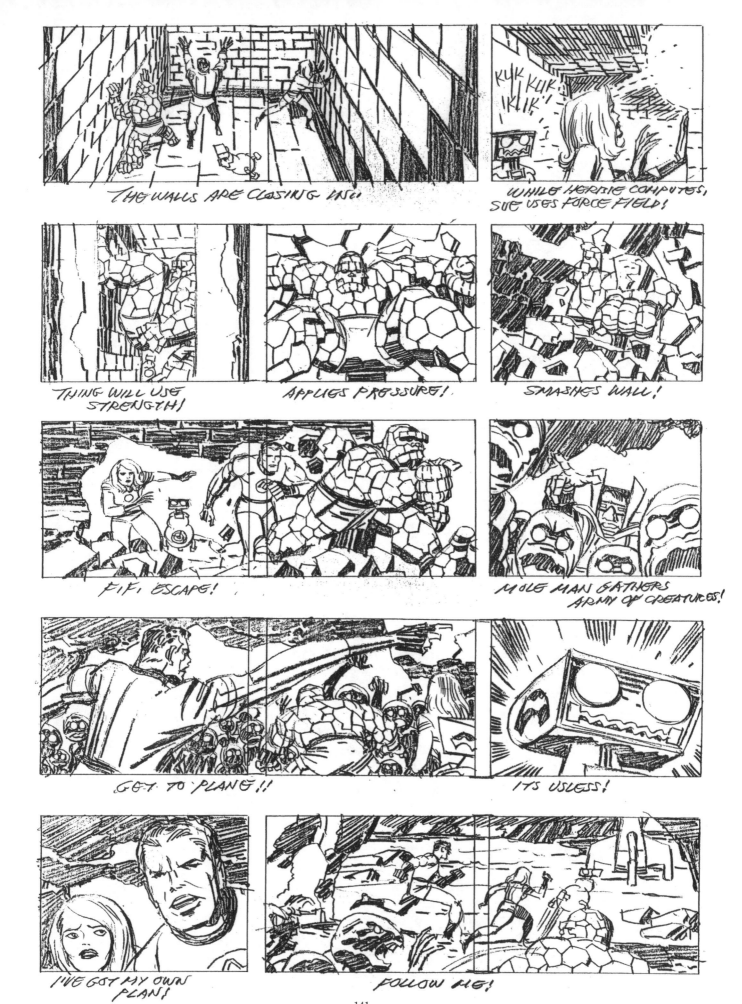

THE WALLS ARE CLOSING IN!

WHILE HERBIE COMPUTES, SUE USES FORCE FIELD!

THING WILL USE STRENGTH!

APPLIES PRESSURE!

SMASHES WALL!

FIFI, ESCAPE!

MOLE MAN GATHERS ARMY OF CREATURES!

GET TO PLANE!!

ITS USLESS!

I'VE GOT MY OWN PLAN!

FOLLOW ME!

AT PLANE, REED SHIFTS WIRES

SNAPS SWITCH!

LIGHTS FLOOD CAVE!

CREATURES FALL BACK!

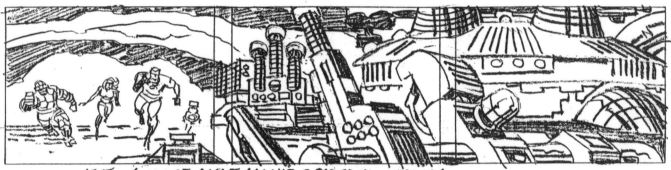

F.F. LOCATE MOLE MAN'S CONTROL UNITS!

REED AND SUE REVERSE PROCESS

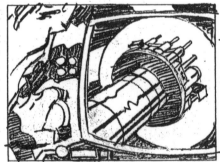

STOLEN POWER PLANTS RISE TO SURFACE!

ALL OVER WORLD, THEY ARE RESTORED IN PLACE!

THEN, BEN TIES UP MOLE MAN'S SWITCHES

CRUMPLES CONTROL PANELS..

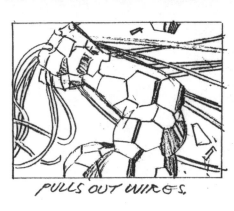

PULLS OUT WIRES.

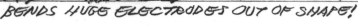

BENDS HUGE ELECTRODES OUT OF SHAPE!

THAT DOES IT!

THERE'S ONE MORE JOB TO DO..

CAPTURE MOLE MAN!

YES, I SUPPOSE SO..

LOOK, REED"

MOLE MAN SITS DISCONSOLATELY IN WRECKAGE..

HE'S BEATEN!

LET'S SHOW COMPASSION!

WHAT'S THE VERDICT?

FIF LEAVE M.M. BEHIND..

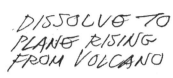

DISSOLVE TO PLANE RISING FROM VOLCANO

FIF. OFF FOR HOME

THEY'VE DONE THEIR JOB.

SUDDENLY VOLCANO ERUPTS!

--IN FULL FORCE!

WHAT A STRANGE COINCIDENCE!

I'LL SAY IT'S STRANGE!

DON'T LOOK AT ME!

OKAY! YOU'RE THE CULPRIT!

I DID IT WITH MY REMOTE CONTROL SWITCH!

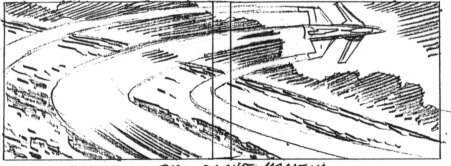

LET'S TAKE THIS PLANE HOME!!!

VOLCANO IS SEALED BY HEATED SLAG!

DISSOLVE TO
FF REPORTING
TO U.N.
COMMITTEE

WAS THERE REALLY A "MONSTER ISLE?"

YES. WE FOUND IT..

BUT IT'S. NO PLACE FOR TOURISTS..

BUT YOU WENT THERE AND DID A GREAT JOB.

THE WORLD OWES YOU MUCH!

THE STORY MUST BE TOLD.

NO. FORGET IT..

MONSTER ISLE MUST REMAIN--

--A LEGEND....

FADE OUT

THE END

145

THIS IS A PLOT?

An examination of Lee and Kirby's Fantastic Four *writing process*

Stan and Jack plot an issue, in FF Annual #5 *(1967), with script and art by Kirby. (below)* FF #7 *and 8 panels.*

Mark Twain once said that all partners do at least 90% of the work.

If one looks back on the history of comic book writer/artist teams, they'll find that most of them, especially in later years, disagree on who contributed what. This goes right back to Superman's creators Jerry Sigel and Joe Shuster.

Roy Thomas put it like this: "It's only later—and this happens with a lot of artists—suddenly 20 years later they start deciding they were the only person that was important in the team. This happened with Stan, and it happened with me. And generally that's bull."

From time to time over the years both Lee and Kirby were prone to make preposterous, self-aggrandizing statements regarding what they individually contributed to Marvel Comics. For example, Stan claims that he created *Sgt. Fury and his Howling Commandos* over a bet with Martin Goodman. Conversely, John Severin said that Sgt. Fury and his squad was an idea that Kirby had for a newspaper strip long before he went back to Atlas in 1956. Stan's occasional attempts to take credit for things he couldn't possibly have created are almost as ridiculous as Jack telling Gary Groth that Lee never co-plotted any of the 1960s Marvel comics and that Stan had "some

guy at the office" do all his dialoguing for him.

Several sources claim that Kirby plotted his post-1964 Marvel stories with almost no input from Lee, after his workload was reduced and he

settled down to concentrate on *Fantastic Four, Thor* and *Captain America.* This gives the impression that all the mind-boggling ideas from *Fantastic Four's* "Cosmic Era" were Kirby's alone. But like the fictional 1961 Goodman/Liebowitz golf game, this claim is a myth—a myth which can easily be disproved.

A funny thing happened on the way to this book. From the outset, a conscious decision was made to avoid any "who did what" debates regarding Jack and Stan's individual contributions to *Fantastic Four.* But with no preconceived agenda whatsoever, we kept finding more and more evidence that shows Stan was actively involved in the plotting of *Fantastic Four,* to some degree or another, during Kirby's entire run on the series.

This is not to say the magazine's storyline was always an equal division of labor. After 1965, Kirby undoubtedly came up with a greater portion of the ideas. Dr. Michael J. Vassallo has always believed that the book was 70% Jack and 30% Stan, and for years he's had to battle legions of Kirby-centric fans online who don't even want to give Stan 30% credit. But "Doc V" also believes the entire success and voice of Marvel as a company was all

from Stan Lee. It should be noted that Flo Steinberg adamantly agrees with this view. Flo, who was there, assures us that Stan "spearheaded the whole thing."

Joe Sinnott, who inked *FF* #5 and worked on the earliest Thor tales in *Journey Into Mystery,* told us that at the dawn of the Marvel Age Kirby was working almost exclusively from Stan's detailed plot outlines. And in retrospect, Lee's input on the early *FF* plots can be detected if one reads the Ayers-era cannon in succession.

For example, one can find repetitive storyline patterns in nearly every *Fantastic Four* tale from issue #7 through #17. Almost all of these stories feature a sequence that begins with a "floating head caption" (i.e., a caption-box at the top of the panel augmented with a tiny headshot of the character who's narrating the sequence). These captions are always followed by a series of panels which describe a string of past or future events.

This repetition in the scripts is indicative of the book's early story-

YOU NEED NOT LOOK SO SURPRISED! MY OFFER OF A MILLION DOLLARS WAS GENUINE ENOUGH! YOU SEE, ALL THE WEALTH OF THE SEA IS MINE!

lines being driven by someone with a formulated writing approach—in other words, Stan Lee.* *[Editor's Note: See the sidebar "Stop The Presses!" on page 150 for an important rebuttal to this.]* Kirby on the other hand almost always flew by the seat of his pants when spinning his superhero tales; seldom resorting to a repetitive or formulary procedure.

Roy Thomas said by the time he arrived at Marvel in mid-1965, Lee and Kirby's method of working together was already changing and would continue to evolve until Jack left for DC in 1970. According to Roy, by 1965 Stan was gradually decreasing the practice of giving Jack plot outlines, choosing instead to meet him at the office for story conferences.

There's only one historical record that shows how *Fantastic Four* was fashioned during Jack and Stan's Silver Age brainstorming sessions. The following is a transcript from a late 1965 Lee/Kirby plot conference recorded by Nat Freeland for the January 9, 1966 edition of *The New York Herald-Tribune:*

"The Silver Surfer has been somewhere out in space since he helped the F.F. stop Galactus from destroying the Earth," begins Lee. "Why don't we bring him back?"

"Ummh," says Kirby.

"Suppose Alicia, the Thing's blind girlfriend is in some kind of trouble. And the Silver Surfer comes to help her." Lee starts pacing and gesturing as he gets warmed up.

"I see," says Kirby. He has kind of a high-pitched voice.

"But the Thing sees them together and he misunderstands so he starts a big fight with the Silver Surfer. And meanwhile, the Fantastic Four is in lots of trouble. Dr Doom has caught them again and they need the Thing's help." Lee is lurching around and throwing punches now.

"Right," says Kirby.

"The Thing finally beats the Silver Surfer but then Alicia makes him realize he's made a terrible mistake. This is what the Thing always feared more than anything else, that he would lose control and really clobber somebody."

Kirby nods.

"The Thing is broken hearted. He wanders off by himself. He is too ashamed to face Alicia or go back home to the Fantastic Four. He doesn't realize how he is failing for the second time...how much the FF needs him." Lee sags back on his desk, limp and spent.

Kirby has leaped out of the chair he was crumpled in. "Great, great." The cigar is out of his mouth and his baggy eyes are aglow.

"AS YOU KNOW, AGES AGO THE DINOSAURS WERE THE LORDS OF EARTH! BUT, UNFORTUNATELY FOR THEM, THEIR BODIES GREW TOO LARGE WHILE THEIR BRAINS REMAINED THE SAME -- UNTIL THEY SIMPLY GREW THEMSELVES OUT OF EXISTENCE!"

(top and above) FF #9 and #10 panels (Dec. 1962 and Jan. 1963).

Naturally, Jack was outraged by this article in which Freeman described him as "someone you might mistake for an assistant foreman in a girdle factory." But never once in the years after the article's publication did Kirby claim the plot conference was staged, or that Stan was grandstanding for the reporter's benefit. Other Marvel insiders have gone on record to say the session that Freeman described was exactly how Stan brainstormed with his artists even when no reporter was present. Therefore, there's no reason to assume that this particular "weekly Friday morning summit meeting" was anything but the genuine approach that Jack and Stan used to develop their *Fantastic Four* storylines throughout that period.

During the plot session that Freeland was privy to (which eventually spawned *FF* #55), it's obvious that Lee was the dominant partner and that Kirby was almost totally passive. Most of the ideas that Stan offered ended up in the finished story except for the appearance of Dr. Doom, which Kirby decided to put on hold until *FF* #57 (Dec. 1966). This proves that Lee was actively co-plotting *Fantastic Four* around the time of *FF* #55. And at that point, all of the book's most enduring characters had already been established.

In plain point of fact, Stan didn't totally discontinue giving Kirby a typed *FF* plot synopsis at any stage. Lee's plot outlines merely got shorter over the years. Oddly enough, while *FF* #55's storyline was spawned from a face to face meeting, the plots for *FF* #57-60 were all typed by Stan and given to Kirby in outline form. These story outlines still exist. They prove that Lee and Kirby's writing process was pretty much arbitrary at any given point.

For what it's worth, here's a list of "top ten reasons" to acknowledge that Stan had substantial input on *Fantastic Four's* storyline during the entire Lee/Kirby run:

1. Stan's *FF* #1 plot outline. Despite the skepticism of a few conspiracy-minded Kirby fans, there's not one shred of evidence to indicate that this synopsis was written after the fact.

2. Stan's *FF* #8 plot synopsis which Kirby followed to the smallest detail (see **AT A GLANCE** *FF* #8).

3. The Neal Kirby interview in *TJKC* #45. Neal recalled going to the Marvel offices with his dad in the 1960s on a regular basis so that Jack could discuss storylines with Stan.

4. Roy Thomas' recollection that the plot for *FF* #30 was devised while Lee and Kirby were stuck in traffic.

5. Sol Brodsky told Roy Thomas that the creation of the Silver Surfer (i.e. Jack making him up with no input from Stan) was an anomaly. And that to his knowledge, the great majority of the characters were joint efforts.

6. Mark Evanier told us that he has all the Stan Lee plot outlines from the astounding Dr. Doom/Silver Surfer story cycle that spanned *FF* #57-60. These plot outlines prove that at this majestic phase Stan was still making solid contributions to the storylines.

7. *FF Annual* #5 featured a parody of Jack and Stan's 1967 story conferences called "This Is a Plot?" which was written solely by Kirby with no input from Lee. Why would Jack amplify the duo's cooperative plot sessions if he and Stan weren't collaborating on

Fantastic Four's storyline at that point? So, according to Kirby himself, the Lee/Kirby writing team was still alive and flourishing in 1967 (albeit butting heads the whole way).

8. The four-issue Silver Surfer tale in *FF* #74-77 which served as a precursor to the Lee/Buscema *Silver Surfer* series was obviously Stan's brainchild. Kirby wouldn't have initiated the idea of a grand, multi-issue lead-in to a series which he was passed over on—a series which made him feel he had lost the Silver Surfer entirely. Ergo, Lee must have been the driving force behind that story arc.

9. In 2010, Flo Steinberg told us that the entire time she was at Marvel (1963-68), Lee and Kirby conducted joint plot conferences and had a totally harmonious relationship. Steinberg is quite certain about this. As Flo recalled, "I don't ever remember Jack *not* coming in for plot conferences. They would discuss the storylines and act-out and laugh—Stan and Jack's synergy was amazing. There was never any acrimony or hard feelings between them during my time there."

10. In July 1969, when Mark Evanier was visiting Kirby for the first time, Jack got a phone call from Stan Lee. According to Mark, "We got to listen in on Jack's end of a plot conference which lasted only a minute or two—though after it, Jack made a point of telling us that, on earlier issues, they'd spent more time talking." During Evanier's first visit, Kirby was drawing *FF* #97. Jack and Stan were still plotting the book jointly at this juncture, and Kirby's tenure on the series was only five issues away from being over.

All of the above particulars point to Lee being involved with *Fantastic Four's* storyline throughout every phase of the magazine from *FF* #1 until at least *FF* #97. The only instances when Kirby created *Fantastic Four* stories by himself appear to be rare cases like *FF* #80, where Jack either forgot or disregarded the plot points that he and Stan had discussed beforehand.

Eventually things did change. At some point after 1968, Jack and Stan's regular Friday morning summit meetings came to an end. Even before Kirby moved west, both he and Stan found it increasingly difficult to get together and brainstorm on the book's storyline. There simply wasn't enough time. Both men had too many pages to produce. By 1969, the duo's joint plot conferences had become so infrequent that it didn't matter much when Kirby uprooted his family and moved to California. But even after Kirby's relocation, the King wasn't creating the book entirely on his own. He still received regular input from Lee, even if it was only a brief, long-distance phone call.

Under the harsh light of retrospection, it appears that when the duo's synergetic face to face story conferences ended, the trouble began. Why? Because the less input Stan had on a *FF* story before the fact, the more he felt inclined to change Jack's storyline after the fact. Mike Gartland, who authored *The Jack Kirby Collector's* "Failure To Communicate" series, put it like this: "I believe that Lee and Kirby created the FF together, and had plotting sessions together, but later on (around *FF* #39 and up), the plots were mostly driven by Kirby with less input from Stan, but more changes by him afterwards."

Stan freely admits his proclivity to revise Kirby's *FF* storylines. According to Lee, "In the beginning I'd give him written-out plots, like the outline for the first *Fantastic Four*. After awhile, I would just tell him what I thought the story ought to be. Then after awhile, I would just give him a few words. He could practically do the whole thing by himself, y'know? Very often I didn't even know what the hell he was going to give me. I'd get some pages of artwork, and I wrote the copy and turned it into whatever story I wanted it to be."

Some Kirby fans may find the above statement by Lee to be sacrilegious, but Stan wasn't the only member of the duo who made story changes. Jack would seldom walk away from a Lee/Kirby brainstorming session and draw a book that followed the predetermined plot points to the letter. Jack's addition of the Silver Surfer to the Galactus tale is one well-known example of this. Another example can be found in *FF* #55, where Jack added a Human Torch/Wyatt Wingfoot subplot that wasn't mentioned in the conference that preceded it. Like Stan said, "Jack's pages typically included things that Jack would have added that we never discussed which were all wonderful."

To be fair, Lee's alterations of Kirby's storylines and dialogue suggestions weren't implemented because Stan doubted Jack's talent. Stan simply had his own way of doing

(top) FF #11 panel. (above) FF #12 panel. (center) Tales of the Unexpected #16 (Aug. 1957)—an early Kirby Thor at DC.

things; his own style of writing. And even though it was Lee's editorial prerogative to revamp Jack's story ideas, Kirby saw Stan's changes as a galling betrayal of his artistic intent; especially when Stan ordered him to redraw pages, with no additional pay, to make the story go Stan's way.

As far as Kirby was concerned, the final straw came with *Fantastic Four* #66. After the King saw what Stan had done to his "cocoon" story, he pretty much threw in the towel, creatively speaking. For the rest of his run on the series, he co-produced the book with notably diminished enthusiasm.

In recent years, in an effort to give Jack Kirby the credit he deserves, some overzealous writers have practically portrayed Stan Lee as the man who rode Kirby's back to fame and fortune. The reason for this is almost comprehensible. It's easy to see what Kirby contributed to Marvel Comics. The King's offerings leap right off the pages, where Stan's are less conspicuous.

Another reason for Jack's current status as the "real" creator of Marvel is fandom's empathy for Kirby The Underdog; an image that was fostered in the 1980s when Kirby played David to Marvel's Goliath during the infamous battle for his original art. This too is understandable. But the fact that Lee ended up a multi-millionaire while Kirby only received page-rates doesn't mean that Stan's contributions should be under-credited or disregarded entirely, as they've often been in recent years.

Out of genuine love for Jack Kirby, comic fandom has almost gone overboard. These days the comic book community is so rabidly pro-Kirby that Stan often comes off looking like Doctor Doom. This is entirely unfair, and even Kirby's strongest supporters, John Morrow and Mark Evanier, have called for an end to Lee-bashing. More power to them.

There's no point in trying to ascertain which *Fantastic Four* ideas were Stan's and which were Jack's. Most of them were spawned from the regular story conferences that the duo had right up to the very end of their collaboration, either in person or by phone.

Marvel Comics wouldn't have happened if Jack Kirby had been working with any other writer/editor than Stan Lee. Nor would

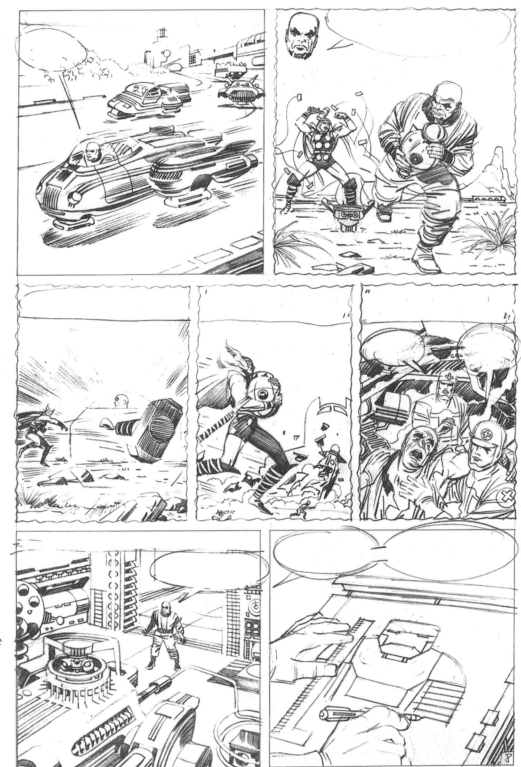

In Journey Into Mystery *#101 (FEb. 1964), Kirby used his time-tested "talking head" flashback technique.*

Marvel have materialized if Lee had tried to launch a superhero-driven comics line with any other artist than Jack Kirby. Although Kirby was the main creative force, Lee's talent for radically modernized characterization and dialogue, along with his tireless efforts to promote the Marvel brand, contributed enormously to the company's success.

Fantastic Four soared on a combination of Jack Kirby action and Stan Lee angst. Both men, together, created the greatest superhero series of the 20th Century. ★

149

*Stop The Presses!

A rebuttal by editor John Morrow

As much as I admire Mark's research into the Lee/Kirby working process, he's reached the wrong conclusion on one point—but in light of his passing, I'm not editing it out of this book. Yes, there are recurring "flashback" panels throughout the early Lee/Kirby issues, featuring a tiny talking head conveying narration for the reader. However, a little further research shows that Kirby was using this storytelling device long before *Fantastic Four* #1 ever appeared.

A year earlier, in Marvel's *Journey Into Mystery* #62 (Nov. 1960), Jack used this device in "I Was A Slave of the Living Hulk!" in conjunction with Stan Lee (and possibly Larry Lieber scripting), and likely many other "Atlas monster" stories. But also shown here are even *earlier* examples from his "Challengers of the Unknown" work (in both DC's *Showcase* in 1957-58, and the solo *Challengers* book in 1958), showing the *exact same device used on numerous occasions.* Challs is the closest forerunner to the FF in terms of concept and execution, but I was also able to quickly find instances of this technique in Jack's work on the "Green Arrow" strip in DC's *Adventure Comics* (1958-59), and even one from *Adventures of the Fly* #1 for Archie Comics (1959). Based on how easily I was able to track these earlier examples down, I'm certain there are many more as well, prior to *FF* #1 in 1961, such as the DC Comics "Thor" example on page 148.

So by Mark's logic, yes, there are repetitive storyline patterns in the early Marvel stories that Stan and Jack worked on together. The Mole Man is even presented this way on page 22 of *Fantastic Four* #1. But since those same patterns exist years earlier, for work done for at least two other publishers, the only common link between them all is Kirby himself. Don't forget: by the time Kirby returned to Marvel to work with Stan in the 1950s, he had likely written as many comics as Stan had. So if this proves that all the early Marvel books' storylines were being driven by someone with a formulated writing approach—a theory I'm not 100% sold on—that person would be *Jack Kirby,* not Stan Lee.

(above) Showcase #7 and #11 panels from 1957. *(below)* Showcase #12 and Challengers #1 examples (1958).

(above) Panels from Challengers of the Unknown #2 and Adventures Comics #253 (1958), both for DC Comics.

(above) Journey Into Mystery #62 (Nov. 1960) and Fantastic Four #1 (Nov. 1961), both for Marvel Comics.

A later, more evolved example of Kirby's "talking head" flash-back technique (which he modified as his style changed) for the 1978 Silver Surfer Graphic Novel, his last comics work done in conjunction with Stan Lee.

Kirby's career comes symbolically full-circle, on this cover for 1976's FF Annual #11 (1976), as he depicts Timely Comics' "big three"—Captain America, Sub-Mariner, and the Human Torch—with the FF.

AFTERWORD

by Mark Alexander

When compiling a book like this one, discovers why most authors prefer to write fiction.

Wading through the quagmire of contradictory information to get to the truth (or what's left of it) can be utterly exasperating. After six solid months of studying the Atlas period, several examples could be sighted where knowledgeable sources disagree on the company's annals and timelines. These events transpired in the 1950s, but they seem almost as obscure as ancient history.

The exasperation multiplies when the old gents from Timely Comics are questioned about any specific year. Obviously, time and age will distort a person's remembrances. In interview after interview, many of the Timely/Atlas crew tended to contradict each other. For example, some of the vets from Goodman's staff claim the Timely Bullpen was shut down as early as 1947. Others remember themselves being there as late as 1959.

In the end it was decided to only use dates which were compiled by comic book historians. Individuals like Tom Lammers, Dr. Vassallo and Jim Vadeboncoeur have more insight into the chronology of Timely/Atlas events than the people who lived them. Simply, the historians have researched those dates more meticulously than the men and women who made those dates worth researching.

Readers who aren't particularly intrigued by the Timely/Atlas era may find chapters 1 through 3 somewhat redundant to the Lee/Kirby "Wonder Years," but here's the thing: In order to understand how Goodman, Lee and Kirby all ended up in the same place in that fateful spring of 1961 when *Fantastic Four* was conceived, one needs to know the pre-1961 backgrounds of those three men. And when rooting out the Marvel phenomenon, it's essential to understand that Atlas was once the largest comics company that ever existed. When it self-destructed in 1957, it left Goodman with a greatly scaled-down operation. In the years immediately after the Atlas implosion, Independent News held Goodman's comics at a level where it was feasible for one man (Stan Lee) to actually control the content of all the books. Stan couldn't get bigger, which had been Goodman's goal for the past seventeen years, so instead he got better.

(top right) Cover of FF *#108, which featured remnants of an unused Kirby story originally planned for #102.*
(above) While Kirby wouldn't return to Fantastic Four *in the 1970s, he did several issues' covers, such as #190 shown here (1978).*

In one of the Stan Lee/FF interviews conducted for this book, we got an interesting tidbit from Stan the Man which didn't seem to fit anywhere in the main text, so it will be reported here. One of the most intriguing things about Lee's FF #1 plot-synopsis is that, near the end of the paragraph about Sue's invisibility, Stan addresses the artist, and a word is typed out before Lee typed "Jack." Over the years many historians, including Roy Tomas, have wondered if Lee had originally considered a different illustrator for the strip other than Kirby.

When we asked Stan about this, he was quite adamant: *"Jack was our top superhero action artist at the time. He was always my first choice for any new superhero book if he had the time to do it."*

Regarding the **AT A GLANCE** pages, instead of using the forum to relate a blow-by-blow synopsis of each issue, it was decided to examine the more abstract and peripheral aspects of the stories. Anyone reading this text is probably familiar with the storylines already. Anyone who wants a dry, detailed summation of FF #1-102 should pick up back issues of *The Official Marvel Index to the Fantastic Four*. High-grade copies sell for less than a buck apiece.

Because *Fantastic Four #108* (March 1971) was an unfinished Lee/Kirby effort, the Lee/Kirby/Buscema/Romita hodgepodge which resulted was not addressed in the **AT A GLANCE** section. The author doesn't consider it to be a genuine branch of the Lee/Kirby *Fantastic Four* omnibus. The same applies to *Fantastic Four: The Lost Adventure* (April 2008), with or without the missing page that later surfaced.

Next, with all due respect to Mark Evanier, whose information contributed enormously to this book, I tend to disagree with his opinion that if Kirby had received a decent contract from Marvel in the late 1960s, he and Stan could have produced another 100 issues of worthwhile *Fantastic Four* stories.

If the King had received an acceptable contract, and recommenced contributing great characters and concepts, I think it would have all played out the same. Stan would have continued to change Jack's stories, Jack still would've gotten pissed off, and his enthusiasm would have eventually waned. By 1970, Jack Kirby needed to create his own stories and dialogue. He needed to tell his tales *his* way. At that point he could no longer suppress his aspirations to write, or have Lee override them.

Undoubtedly, Jack and Stan could have produced another 100 issues of kitsch, where the FF battle mediocre villains and Dr. Doom returns 30 times, but comic fandom is probably better off that it didn't happen. It would have become an agonizing endurance test for the creators and readers alike.

Without going into too much detail, during the writing of this text the author acquired an entirely new admiration for Stan Lee. It's my gut feeling that Stan had more to do with the initial genesis of the FF than Kirby; and then later, the issues after *FF #38* seemed to signal an emerging predominance of Kirby-driven storylines. Jack's art in *FF #1* and 2 doesn't look like the King initially had much enthusiasm for the series. It gets noticeably better in *FF #3*, by which time Kirby would have known from the fan letters that the book was a hit.

(this page) Lee and Kirby in the 1970s.

So here's the paradox: all the Lee-bashing Kirby-centric zealots who claim that Stan practically rode Jack's coattails to fame and fortune *weren't there at the time*. All the Marvel insiders that we interviewed—who *were* there—are quite adamant that the "Anti-Stan" legions have a warped view of reality.

Stan Lee is a National Treasure folks. We're gonna miss him when he's gone.

At this point I have a confession to make. Although I've no proof, my instincts tell me the story about Martin Goodman being a hobo in 1929 is just another comic history myth like the 1001 tall tales which surround Harry Donenfeld, the founder of DC Comics.

The only source of this rumor was Jerry Perles, Martin's life-long friend and legal advisor. No book on comics has ever questioned the story, but it simply doesn't ring true. The idea that someone could be a tramp one minute and a publishing mogul the next is just too hard to swallow. As Hemmingway once wrote, "It isn't the sort of thing one does." It was kept in because it gives the story flavor, and who knows; it *might* be true.

Isn't suspension of disbelief the key to enjoying comic books in the first place?

In closing, when you look back, you always make things better than they really were. That's a cliché by now. But with that in mind, I'd still say the 1960s Marvel Age of comics was an immensely exciting era to live through. Comics were better than they'd ever been; better than they're ever likely to be again.

I consider myself truly blessed to have seen it all unfold through the eyes of a young boy who loved superheroes.

If anyone knows more about Martin Goodman's past, please write me at P.O. Box 4, Oreana, IL 62554. All correspondences will be answered. Comments and criticisms about this book are most welcome as well.

Mark Alexander, May 2011

[Editor's Note: In light of Mark's passing before the publication of this book, please send your comments to the publisher instead at twomorrow@aol.com] ★

SOURCE NOTES

Since the Marvel Age was an era of relatively recent history, many of the participants in the events described were available to provide firsthand accounts. However, writing under the grim specter of deadline pressure made it necessary for the author to enlist the aid of the inimitable Paula Ruffini (lead guitarist of Modesty Blaze) to conduct several e-mail and snail-mail interviews for this book. Paula's efforts in this regard proved invaluable.

Equally invaluable were the contributions of Mark Evanier. The amount of e-mail info he was willing to provide via Rhonda Rade was generous beyond belief; especially when one considers his intensive writing schedule and the deadlines that go along with it.

Besides Mark's e-mail info, an enormous amount of material in this book regarding Marvel Comics circa 1965-66 was gleaned from Evanier's *Jack Kirby Collector* columns. Anyone who's interested in Jack Kirby—or comics in general—should purchase any book that Mark writes or co-authors. He is, and will remain, the world's leading authority on The King of Comics.

Chapter I: *The Knock-off Champion:*

1. Physical description of Martin Goodman provided by Flo Steinberg in a letter to Paula Ruffini. Further details were gleaned from the Martin Goodman Wikipedia bio.

2. Details regarding the ANC/Hearst rivalry were culled from *The Chief: the Life of William Randolph Hearst* by David Nasaw. Supplementary information was acquired from the Wikipedia bios of Moe and Max Annenberg.

3. "If you get a title"—Martin Goodman quote from *Five Fabulous Decades of the World's Greatest Comics* by Les Daniels.

4. Descriptions of the Timely Comics West 42 St. offices were gathered from *Excelsior! The Amazing Life of Stan Lee* by Stan Lee and George Mair. Additional details were taken from *The Comic Book Makers* by Joe Simon with Jim Simon, and the Marie Severin interview conducted by Jon B. Cooke for *TJKC* #18.

5. "The next time I see that little s.o.b. I'm gonna kill him" –quoted from the Joe Simon panel at the 1998 San Diego Comicon International. Transcribed by Glen Musial for *TJKC* #25.

Chapter II: *Winds of Change: The 1950s*

1. Description of the Timely Comics Empire State Building headquarters was gleaned from Marie Severin's interview conducted by Jon B. Cooke in *TJKC* #18. Further details were taken from the Wikipedia bio on Valerie Barclay and interviews with ex-Timely employees that were found on various internet sites.

2. "Rat Rico"—from the Wikipedia bio on Don Rico.

3. The firing of the Timely Bullpen tied to a change in New York State law was revealed in an exclusive 2010 e-mail from Mark Evanier to Paula Ruffini.

4. "They felt they could save some money"—Gene Colan quote from *Five Fabulous Decades of the World's Greatest Comics* by Les Daniels.

5. "Artists who I have interviewed from that time period" – Dr. Michael J. Vassallo quote from an exclusive 2010 e-mail to Paula Ruffini.

6. "When Martin learned of all the material" –Stan Lee quote from *Excelsior! The Amazing Life of Stan Lee.*

7. Description of the Atlas Park Avenue offices were culled from Stan Lee's quote in *There Goes The Neighborhood* by Martin Bartolomeo, published in *TJKC* #53. Additional details were gleaned from a picture of Stan in his Park Avenue office which Flo helped us identify.

8. "the first with anything"—Stan Lee quote from *Tales To Astonish* by Ronin Ro.

Subhead: *Abandon Ship*

1. "fix those bastards" –Bill Gaines' quote from *The Ten-Cent Plague* by David Hajdu.

2. Description of Simon & Kirby watching the Senate hearings—ibid.

3. "Stupid, stupid, stupid"—Joe Simon quote ibid.

4. "We couldn't get a decent distributor" "—Joe Simon quote from *The Comic Book Makers.*

5. "rarely publicized" –Stan Lee quote from *Excelsior! The Amazing Life of Stan Lee.*

6. Details about Monroe Froelich persuading Goodman to close Atlas News are from *The Great Atlas Implosion* by Jim Vadeboncoeur, published in *TJKC* #18.

7. Details regarding the lawsuit against ANC were gleaned from *Tales of the Implosion* by Thomas G. Lammers, and from e-mail correspondences conducted in 2010 with author Gerard Jones.

8. "a closet"—Gene Colan quote from Five *Fabulous Decades of the World's Greatest Comics* by Les Daniels.

9. "They were in shock" –Stan Lee quote from *Excelsior! The Amazing Life of Stan Lee.*

10. "Stan called me"—Joe Sinnott quote from *Alter Ego* #26, July 2003. The specific date of this call was culled from Joe Sinnott's 1957 work-log, which was originally reported by Dr. Vassallo.

11. "I thought I would never be in comics again" – John Romita quote from a 5/19/98 interview published in *The Comic Book Artists.*

12. "That was the real low point" –Dick Ayers quote from the Ayers interview conducted by James Cassara in *TJKC* #13.

13. "the dark days"—Stan Lee quote from *Excelsior! The Amazing Life of Stan Lee.*

14. Bruce Jay Friedman's opinion of the relationship between Stan and Goodman was gleaned from *Stan Lee: the Rise and Fall of The American Comic Book* by Jordan Raphael and Tom Spurgeon.

Chapter IV: *Genesis*

1. "It was the start" –Roy Thomas quote from *TJKC* #33.

2. Sol Harrison's take on how Goodman learned about the JLA's sales figures was reported by Michael Uslan in a letter published in *Alter Ego* #43 (Dec. 2004).

3. "largely apocryphal"—Martin Goodman quote from *Stan Lee the Rise and Fall of the American Comic Book* by Jordan Raphael and Tom Spurgeon.

4. "You know Stan," –Stan Lee quote reported by Will Murray in *The Formative Fantastic Four,* published in *TJKC* #54.

5. "After I had nailed down the concept" –Stan Lee quote from *Fantastic Firsts*

6. Goodman's aborted plan to replace *Fantastic Four* with a Western title was confirmed by Mark Evanier in an exclusive 2010 e-mail to Paula Ruffini.

7. "an outright lie" –Jack Kirby quote from an interview conducted by Gary Groth for *The Comics Journal* #134 (Feb. 1990).

8. "In the early days"—Joe Sinnott quote from the interview conducted by Jim Amash for *TJKC* #36.

9. "It wasn't until Marvel"—Gil Kane quote from the interview conducted by Jon B. Cooke for *TJKC* #21.

10. "You can't expect a guy" –quote from Stan Lee's introduction to *The Photo-Journal Guide To Marvel Comics Vol. 3* by Ernst Gerber.

11. "They were worried"—Jack Kirby quote from *The Art of Jack Kirby* by Ray Wyman Jr. and Catherine Hohlfeld.

12. "It was a losing field"—Jack Kirby quote from *Five Fabulous Decades of the World's Greatest Comics* by Les Daniels.

13. "Doc Savage"—Stan Lee quote from *Marvel Comics In The 1960s* by Pierre Comtois.

14. "A very safe bet" – Stan Lee quote from *Secrets Of The Fantastic Four* by Will Murray published in *TJKC* #47.

15. "It all fits too neatly"—Stan Lee quote ibid.

16. "Kirby's greatest creation"—Joe Sinnott quote from *Jack Kirby's Heroes and Villains (Black Magic Edition)*.

17. "When I first drew the Thing"—Jack Kirby quote ibid.

Chapter V: *The Early Years*

1. Greg Theakston's theory on the early *Fantastic Four* was gleaned from *Tales To Astonish* by Ronin Ro.

2. "There's no way we could have snuck it in"—Stan Lee quote from an exclusive 2010 e-mail interview conducted by the author.

3. "655 Madison Avenue"—Flo Steinberg quote from an exclusive 2010 correspondence to Paula Ruffini. Descriptions of Goodman's 655 Marvel offices were provided by Flo, as were detailed maps of all the 1960s Marvel offices.

4. Details regarding Marvel's use of the U.S. Postal Service were provided by Flo Steinberg in an exclusive correspondence to Paula Ruffini. Additional info was gleaned from the Dick Ayers interview conducted by James Cassara for *TJKC #13*.

5. "At Magazine Management"—Dorothy Gallagher quote from the Marvel Comics Database bio of Martin Goodman.

6. "They always wanted to have tours"—Flo Steinberg quote from *Five Fabulous Decades of the World's Greatest Comics* by Les Daniels.

Chapter VI: *Momentus*

1. "revoltin' development" origin provided by Gerard Jones in an exclusive 2010 e-mail to Paula Ruffini.

2. "The pinnacle" –Stan Lee quote from *Five Fabulous Decades of the World's Greatest Comics* by Les Daniels.

3. "Nobody expected it"—Flo Steinberg quote from *Five Fabulous Decades of the World's Greatest Comics* by Les Daniels.

4. Descriptions of the 625 Madison Ave. Marvel offices were provided by Flo Steinberg in an exclusive 2010 correspondence to Paula Ruffini. Additional insights were gleaned from an exclusive hand-drawn map provided by Roy Thomas.

5. "Goodman started pressuring Stan"—Leon Lazarus quote from the Leon Lazarus Wikipedia bio.

Chapter VII: *Apotheosis*

1. Details on how Vince Colletta became the inker of *Fantastic Four* were culled from Mark Evanier's "Jack F.A.Q.s." column in *TJKC #34*.

2. "I devoted as much time" –quote from Stan Lee's introduction to *The Photo-Journal Guide To Marvel Comics Vol. 3* by Ernst Gerber.

3. "I created the Inhumans"—Jack Kirby quote from a 1976 edition of *The Nostalgia Journal*.

4. The author's opinions regarding *Fantastic Four's* ordinary human moments and the book's extraordinary 1966 supporting characters were greatly enhanced by a tremendous article published in *TJKC #9* called *The World's Greatest Comic Magazine!* by John Shingler.

Chapter VIII: *Decline*

1. "I think when Stan"—Martin Goodman quote from *Secrets Of The Fantastic Four* by Will Murray published in *TJKC #47*.

2. "We still needed a lot of young kids" –Stan Lee quote from the 1975 San Diego Comics Con Stan Lee panel. Transcribed in *TJKC #18*.

3. Description of the 635 Madison Avenue Marvel offices provided by Flo Steinberg in an exclusive 2010 correspondence to Paula Ruffini. Flo drew a map as well.

4. "I was just tired" – Flo Steinberg quote from the Flo Steinberg Wikipedia bio.

5. "I think the stupidest thing Marvel ever did"—Marie Severin quote ibid.

6. "I had worked for Timely/Atlas"—Joe Sinnott quote from an exclusive 2010 e-mail to Paula Ruffini.

This Is A Plot?

1. "It's only later"—Roy Thomas quote from a 1997 interview conducted by Jim Amash published in *TJKC #18*.

2. "some guy at the office" –Jack Kirby quote from an interview conducted by Gary Groth for *The Comics Journal #134* (Feb. 1990).

3. "70% Jack"—Dr. Michael J. Vassallo quote from an exclusive 2010 e-mail to Paula Ruffini.

4. Mark Evanier's revelation regarding the original *FF #57-60* plot-outlines was relayed in an exclusive 2011 e-mail to Rhonda Rade.

5. "I don't ever remember Jack *not* coming in"—Flo Steinberg quote from an exclusive 2010 correspondence to Paula Ruffini.

6. "We got to listen" –Mark Evanier quote from Evanier's "Jack F.A.Q.s." column in *TJKC #49*.

7. "I believe that Lee and Kirby created the FF together"—Mike Gartland quote from an exclusive 2010 e-mail to the author.

8. "In the beginning" –Stan Lee quote from *The Stan Lee Interview* conducted by Jon B. Cooke for *TJKC #33*.

AT A GLANCE *FF #13:*
"We're gonna do more apes"—Irwin Donenfeld quote from *The Comic Book Heroes* by Will Jacobs and Gerard Jones.

AT A GLANCE *FF #25:*
"Can you see anything"—Mark Evanier quote from Evanier's "Jack F.A.Q.s." column in *TJKC #46*.

AT A GLANCE *FF #24:*
"I thought they were a visual distraction"—Joe Sinnott quote from the interview conducted by Jim Amash for *No Ordinary Joe* published in *TJKC #38*.

AT A GLANCE *FF #29:*
"We would fight anywhere" –Jack Kirby quote from *Childhood Stories Part* 1 by Ray Wyman Jr., published in *TJKC #45*.

AT A GLANCE *FF #33:*
"Collages were another way" –Jack Kirby quote reprinted in *Kirby FIVE-OH! Celebrating 50 Years of the King of Comics*.

AT A GLANCE *FF #48:*
"When I created Galactus"—Jack Kirby quote from *The Lost Kirby Interview* conducted by Annie Baron-Carvais published in *TJKC #32*.

AT A GLANCE *FF #50:*
"The Silver Surfer looked so noble"—Stan Lee quote from his intro to *Marvel Masterworks Vol. 25*.

AT A GLANCE *FF #51:*
"I didn't know" –quote from Stan Lee's introduction to *The Photo-Journal Guide To Marvel Comics Vol. 3* by Ernst Gerber.

AT A GLANCE *FF #68:*
"Make the stories simpler"—Martin Goodman as quoted by Stan Lee, during the 1975 San Diego Comics Con Stan Lee panel. Transcribed in *TJKC #18*.

AT A GLANCE *FF #77:*
"The finest series I know"—Stan Lee quote from *The Comic Book Heroes* by Will Jacobs and Gerard Jones.

AT A GLANCE *FF Annual #6:*
"It was the first comic book story"—Stan Lee quote from the intro to *Fantastic Four Vol. 8 Marvel Masterworks* series.

AT A GLANCE *FF #82:*
"too homosexual" –quote from *Tales To Astonish* by Ronin Ro.

AT A GLANCE *FF #92:*
Mike Gartland's hypothesis regarding the FF's lack of uniforms (in the final Kirby issues) was culled in an exclusive 2010 e-mail from Gartland to the author.

AT A GLANCE *FF #97:*
"Maybe we should do a *Creature From the Black Lagoon* story!" –this is *not* an actual Martin Goodman quote: It was fictionalized by the author to make a (hopefully) amusing point; and it was clearly stated as such.

CHARACTER PROFILE: *Karnak the Shatterer*
"It was a judo-type uniform"—Jack Kirby quote from *The Comics Journal Library Volume One: Jack Kirby*.

CHARACTER PROFILE: *Galactus*
"I told him I wanted a character called Galactus" –Stan Lee quote from the Stan Lee interview conducted by Jon B. Cooke for *TJKC #33*.

CHARACTER PROFILE: *The Black Panther*
Stan's regret over the common name shared by T'Challa and the 1960s militant political party was reported in *Marvel Universe* by Peter Sanderson.

POSTSCRIPT

by Cheryl (Alexander) Urbanczyk

It was a beautiful day in early September of 1964 in the city of Milwaukee, Wisconsin. My brother Mark, my Aunt June and I were standing on the corner waiting for the light to change. We heard the sirens—loud and coming down the street in front of us. I expected to see fire engines, but instead it was lots of Milwaukee motorcycle police riding in front and on the sides of four shiny black limousines. The Beatles had arrived! We knew it was them because we lived by the airport and the newspaper had said they were arriving at Mitchell Field. Of course the windows were tinted black and we never saw their faces, but that scene would be permanently etched in our minds forever.

My brother was nine and I was eleven, so of course we wouldn't be going to the Beatles Concert. We were still young and protected. We lived in a quiet neighborhood at the very end of the city. The railroad tracks were behind our house, so the only cars that came down our block were of the people that lived there. At night the kids took over the street. There was always a softball game going on or Hide 'n' Seek or some other neighborhood activity. We spent our summers swimming at the county pool, building forts, collecting bugs, and every Saturday morning, all the neighborhood kids walked to the Saturday Matinee to watch Godzilla take over Tokyo, and maybe a Bugs Bunny cartoon or two.

And then there was my brother and his comic books. My mother swore he knew how to read at three years old, because he loved to have people read to him. Ordinary books didn't do—he had been hooked on comic books at an early age. What could compare to all those bright colored pages of superheroes saving Manhattan, or the universe, or wherever earthlings needed saving?

Mark loved to draw, and copied all the pictures of the superheroes. He sent pictures to the guys at Marvel and to his delight they sent back postcards. "Keep up the good work, Mark" one said and was signed by Stan Lee. He did keep up the work—his love for art and comic books stayed with him. He loved music too, and as soon as he got his first guitar, he learned every Beatles song he had time to learn, and played in local bands most of his life.

Those happy childhood days soon passed. My first year of high school was 1968—the most violent year in the history of the United States. At age 14, I was already hearing about race riots, the assassinations of Robert Kennedy and Dr. Martin Luther King, and already knew people that had older brothers going off to war in Vietnam. The end of the sixties changed America forever. I'm not saying that those years were all bad—we had Woodstock and hippies and Jimi Hendrix, but the damage was done; the true innocence of childhood was lost forever.

My brother passed away before this book came into print. He did, however, know that it was being published, and that made him extremely proud. I am so happy that he can share with you the story behind the scenes of Marvel Comics' Silver Age. I'm sure it will take you back to a very happy time in history—the Fab 4 and the Fantastic Four—a time that may never be equaled again. ★

(above) Author Mark Alexander in 1964 with his uncle and favorite comic book, Fantastic Four *#26.*

THE JACK KIRBY COLLECTOR

The JACK KIRBY COLLECTOR magazine (edited by JOHN MORROW) celebrates the life and career of the "King" of comics through **INTERVIEWS WITH KIRBY** and his contemporaries, **FEATURE ARTICLES, RARE AND UNSEEN**

DIGITAL EDITIONS AVAILABLE FOR ONLY $1.95 - $3.95

KIRBY ART, plus regular columns by **MARK EVANIER** and others, and presentation of **KIRBY'S UNINKED PENCILS** from the 1960s-80s (from photocopies preserved in the **KIRBY ARCHIVES**). Now in **OVERSIZED TABLOID FORMAT**, it showcases Kirby's amazing art even larger!

Go online for an ULTIMATE BUNDLE, with issues at HALF-PRICE!

KIRBY COLLECTOR #31
FIRST TABLOID-SIZE ISSUE! MARK EVANIER's new column, interviews with KURT BUSIEK and JOSÉ LADRONN, NEAL ADAMS on Kirby, Giant-Man overview, Kirby's best 2-page spreads, 2000 Kirby Tribute Panel (MARK EVANIER, GENE COLAN, MARIE SEVERIN, ROY THOMAS, and TRACY & JEREMY KIRBY), huge Kirby pencils! Wraparound KIRBY/ADAMS cover!

(84-page tabloid magazine) **$9.95**
(Digital Edition) **$3.95**

KIRBY COLLECTOR #32
KIRBY'S LEAST-KNOWN WORK! MARK EVANIER on the Fourth World, unfinished THE HORDE novel, long-lost KIRBY INTERVIEW from France, update to the KIRBY CHECKLIST, pencil gallery of Kirby's least-known work (including THE PRISONER, BLACK HOLE, IN THE DAYS OF THE MOB, TRUE DIVORCE CASES), westerns, and more! KIRBY/LADRONN cover!

(84-page tabloid magazine) **$9.95**
(Digital Edition) **$3.95**

KIRBY COLLECTOR #33
FANTASTIC FOUR ISSUE! Gallery of FF pencils at tabloid size, MARK EVANIER on the FF Cartoon series, interviews with STAN LEE and ERIK LARSEN, JOE SINNOTT salute, the HUMAN TORCH in STRANGE TALES, origins of Kirby Krackle, interviews with nearly EVERY WRITER AND ARTIST who worked on the FF after Kirby, & more! KIRBY/LARSEN and KIRBY/TIMM covers!

(84-page tabloid magazine) **$9.95**
(Digital Edition) **$3.95**

KIRBY COLLECTOR #34
FIGHTING AMERICANS! MARK EVANIER on 1960s Marvel inkers, SHIELD, Losers, and Green Arrow overviews, INFANTINO interview on Simon & Kirby, KIRBY interview, Captain America PENCIL ART GALLERY, PHILIPPE DRUILLET interview, JOE SIMON and ALEX TOTH speak, unseen BIG GAME HUNTER and YOUNG ABE LINCOLN Kirby concepts! KIRBY and KIRBY/TOTH covers!

(84-page tabloid magazine) **$9.95**
(Digital Edition) **$3.95**

KIRBY COLLECTOR #35
GREAT ESCAPES! MISTER MIRACLE pencil art gallery, MARK EVANIER, MARSHALL ROGERS & MICHAEL CHABON interviews, comparing Kirby and Houdini's backgrounds, analysis of "Himon," 2001 Kirby Tribute Panel (WILL EISNER, JOHN BUSCEMA, JOHN ROMITA, MIKE ROYER, & JOHNNY CARSON) & more! KIRBY/MARSHALL ROGERS and KIRBY/STEVE RUDE covers!

(84-page tabloid magazine) **$9.95**
(Digital Edition) **$3.95**

KIRBY COLLECTOR #36
THOR ISSUE! Never-seen KIRBY interview, JOE SINNOTT and JOHN ROMITA JR. on their Thor work, MARK EVANIER, extensive THOR and TALES OF ASGARD coverage, a look at the "real" Norse gods, 40 pages of KIRBY THOR PENCILS, including a Kirby Art Gallery at TABLOID SIZE, with pin-ups, covers, and more! KIRBY covers inked by MIKE ROYER and TREVOR VON EEDEN!

(84-page tabloid magazine) **$9.95**
(Digital Edition) **$3.95**

KIRBY COLLECTOR #37
"HOW TO DRAW COMICS THE KIRBY WAY!" MIKE ROYER interview on how he inks Jack's work, HUGE GALLERY tracing the evolution of Jack's style, new column on OBSCURE KIRBY WORK, MARK EVANIER, special sections on Jack's TECHNIQUE AND INFLUENCES, comparing STAN LEE's writing to JACK's, and more! Two COLOR UNPUBLISHED KIRBY COVERS!

(84-page tabloid magazine) **$9.95**
(Digital Edition) **$3.95**

KIRBY COLLECTOR #38
"HOW TO DRAW COMICS THE KIRBY WAY!" PART 2: JOE SINNOTT on how he inks Jack's work, list of the art in the KIRBY ARCHIVES, MARK EVANIER, special sections on Jack's technique and influences, SPEND A DAY WITH KIRBY (with JACK DAVIS, GULACY, HERNANDEZ BROS., and RUDE) and more! Two UNPUBLISHED KIRBY COVERS!

(84-page tabloid magazine) **$9.95**
(Digital Edition) **$3.95**

KIRBY COLLECTOR #39
FAN FAVORITES! Covering Kirby's work on HULK, INHUMANS, and SILVER SURFER, TOP PROS pick favorite Kirby covers, Kirby ENTERTAINMENT TONIGHT interview, MARK EVANIER, 2002 Kirby Tribute Panel (DICK AYERS, TODD McFARLANE, PAUL LEVITZ, HERB TRIMPE), pencil art gallery, and more! Kirby covers inked by MIKE ALLRED and P. CRAIG RUSSELL!

(84-page tabloid magazine) **$9.95**
(Digital Edition) **$3.95**

KIRBY COLLECTOR #40
WORLD THAT'S COMING! KAMANDI and OMAC spotlight, 2003 Kirby Tribute Panel (WENDY PINI, MICHAEL CHABON, STAN GOLDBERG, SAL BUSCEMA, LARRY LIEBER, and STAN LEE), P. CRAIG RUSSELL interview, MARK EVANIER, NEW COLUMN analyzing Jack's visual shorthand, pencil art gallery, and more! Kirby covers inked by ERIK LARSEN and REEDMAN!

(84-page tabloid magazine) **$9.95**
(Digital Edition) **$3.95**

KIRBY COLLECTOR #41
1970s MARVEL WORK! Coverage of '70s work from Captain America to Eternals to Machine Man, DICK GIORDANO & MARK SHULTZ interviews, MARK EVANIER, 2004 Kirby Tribute Panel (STEVE RUDE, DAVE GIBBONS, WALTER SIMONSON, and PAUL RYAN), pencil art gallery, unused 1962 HULK #6 KIRBY PENCILS, and more! Kirby covers inked by GIORDANO and SCHULTZ!

(84-page tabloid magazine) **$9.95**
(Digital Edition) **$3.95**

KIRBY COLLECTOR #42
1970s DC WORK! Coverage of Jimmy Olsen, FF movie set visit, overview of all Newsboy Legion stories, KEVIN NOWLAN and MURPHY ANDERSON on inking Jack, never-seen interview with Kirby, MARK EVANIER on Kirby's covers, Bongo Comics' Kirby ties, complete '40s gangster story, pencil art gallery, and more! Kirby covers inked by NOWLAN and ANDERSON!

(84-page tabloid magazine) **$9.95**
(Digital Edition) **$3.95**

KIRBY COLLECTOR #43
KIRBY AWARD WINNERS! STEVE SHERMAN and others sharing memories and never-seen art from JACK & ROZ, a never-published 1966 interview with KIRBY, MARK EVANIER on VINCE COLLETTA, pencils-to-Sinnott inks comparison of TALES OF SUSPENSE #93, and more! Covers by KIRBY (Jack's original '70s SILVER STAR CONCEPT ART) and KIRBY/SINNOTT!

(84-page tabloid magazine) **$9.95**
(Digital Edition) **$3.95**

KIRBY COLLECTOR #44

KIRBY'S MYTHOLOGICAL CHARACTERS! Coverage of DEMON, THOR, & GALACTUS, interview with KIRBY, MARK EVANIER, pencil art galleries of the Demon and other mythological characters, two never-reprinted BLACK MAGIC stories, interview with Kirby Award winner DAVID SCHWARTZ and F4 screenwriter MIKE FRANCE, and more! Kirby cover inked by MATT WAGNER!

(84-page tabloid magazine) **$9.95**
(Digital Edition) **$3.95**

KIRBY COLLECTOR #45

Jack's vision of PAST AND FUTURE, with a never-seen KIRBY interview, a new interview with son NEAL KIRBY, MARK EVANIER's column, two pencil galleries, two complete '50s stories, Jack's first script, Kirby Tribute Panel (with EVANIER, KATZ, SHAW!, and SHERMAN), plus an unpublished CAPTAIN 3-D cover, inked by BILL BLACK and converted into 3-D by RAY ZONE!

(84-page tabloid magazine) **$9.95**
(Digital Edition) **$3.95**

KIRBY COLLECTOR #46

Focus on NEW GODS, FOREVER PEOPLE, and DARKSEID! Includes a rare interview with KIRBY, MARK EVANIER's column, FOURTH WORLD pencil art galleries (including Kirby's redesigns for SUPER POWERS), two 1950s stories, a new Kirby Darkseid front cover inked by MIKE ROYER, a Kirby Forever People back cover inked by JOHN BYRNE, and more!

(84-page tabloid magazine) **$9.95**
(Digital Edition) **$3.95**

KIRBY COLLECTOR #47

KIRBY'S SUPER TEAMS, from kid gangs and the Challengers, to Fantastic Four, X-Men, and Super Powers, with unseen 1960s Marvel art, a rare KIRBY interview, MARK EVANIER's column, two pencil art galleries, complete 1950s story, author JONATHAN LETHEM on his Kirby influence, interview with JOHN ROMITA, JR. on his Eternals work, and more!

(84-page tabloid magazine) **SOLD OUT**
(Digital Edition) **$3.95**

KIRBY COLLECTOR #48

KIRBYTECH ISSUE, spotlighting Jack's high-tech concepts, from Iron Man's armor and Machine Man, to the Negative Zone and beyond! Includes a rare KIRBY interview, MARK EVANIER's column, two pencil art galleries, complete 1950s story, TOM SCIOLI interview, Kirby Tribute Panel (with ADAMS, PÉREZ, and ROMITA), and covers inked by TERRY AUSTIN and TOM SCIOLI!

(84-page tabloid magazine) **$9.95**
(Digital Edition) **$3.95**

KIRBY COLLECTOR #49

WARRIORS, spotlighting Thor (with a look at hidden messages in BILL EVERETT's Thor inks), Sgt. Fury, Challengers of the Unknown, Losers, and others! Includes a rare KIRBY interview, interviews with JERRY ORDWAY and GRANT MORRISON, MARK EVANIER's column, pencil art gallery, a complete 1950s story, wraparound Thor cover inked by JERRY ORDWAY and more!

(84-page tabloid magazine) **$9.95**
(Digital Edition) **$3.95**

KIRBY FIVE-OH!
CELEBRATING 50 YEARS OF THE "KING" OF COMICS

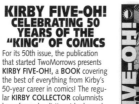

For its 50th issue, the publication that started TwoMorrows presents KIRBY FIVE-OH!, a BOOK covering the best of everything from Kirby's 50-year career in comics! The regular KIRBY COLLECTOR columnists have formed a distinguished panel of experts to choose and examine: The BEST KIRBY STORY published each year from 1938-1987! The BEST COVERS from each decade! Jack's 50 BEST UNUSED PIECES OF ART! His 50 BEST CHARACTER DESIGNS! And profiles of, and commentary by, the 50 PEOPLE MOST INFLUENCED BY KIRBY'S WORK! Plus there's a 50-PAGE GALLERY of Kirby's powerful RAW PENCIL ART, and a DELUXE COLOR SECTION of photos and finished art from throughout his entire half-century oeuvre. This TABLOID-SIZED TRADE PAPERBACK features a previously unseen Kirby Superman cover inked by "DC: The New Frontier" artist DARWYN COOKE, and an introduction by MARK EVANIER, helping make this the ultimate retrospective on the career of the "King" of comics! Takes the place of JACK KIRBY COLLECTOR #50.

(168-page tabloid-size trade paperback) **$19.95**
(Digital Edition) **$5.95**
ISBN: 9781893905894
Diamond Order Code: FEB084186

KIRBY COLLECTOR #51

Bombastic EVERYTHING GOES issue, with a wealth of great submissions that couldn't be pigeonholed into a "theme" issue! Includes a rare KIRBY interview, new interviews with JIM LEE and ADAM HUGHES, MARK EVANIER's column, huge pencil art galleries, a complete Golden Age Kirby story, two COLOR UNPUBLISHED KIRBY COVERS, and more!

(84-page tabloid magazine) **$9.95**
(Digital Edition) **$3.95**

KIRBY COLLECTOR #52

Spotlights Kirby's most obscure work: an UNUSED THOR STORY, BRUCE LEE comic, animation work, stage play, unaltered pages from KAMANDI, DEMON, DESTROYER DUCK, and more, including a feature examining the last page of his final issue of various series BEFORE EDITORIAL TAMPERING (with lots of surprises)! Color Kirby cover inked by DON HECK!

(84-page tabloid magazine) **$9.95**
(Digital Edition) **$3.95**

KIRBY COLLECTOR #53

THE MAGIC OF STAN & JACK! New interview with STAN LEE, walking tour of New York where Lee & Kirby lived and worked, re-evaluation of the "Lost" FF #108 story (including a new page that just surfaced), "What If Jack Hadn't Left Marvel In 1970?," plus MARK EVANIER's regular column, a Kirby pencil art gallery, a complete Golden Age Kirby story, and more, behind a color Kirby cover inked by GEORGE PÉREZ!

(84-page tabloid magazine) **$10.95**
(Digital Edition) **$3.95**

KIRBY COLLECTOR #54

STAN & JACK PART TWO! More on the co-creators of the Marvel Universe, final interview (and cover inks) by GEORGE TUSKA, differences between KIRBY and DITKO'S approaches, WILL MURRAY on the origin of the FF, the mystery of Marvel cover dates, MARK EVANIER's regular column, a Kirby pencil art gallery, a complete Golden Age Kirby story, plus Kirby back cover inked by JOE SINNOTT!

(84-page tabloid magazine) **$10.95**
(Digital Edition) **$3.95**

KIRBY COLLECTOR #55

"Kirby Goes To Hollywood!" SERGIO ARAGONÉS and MELL LAZARUS recall Kirby's BOB NEWHART TV show cameo, comparing the recent STAR WARS films to New Gods, RUBY & SPEARS interviewed, Jack's encounters with FRANK ZAPPA, PAUL McCARTNEY, and JOHN LENNON, MARK EVANIER's regular column, a Kirby pencil art gallery, a Golden Age Kirby story, and more! Kirby cover inked by PAUL SMITH!

(84-page tabloid magazine) **$10.95**
(Digital Edition) **$3.95**

KIRBY COLLECTOR #56

"Unfinished Sagas"—series, stories, and arcs Kirby never finished. TRUE DIVORCE CASES, RAAM THE MAN MOUNTAIN, KOBRA, DINGBATS, a complete story from SOUL LOVE, complete Boy Explorers story, two Kirby Tribute Panels, MARK EVANIER and other regular columnists, pencil art galleries, and more, with Kirby's "Galaxy Green" cover inked by ROYER, and the unseen cover for SOUL LOVE #1!

(84-page tabloid magazine) **$10.95**
(Digital Edition) **$3.95**

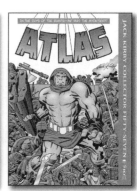

KIRBY COLLECTOR #57

"Legendary Kirby"—how Jack put his spin on classic folklore! TONY ISABELLA on SATAN'S SIX (with Kirby's unseen layouts), Biblical inspirations of DEVIL DINOSAUR, THOR through the eyes of mythologist JOSEPH CAMPBELL, a complete Golden Age Kirby story, rare Kirby interview, MARK EVANIER and our other regular columnists, pencil art from ETERNALS, DEMON, NEW GODS, THOR, and Jack's ATLAS cover!

(84-page tabloid magazine) **$10.95**
(Digital Edition) **$3.95**

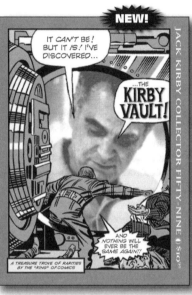
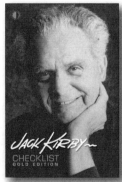